KU-218-941

Cuba
A Different Story

Editorial Capitán San Luis
La Habana, Cuba, 2013

Cover Design: Eugenio Sagués
Computerization: Norma Ramírez Vega
Translation: J. F. Vera

Original Title in Spanish: *Contar a Cuba. Una historia diferente*

ISBN: 978-959-211-388-6

Editorial Capitán San Luis, Ave. 38 No. 4717, entre 40 y 47, Kohly, Playa, La Habana, Cuba.

Email: direccion@esanluis.rem.cu

Index

I

A FRIEND IN NEED…

Did you know that Cuba played a decisive role in the independence of the Thirteen American Colonies? George Washington could fight and defeat the English in Yorktown, on the coast of Virginia, thanks to the funds he received from Cuba and the assistance provided by troops from Havana and Haiti. As the saying goes, a friend in need is a friend indeed. But, this is a forgotten story. No plaque marks an event that is not even mentioned in the large *Outline of the History of the United States* produced by the State Department in Washington and generously given away by US diplomatic missions around the world. The support of Cubans helped to simultaneously displace England from many of its key enclaves in the Caribbean and cleared the affront of 1762 when English troops took over Havana. It was the first time that Cubans left their land to fight for the independence of another nation, albeit the protagonist of that heroic deed was Francisco de Miranda, a Venezuelan who heralded the independence of Latin America.

Rum: the fuel of the war

One of the forerunners of the American independence and second President of the United States of America, John Adams, used to say that there was no reason to be embarrassed by the admission that molasses played a major role in the independence of the United States.

The wise Cuban historian Eduardo Torres-Cuevas has written: *"The development of a complex system of trade relations between Havana and the Thirteen Colonies created a bilateral connection that transcended the interests of their respective metropolises. In the decade of 1760-1770, Cuban molasses found its way to thirty distilleries in Rhode Island with an annual production of 1400 barrels of the already famous, 'Antillean Rum,' just for export to Africa. At the same time, the smugglers who moved between the three regions brought to Cuba major shipments of slaves that they often paid for with the rum produced in North America using molasses from the Cuban sugar mills.*

"But, in 1764, just when such trade was growing faster, England enforced the Sugar Duties Act. One of the consequences of this action was the interruption of the molasses trade with the Hispanic and French Antilles. Soon the conflict broke out between London and the American rum manufacturers."

In 1776, Americans proclaimed their separation from Great Britain and set out to establish relations with the Spanish authorities in Cuba. Following the old dictum that 'my enemy's enemy is my friend', Spanish King Carlos III welcomed this move and took steps to secretly help them. Weapons and ammunition left Spain for Havana, from where they were transferred to New Orleans and subsequently to the rebels.

It was really an exchange because the Peninsula received tobacco and other commodities from the colonies involved in the conflict, while Spain braced up for the war against Great Britain. In the spring of 1779, Carlos III decided to start the fight and gave London an ultimatum demanding the return of Gibraltar and Minorca, the withdrawal from Honduras and the evacuation of Bahamas, Jamaica and other British possessions, as well as the reversal of the privilege to extract dyewoods from Campeche. Subsequently, the Spanish monarch signed with France –which was already at war with England and also contributed to the cause of the Thirteen Colonies— a secret pact with the pledge of joining the conflict if his demands were not met. London did not accept Madrid's diktats and hostilities broke out on June 23, 1779. It took almost a month for the news to reach Cuba where the event was proclaimed on the streets of Havana. Spain was at war with England.

Havana then became a source of supplies for the American independence fighters. War provisions arriving in the Island from Mexico and the Corunna were re-embarked in Havana and sent to the rebels. Meanwhile, commerce grew between Philadelphia and the capital of Cuba. Two businessmen were behind both operations: on the continent, a slave smuggler by the name of Robert Morris, *'the financial mind of the United States' Independence War,'* as he was called; on the Island, Juan Miralles, a Havana resident who represented Spain in its dealings with the rebels. Years later Miralles passed away at the residence of George Washington, who said on the occasion that *"he was universally loved in this country and thus his death will be lamented."* The assistance arranged by Morris and Miralles included the repair and supply of the squadron under the rebel Commodore Alexander Gulon at the Havana shipyard and arsenal.

On August 27, two months after the declaration of war, Spanish General Bernardo Gálvez advances on Florida leading an army of Cuban *criollos*[1] from one victory to another and, between September 7 and 21, he forces the enemy to surrender at Manchac, Panmure and Baton Rouge. He is then reinforced with members of the Regular Regiment and the Battalion of Blacks and Mulattos from Havana, and with these additional forces the following year he assaults and occupies Mobile, on February 12. One year later, Gálvez lays siege to Pensacola, again with the support of Cuban troops. This time the troops are led by a Cuban: General Juan Manuel Cajigal, who would be the first to enter that city. Both officers provide cover to the Mississippi river ensuring supplies to the rebels and spoiling the English plans to

[1] *Criollos*, in colonial Cuba, those born on the island to Spanish parents and their descendants.

surround the independence fighters from their positions in the west. "*The victories thus attained had other strategic features: they fueled the confrontation of the American native tribes with the English; the Bahamas Canal route was dismantled; the enemy lost its positions on the American Caribbean and Mexican coast and the operational capability of its forces was diminished as it had to use a significant number of troops in the confrontations,*" writes Dr. Torres-Cuevas.

For his war merits, in 1781 Cajigal is appointed Captain General of Cuba thus becoming the first *criollo* to hold such senior position. He organizes an expedition against the Bahamas and rather easily seizes those islands, while the triumphant Gálvez is sent to occupy Jamaica, a mission intended to deal the British Empire a *coup d'grâce* in the Caribbean. But his mission fails. France and Spain make plans to concentrate in Cap-Haitien fifty-five battleships and 20,000 men. The British squadron under Admiral Rodney receives final instructions to prevent at all costs such concentration that could prove deadly to the fate of Jamaica and the British squadron. Eventually, he manages to catch up with the French and drag them into the naval battle of *Los Santos*, on April 12, 1782. This ends up in disaster for the French and Spanish troops, as the attack on Jamaica is cut short and the British reassert their domain on the Caribbean Sea. A few months later, in August, Rodney shows up in front of Havana but realizing that its numerous defenses make the city unassailable, he abandons the area quietly leaving the city untouched.

Francisco de Miranda

Alongside Cajigal we find Francisco de Miranda, a Venezuelan with the rank of Lieutenant Colonel of the Spanish Army and Aide de Camp of the Captain General.

Miranda (1750-1816) is the first Latin American of world historic dimensions. He is a learned man and a restless traveler who speaks several languages. He has a double virtue: he knows everything worth knowing and is not considered a foreigner in any country. He leaves Caracas at the age of 23 and his curiosity takes him to Moscow, Prague, Saxony, Stockholm and elsewhere. He fights the Moors in Morocco and the pirates in Algeria. A General in the armies of the French Revolution and a precursor of Latin American independence, Miranda ends up rotting in a Spanish jail. He makes an impressive physical presence but love to him is meant only to let off steam and never to get in the way of his most ambitious plans. His lovers, including the Czarina of Russia, Catherine the Great, can be counted by the dozen; and from every one of them he keeps a tuft of pubic hair, properly identified. In the first decades of the 20th century, the bizarre collection finds its way to the Venezuelan Academy of History where the Archbishop of Caracas would have it incinerated.

Cajigal and Miranda get along very well but such empathy barely conceals the predominance of the young *criollo* over the experienced veteran. Cajigal is the first to defend him, even when his former aide de camp becomes a conspirator. Miranda outstands as an officer in the siege of Pensacola but also as a skillful negotiator and diplomat in the discussion of the agreements leading to the incorporation of the Bahamian Islands to the Spanish crown. Furthermore, he becomes a champion fundraiser for George Washington who needs the money to continue fighting the English.

That money could only be raised in Cuba. Informed of the situation, Cajigal sends Miranda to meet with Washington to be apprised of the details and make the arrangements that would make possible such assistance. Torres-Cuevas has written about it: "*On his return, the Venezuelan would start pooling the necessary resources. A large amount of funds come from public contributions in the Island, including Havana where women from important families relinquish part of their jewelry to support American independence. The money collected, amounting to one million eight-hundred thousand pesos of eight reales*[2]*, is handed over in Havana to the young French officer Claudio Enrique de*

[2] *Real,* a17th century coin worth a quarter of a peseta.

Saint-Simon who would later become a celebrated author and a utopian socialist...

"Once the (French) troops receive their service pay and the expenses are covered Washington, reinforced with troops from Havana and Haiti, marches against the forces of British General Cornwallis in the Virginian area of Yorktown. After several days of combat the British surrender." This is not the end of the war but the decisive victory certainly paves the way to independence.

There is rivalry between Gálvez and Cajigal. Additionally, the success of both generals arouses jealousy in the Court. Cajigal would soon find himself entangled in some messy imbroglio. It was said that on his return from Jamaica, Miranda, who had traveled there as a spy but pretending to be a Cuban merchant, had smuggled contraband by Surgidero de Batabanó, something very common at the time but that in this particular case could not be proven. Is it a conspiracy to move them out of the way? Miranda and his patron are detained. Cajigal, who defends his subordinate, is sent to Spain as a prisoner; Miranda manages to escape. The long trial that follows ends in acquittal in 1799 when Francisco de Miranda is already a personality of international renown and an irreconcilable enemy of Spain.

January 24, 2010

PLACIDO, TWO CENTURIES LATER

If *The Cucalambé* is the only Cuban poet to have become an indivisible part of the true essence of the people, since the line separating what he wrote from what he is said to have written is blurred, Plácido, alongside Heredia, is the first to be liked by both the highly educated and the not so learned. As Lezama Lima put it, he combined spontaneity with a refinement whose essence is as pervasive as it is unknown. According to Lezama, *"He was the joy of the house and the party, the guitar and the melancholy of the night. He held the key to the fête and the imaginary."*

The editions of his poems exceeded Heredia's; he was the most publicized Cuban poet in the 19th century. He produced occasional poems made to order but his extemporizations make up the substance of his work. At parties and soirées that he was asked to attend, it was a common occurrence to give him a phrase from which he would easily improvise a poem. Citio Vitier has defined him as a minstrel but he was also a chronicler. Many of his verses, even those he composed ad-lib, are natural and clear. The spontaneity of his *letrillas*[3] is beautiful and delicate, and his erotic sonnets, particularly the one entitled *A una ingrata*, reveal a strange quality. He composed odes of pure resonance and his ballads oozed his Cuban identity...

Spanish critic Marcelino Menéndez Pelayo, who missed or could not appreciate the genuinely local and youthful pieces of this author, still praised him when he said that *"The writer of the masterly and exquisite romance Jicotencal, which Góngora would not mind to call his own; the beautiful descriptive sonnet La muerte de Gessler; the gracious letrilla La flor de la caña; and the inspired prayer he recited on his way to death, does not need to be a mulatto or to have been executed to be remembered by posterity..."* It's true, but as Cintio Vitier would say, we also remember him as the mulatto who was executed by firing squad due to the stupidity of Spanish colonialism and the ever-present racism.

Plácido became a very well known and popular figure of society in the province of Matanzas. People of all social classes demanded his presence in parties and celebrations. But, this same popularity would bring about his misfortune since the Spanish authorities felt that he had the capacity to lead one of the real or alleged conspiracies of blacks and mulattos shaking the Island in the 1840s. He was thus accused of being a member of one of them –the so-called *La Escalera Conspiracy*— and sent to prison, and although the accusations could not be proven, he was sentenced to death. He was executed by firing squad in the city of Matanzas in 1844.

[3] *Letrilla*, is a short poem where the same line is repeated at the end of every stanza giving it a certain musicality.

A biography

Plácido was born on March 18, 1809 in Havana, at a house on the Bernaza Street, in front across of what is today *La Moderna Poesía* bookstore. He was the son of Concepción Vázquez, a Spanish dancer born in Burgos, and Diego Ferrer Matoso, a mulatto hairdresser. They had met at the Principal Theater where both worked. The mother chose to have her baby in secret and soon abandoned him at the Orphans House located on Muralla and Oficios streets. Still, she gave him a name. In a note accompanying the infant, it could be read that his name was Diego Gabriel de la Concepción, to which the last name Valdés was added. This was common to all the children brought up in orphanages in Cuba. His godfather was a drugstore owner, Plácido Fuentes, whose name the poet would use as his famous pseudonym, although some say that he took it from the novel *Plácido and Blanca* written by the Countess of Genlis.

Little is known of the dancer's romance with the hairdresser. She made money with her trade and kept in touch with her son –who was taught to address her as "Madame"— but she always suppressed any expression of maternal love and saw him walk to his death without as much as a gesture of desperation that could erase her lifelong indifference. In his sonnet with the title *Fatalidad* Plácido wrote: *"Between the mother bed and the cradle/ an iron wall of honor you raised..."*

In his book named *Plácido, el poeta infortunado*[4], Leopoldo Horrego Estuch wrote that aside from the social challenge it meant for a white woman to have a baby born out of wedlock and fathered by a mulatto, Concepción, who wrote poems and even published them, wanted to devote all of her time to art. The hairdresser, on the other hand, felt remorse over the fate of the little boy and eventually took him out of the orphanage and had his mother and sisters care for him.

The resources of the Ferrer Matoso family were limited and Diego, who could win a carriage today on a bet and lose it the

[4] *Plácido, the Unfortunate Poet.*

following day to another, was reckless and short-sighted. He loved his son but usually neglected his duties to the little boy. And so it was that the family's financial difficulties and the father's indifference affected the future poet who could not attend school until the age of ten. But then the hairdresser left Cuba and set residence in Mexico. Plácido studied in various schools, including the Colegio de Belén, which only admitted black and mulatto boys in its section for the poor. His teachers found him to be an amazing boy for he was lively and smart and popular among his peers, even though his discipline left much to be desired. He would eventually become a skilful and daring swimmer.

Diego attended school for only two years. At the age of twelve, when he already improvised *décimas*[5] and *cuartetas* with particular ease, he started working at a carpenter's workshop. From there he went on to work as an apprentice with the celebrated portraits painter Vicente Escobar and later with José Severino Boloña in a printing shop where he found a favorable ambiance for his poetry as he trained in the craft of typographer. Later on, his low income at the printing shop led Plácido to become an ornamental-comb manufacturer. This was a rather lucrative job at the time since in Cuba, the same as in Andalusia, women considered the ornamental-comb an indispensable accessory. In just a few months, at Misa's silversmith workshop on Dragones street, he became an expert artist of the tortoiseshell, which his hands transformed into elegant canes, ornamental-combs with graceful arabesques, and delicate bracelets.

The Poet

The ornamental-comb maker evolves into Plácido, the poet. On the table of the silversmith shop, by his working tools, he keeps a book and a sheet of paper where he writes down his improvisations. From his days at the Boloña printing-shop, he is admired not only by those who listen to his impromptu poems

[5] *Décimas* and *cuartetas*, poetic compositions with stanzas of ten and four verses, respectively, very popular in the Cuba up to this day.

but also by friends and colleagues who ask him to write sonnets and quartets which are then widely copied and circulated.

In 1836, he goes to Matanzas to work as an editor for the newspaper *La Aurora*. There he is in charge of the poetry section, a very important one in those years. He should publish one poem in every newspaper edition for a monthly salary of 25 pesos but Plácido supplements his income with special verses he writes and sells for weddings, birthdays and baptisms. It is said that he earned several gold ounces for some of his laudatory poems, which he offered printed in silk and framed with filigree and vignette, both very common at the time. And it was not unusual for lovers to ask and pay for a poem that they would later offer as their own.

Many criticized Plácido for trading his compositions, and for years some said that José Jacinto Milanés had drawn inspiration from this to write *El poeta envilecido*, a poem whose main character delights with his improvisations the guests of a party who pay him with the leftovers of the banquette that he must share with the house dog. But this is not true. Milanés always spoke of Plácido with respect and admiration, and the abovementioned poem, whether abstract or allegoric, was written without a particular person in mind. That much was stated in writing, in 1880, by José Jacinto's brother Federico Milanés; and nearly ninety years later Cintio Vitier was glad to rectify such mistake: " *Plácido was ill-treated by all his critics, from Del Monte to Sanguily, however, it is worth saving Milanés from such an accusation of unfairness,*" since he was very much praised by the poet.

In 1836, Plácido published his first book *Poesía*[6], and four years later he published *El Veguero*[7], containing *letrillas* and epigrams. In 1834, he contributed the poem *La siempreviva* to the *Aureola Poética* dedicated to Spanish poet Francisco Martinez de la Rosa, who was also a minister of the Crown. Then this and another poet, Juan Nicasio Gallego, invited the Cuban bard to travel to Spain but Plácido declined. He felt he needed to stay in his own scenery.

[6] *Poetry*
[7] The Tobacco Grower

About Plácido's poetry, Lezama Lima wrote: "*Plácido adds to our poetry a minstrel's flair. Our poetry is leaving behind the drag of neoclassicism to enter the excesses of romanticism, and in comes Plácido's smiling grace and joviality. No one can deny that his poetic verb describes many of the conditions found in our nature: transparency, water games, fine and subtle links. It's difficult to find a poem, even among those written for the occasion, without a funny turn, an irate metaphor and like the mysterious presence of the four elements of our roots...He is a part of our own nature; he is delicate, sensual and moderate. He has a quality of the fine valleys of the Western provinces...*"

Executed by firing-squad

Plácido's girlfriend named Fela dies in 1833, during the cholera epidemic in Havana. Later, the poet moves to Matanzas where he marries María Gila Morales. He seldom visits the capital and when he does he stays with his mother. Then, in search for a better job he goes to Santa Clara with his wife. In 1843 he is in Trinidad, when on April 1st an anonymous note is addressed to the Political Governor of Las Villas –a document full of misspelled words that Horrego Estuch reproduces in his previously mentioned book— accusing him of involvement in a rebellion of blacks and mulattos that according to the note would soon break out in various parts of the territory. The anonymous author of the note offers the names of the alleged conspirators and warns that Plácido has come to Santa Clara to make contact with and organize the local rebels. Apparently, the snitch is well informed because he mentions the leader of the plot who he says is hiding in his home 350 pounds of bullets, gunpowder, fuses and rifles. He not only reveals names and other details but also suggests to the Governor how to suppress those involved asking him to act firmly against blacks and mulattos in the area, even if they are not involved in the conspiracy, and to enforce the rule preventing them from meeting and roaming the streets at certain hours.

It is because of this anonymous note that Plácido spends six months in jail in Trinidad. A document signed in that city on

November 15, 1843 certifies that the poet was found innocent and acquitted in the trial before the Military Commission Court. However, the report warns that *"it is advisable that the territorial authorities of the area where he sets his residence remain alert about his behavior and demand him to start working within fifteen days..."* The officials in Trinidad don't think highly of him: *"...his behavior during the time he has remained free here... is quite bad: he is not known to have held any job; the man is a suspect and...his presence in the Island is considered harmful."*

This report seals his fate. A few months later, he is accused of participation in a conspiracy known as *La Escalera*. This time he is doomed. On June 28, 1844, at dawn, he is executed alongside ten other men.

Shortly before his execution the poet writes down his testament. He is so poor that he can only leave *"his regards"* to those who love him and to the poets he admires. During his last hours, he also writes a few poems, including *Adiós a mi lira, Plegaria a Dios,* and one dedicated to his mother. The poet himself hands these manuscripts over to his wife.

Nearly twenty thousand people watch the horrible execution. The slaves from the nearest farms are forced to watch as a lesson but many others are moved by the gruesome curiosity of seeing the poet executed. Plácido, who during the interrogations did not tire of claiming his innocence, recites his poem *Plegaria...* in a clear voice as he walks to his death, but a drum roll drowns his powerful voice as a platoon of forty four soldiers with their chiefs is aligned facing those sentenced to death. Four soldiers are assigned to each prisoner; two aiming at the head and two at the chest, and a priest for every man to be executed. The priests and the condemned say their prayers and Plácido still finds enough courage in him to challenge his prosecutors and executioners in the eyes of God and call their names. The order to open fire is given; *"Good-bye, my beloved homeland..."* he says. But, the first round hits him on the shoulder, and four soldiers are ordered to shoot again. This time they blow up his head.

March 1, 2009

MARTI IN THE EYES OF A SPANISH JOURNALIST

She lived in Cuba during the final stage of the War of Independence, 1895 to 1898, when she gave free reign to her extreme fundamentalism. She was a secretary of the Red Cross and as a journalist she visited the battlefield in the area from Júcaro to Morón to write with other reporters *El álbum de la Trocha* dedicated to Valeriano Weyler and published in 1897. In her articles, she had no qualms to praise that bloody officer while she harshly carried on against the Cuban patriots. After the Spanish defeat in Cuba, which she took as a personal disaster, she left Havana and was never embarrassed to recall that *"she wept profusely almost the entire voyage"* back to Spain.

But in 1914, Eva Canel, the journalist, fiction and drama author, returns to Cuba at the invitation of some Spanish friends. This time she tours the Island with the purpose of writing about the former colonial enclave. But she has an obsession; she wants to visit the tomb of José Martí. In Havana, Mrs. Canel inquires into the rumors of his burial place but can't find an answer. Someone tells her that perhaps in Camagüey. She travels to Santiago and at the Santa Ifigenia cemetery, after praying on behalf of the Spanish mothers for the soldiers killed at El Caney and San Juan, she resumes her quest.

In Santiago de Cuba, the watchman of the necropolis points out a place and says, *"There, that's Martí's tomb."* Then she approaches the site, weeps and says prayers.

In 1891, the Apostle of the Independence of Cuba and the future inflexible advocate of the Spanish cause met in New York City and struck up a fleeting but close friendship. Martí helped her with the English language and opened the way to the great city for the journalist. He comforted her on the pain of leaving her son in a boarding school; it was the first time they were separated. It was easy for Martí to sympathize with such pain for he was living away from his own child. One day, as they had planned to go out together, he wrote her a note indicating the place of the rendezvous on the other side of the river, and in the short message he included this irresistible courtesy: *"On my way there, I'll be telling the flowers to dress up for you..."*

The last time they met, Martí took to the rendezvous a beautiful box of chocolates.*"Don't write to me. I won't write to you either," Martí said. "But, why Martí?" she asked. And he answered, "Because I don't write to those I love. It could be compromising. I don't write to my mother, either, and see that I'm putting you on a level with her."*

Eva Canel wrote: "*At the moment, I did not understand his generous decision, but I did later. I was heading for Cuba and he was preparing the revolution with the patience of a Benedictine friar that prevailed over his will beyond all troubles and disappointments."*

Lo que vi en Cuba[8]

At that time, Eva Canel, the woman from Asturias, was thirty-four years old, four years younger than Martí and a widow from the age of twenty-seven. Her real name was Agar Eva Infanzón Canel. At the age of fifteen, she had married in Madrid author Eloy Perillán Buxó. His political ideas were the cause of Perillán's exile, first in Bolivia and later in Peru and Argentina where the couple led an intense life in the area of journalism. Perillán was a Republican, and so was Eva, seemingly, but she leaned towards conservatism and after her husband's death she definitely sided with a nationalist and royalist right wing.

In 1891, she is in Havana collaborating with the *Diario de la Marina* newspaper and other publications. She is determined to find her way writing fiction and drama. She travels to the United States of America to cover the Universal Exhibition of Chicago for various newspapers and upon returning she is accused of publishing under her name several unedited novels written by Perillán. She then founds *La Cotorra* magazine of which she said: "*As she cannot use the saber...she defends by pecking."*

[8] What I Saw In Cuba.

The publication wrapped up in 1893, the same year that saw the premiere of the play *La mulata*, which just like *El indiano* –that opened the following year— brought the author the enthusiastic applause and support of the audience.

Then the War of Independence breaks out. Her reports from the Júcaro-Morón Trail extol the courage and the sense of duty of the Spanish troops deployed along that fortified line. The invasion of the western part of the Island by the Ejército Libertador de Cuba [Cuban Liberation Army] elicits hard criticisms about the efficacy of that fortified trail built to hold back the advance of the independence fighters, that is, the *mambises*[9], and places the Spanish high command in Cuba in a very tight spot.

Subsequently, Captain General Martínez Campos is replaced by [Valeriano] Weyler who, in an effort to annihilate the rebellion and the civilian population, issues the *Edict of the Concentration* forcing the farmers into concentration camps in the urban areas, where many would starve to death or perish of various illnesses, the idea being to deprive the *mambises* of any help. Mrs. Canel tries to show in her reports that the trail is almost a paradise and that the decimated troops are happy of serving Spain. In 1898, she publishes the deeply anti-Cuban journal *El Correo* and is a contributor to other journals that defend the interests of the advocates of autonomist ideas.

Researcher Jorge Domingo contends that somehow the journalist found herself involved in the explosion of the battleship *Maine* in the Havana harbor, although the charges against her failed to materialize. Anyway, by that time, her days in Cuba were numbered.

After spending some time in Spain, Mrs. Canel returns to the Americas and settles in Buenos Aires, where she becomes the owner of a printing shop and the founder of such magazines as *Kosmos* (1904) and *Vida Española* (1907). Additionally, she contributes to major continental publications and lectures while cultivating her talents as a novelist and a playwright.

[9] *Mambises*, local name given to Cuban independence fighters.

Back in Cuba, she embarks on a long trip throughout the country. She leaves Havana on a small ship that takes her to Santiago de Cuba with short calls on some ports along the northern coast, and from there she goes on to Guantánamo by train; then, again by train, she comes back west up to Havana. She had previously visited Pinar del Río.

The result of such a long journey is reflected in *Lo que vi en Cuba*[10], an over three-hundred pages book originally published in Havana in 1916, and recently reprinted by *Editorial Oriente* containing only those chapters dealing with the east of the country –about one-hundred and fifty pages— but enhanced with the introduction and notes of José Abreu Cardet and Elia Sintes Gómez.

During the War of Independence, Mrs. Canel attacks the Cubans fiercely but in 1914 she doesn't feel so bad among them here, where there is no hatred or resentment against the Spaniards, despite the war and the atrocities committed by the *voluntarios*[11], and as a rule there is no rejection of the thousands of men and women from Spain who settle in Cuba after independence. In her writings there are no expressions of grief over the lost colony although for Spain this is not just one more Caribbean island, but *its* island. However, she is very critical of the US hegemony on the economy of the island nation. According to Eva Canel, Martí had advanced such notion during their meetings in New York. In her book *Lo que vi en Cuba*, she includes a chronicle about Martí that she publishes in the journal *El Cubano Libre*, from Santiago de Cuba, at the request of its editor.

America for Humanity

Mrs. Eva Canel says that although they talked much about Spain –literature, personalities, events— Martí never spoke about Spanish politics or its policies in Cuba and Puerto Rico. *"He*

[10] *What I Saw In Cuba*

[11] Voluntarios, Cubans and resident Spaniards who volunteered to act against local advocates of independence from Spain.

avoided politics and, at that time, I lacked the experience to even approach the subject." His main purpose, which he accomplished gracefully, was to teach the Spanish woman the good and the bad things about the United States.

One day he said, *"Let's take advantage of the good never allowing the imposition of the bad."* And he added, *"If the independent life of my country depended on them, I would not want it because I know it would not mean life or independence."* Then, he turned to the woman with a joyful gesture and in a suggestive tone he asked, *"Are you familiar with the story of the friar and the nail?"* As she said she was, Martí commented: *"Well, to Cuba these gentlemen would be the friars and the nail would be the direct protection they would offer."* When she visited the north coast of Cuba, she recalled the nail Martí referred to *"where the nail of the friar was the United Fruit Company, also plunged into Central America and in Santa Marta, Colombia, and in Bocas del Toro, Panama, as well as in every other country where they grow banana, pineapple, coffee, cocoa and sugarcane."* That's why she feels that Martí's intellectual legacy is of paramount importance to perpetuate the Spanish race and character, and its language.

She makes a substantial clarification. The phrase *"America for Humanity"* gallantly said by Sáenz Peña, the Argentinean delegate to the 1st Pan American Conference, opposite that of *"America for Americans"* said by Monroe, is not his but Martí's. *"I heard it from the Apostle –a better qualification could not be given to him— a long time before the Conference."* Martí was the Argentinean Consul in New York and Sáenz Peña was still a young, romantic and determined Hispanophile. Such characteristics, that he held until becoming President of his country, favored his understanding with Martí who had an influence on him and who taught him his dialectics and his perception of what Mr. Blaine intended to accomplish with that conference. This is the reason why Sáenz Peña set obstacles along the road that the US Secretary of State had planned to walk smoothly.

How was Martí in the privacy of friendship? Eva Canel makes reference to this in her chronicle. She writes: *"It was not through his words that Martí revealed to me his character and condition, his talent or soul, but rather through the observation of his very eloquent silences: Ah, the silences of Pepe Martí!*

"Did he suffer? Did he rejoice? Did he doubt? Did he believe? Everything fitted in his mind but he did not show it. He had the powerful gift of letting others judge him without any effort on his part. He was analyzed because an analysis was possible, as he was loved because he incited admiration, and love and admiration combined to give rise to the amazement of finding oneself face to face with a mystic man living within himself. He was not a Saint John of the Cross lost in another time or in a different civilization traveling throughout the centuries to the current age by miraculous reincarnation. He was a hermit Paul in flesh and blood living on the Tabor of infinite eagerness; eagerness for an ideal that not even the independence of his homeland would have quenched."

After the publication of that book and that chronicle, Eva Canel never left Cuba again. She passed away in Havana in 1932.

January 27, 2008

THE WEDDING OF GENERAL JOSE

The story is recounted by General Enrique Loynaz del Castillo in his book *Memorias de la Guerra*[12]. The War of Independence is about to begin in Cuba and General Antonio Maceo insists that his brother José should marry his fiancé Elena Nuñez before the onset of the conflict.

Loynaz arrives in Costa Rica and soon wins the heart of the Maceo family. In his book he writes: *"All of the Maceo brothers, glorious champions of my homeland, decorated with the scars of the liberating struggle, soon compensated with their affection my admiration for their great virtues... But José, in particular, favored me with his confidence. Antonio used to say that José looked through my eyes."*

[12] Memories of the War

It was because of this confidence that General Antonio asked Loynaz to persuade his brother José to get married. Loynaz, who was then only 23 years old, did not waste a second before undertaking the delicate mission that the Titan trusted to his 'diplomatic' talents. One day at the house of Elena's family he called the *Lion of Oriente* aside and said: *"José, why don't you marry this virtuous girl and make her happy before leaving for the war?"* To which the other answered: *"Ah! Antonio has sent you!"* But, Loynaz responded: *"Absolutely not, it just seems to me a very pleasant duty to fulfill. Elena could take care of the farm and in full right look after your interests here in Costa Rica, in addition to the great treasure that a good wife is for a good man."*

General José Maceo listened attentively to the stream of words and remained silent for a few minutes. He seemed persuaded by the reasons given by his friend but then spoke of how little confidence he had in the Spanish priests, such as the one who celebrated mass in Nicoya where his brother Antonio, with a group of Cuban officers, was bent on making a farm prosper in the lands granted by the Costa Rican government.

José also said that he disliked the complications of confession and communion that the church marriage demanded. He simply felt it was "*foolish*." Still, he caved in to Lyonaz's arguments and the latter chose to take him to the priest right away to make the necessary arrangements for the wedding before José had time to change his mind.

After all, it was not as complicated as José had assumed; but still the priest wanted to ask him two or three inevitable questions. First, he asked about the Christian faith of the groom and as José said he embraced it the priest moved on to the thorny issue of the Ten Commandments. The conversation progressed smoothly until the fifth precept, when the prelate said: *"And, of course, my son you have never committed the sin of killing..."* That's when José lost his temper and retorted: *"Look, father, you need to be a guanajo*[13] *to ask such question from a man who has been*

[13] *Guanajo,* a Cuban local term used for *fool.*

engaged in a war for ten years killing Spaniards. And even a priest once fell in my hands." At this point, the priest asked in astonishment: "*You mean you killed a man of God? That's a mortal sin that I can't absolve. We must ask Rome for a waiver!*" To which José Maceo answered in rage: "*It's you who's going to Rome now, through that window!*"

Enrique Loynaz del Castillo writes in his *Memorias de la Guerra* that it was the window that saved the priest from the anger of the Cuban General.

El León de Oriente

By that time, José Maceo had not only known war but also prison.

He had joined the Ten Years War two days after the *Grito de Yara* marked its beginning and was progressively promoted from plain soldier to colonel, a rank he received after the *Protesta de Baraguá*. During the *Short War*, he spent ten months in campaign and was elevated to the rank of Brigadier General. Later, when he was forced to lay down arms, he thought the Spanish government would guarantee his leaving the country and, in fact, he was allowed to abandon the Island but only to be captured in the high seas and taken to Puerto Rico from where he was sent to the Chafarinas prison and two years later, in 1882, he was transferred to Ceuta.

He managed to escape and in Tanger, Morocco, he obtained permission from the American Consul to enter the United States, but during a stopover in Gibraltar he was detained and handed over to the Spanish authorities who took him to Algeciras and then to Ceuta, and subsequently to the prisons of Pamplona and La Estrella.

In 1884, he ran away again, this time from La Mola prison in Mahón, and sought refuge in Algeria. From there he went to France, the United States and Jamaica before joining Antonio in Panama, in December 1886. He would finally settle in Costa Rica where, in 1891, his brother received from the government a concession of lands to be labored by a group of veterans of the War of Independence in Cuba.

According to biographer Raúl Aparicio, General Antonio planned to reunite his entire family at Nicoya, in front of the Pacific Ocean. José would soon join him and the Titan only waited until he had a modicum of conditions to ensure the stay of his wife María. He also dreamed of bringing his mother, Aparicio has said, but Mariana was very attached to Jamaica where she lived with her son Marcos and was not keen on the prospect of making a voyage to the Pacific; she was already eighty years old.

It was from Costa Rica that Antonio and José Maceo came to fight for a free Cuba. On April 28, 1895, José was promoted to Major General, and on October when he was already the chief of the First Army Corps, Antonio handed over to him the command of the eastern province *ad interim*, a position in which he was confirmed by Máximo Gómez. The following year, in April, he was ordered to give up this command to Major General Mayía Rodríguez; he resigned but refused to relinquish power before receiving an explicit order from the General in Chief. He finally surrendered it to Calixto García and remained as chief of the First Corps. On July 5, 1896, a bullet hit him on the chest knocking him off his horse at Loma del Gato. He died four hours later at a farm named Soledad, in Ti Arriba.

For his fervent charges on the enemy and his extraordinary courage, José Maceo was called *El León de Oriente* (The Lion of Oriente).

The wedding's best man

It is said that *guanajo* was a word used by the Cuban aborigines. Anyway, this Cuban word serves to identify the turkey but it's also a colloquial term applied to the fool or silly, while *guanajada* is also a local term synonym with stupidity or silliness. It's not strange then that the priest of Nicoya did not understand what José Maceo had meant by calling him *guanajo;* still, Loynaz could not persuade him that such a word was used in Cuba as a delicate praise. The prelate felt that this explanation did not match up with the angry gestures that accompanied José's phrase.

Patiently and tactfully Loynaz was able to iron out the differences between the envoy of God and the warrior. The priest accepted the 25 pesos he was promised that would spare him the long journey to Rome to ask for a waiver for the mortal sins of the groom.

So, the wedding was announced and the community headed by General Antonio converged at the bride's home on the previously agreed date. The priest arrived and asked Loynaz in a whisper who would be the best man to "*the beast.*" It would be no other than Loynaz, who was then asked to stand by the groom, as the godmother stood by the bride, and the ceremony started; a rather quick ceremony which concluded without the word *amen*. The wedding act seemed too short to Loynaz, and he told the priest who said: "*And what else do you want for 25 pesos?*"

At that moment, the priest took his money and left. He did not even wait for the Champaign to which the bride's family treated their guests.

June 27, 2004

MANUEL GARCÍA, THE KING OF THE CUBAN COUNTRYSIDE

José Martí did not accept the eight thousand pesos that Manuel García offered for the war because they were the result of a kidnapping but the man was not denied the right to fight for the independence of Cuba. In this connection Martí wrote to Máximo Gómez: "*In a sad and submissive letter, Manuel García said that he awaits orders.*" And Gómez himself wrote to Francisco Carrillo, leader of the Revolution in Las Villas: "*Count Manuel García in.*"

But, Manuel García died on February 24, 1895, the day the War of Independence broke out. He was murdered as he marched to join and lead the group of Juan Gualberto Gómez and Antonio López Coloma stationed at Ibarra. It is said that he was joining the forces with the rank of Captain; however, it seems to be true that clubs of Cuban emigrants in Key West had previously given him the star of Major. It has been said that before the onset of the war, Juan Gualberto had given the rank of Colonel to that man who, in his own way and alone, had encouraged subversion in the Island and that with his methods, be them right or wrong, had contributed funds to the insurrection.

Few Cuban personalities are as unsung or as lightly taken as that of *The King of the Cuban Countryside*. Perhaps no other is more controversial and polemic. Up to this day, many think that he was no more than a bandit. But, as he used to take from the rich to give to the poor his life is covered by a romantic and sentimental aura, –an image promoted by literature, films, poems, paintings and even comics— and an increasing number of people are coming around and considering him a patriot.

In 1886, García writes from Key West to Máximo Gómez, *"My General, willing to return to Cuba's countryside…I am at your service as a soldier of the cause of my homeland's independence."* And, in 1891, in a manifesto addressed to the South American republics, and signed at the town of Melena del Sur in Havana, he writes: *"Now, with deep respect, we ask from the foreign governments to remain neutral towards our civil war and if the reasons we have to fight are enough to arouse your solidarity, you may come and help us."* In this document, García describes the reasons leading Cuba to fight for its freedom and announces that the country has declared war on the Spanish monarchy. He then signs it as *'General of the West Department,'* a title that he gave himself, the same as that of *'The King of the Cuban Countryside and of almost the Entire Island of Cuba,'* as he signed the letter he forwarded around the same date to the newspaper *La Lucha*.

A public enemy

Who was this man? Unfortunately, almost everything known about his life was written by his enemies. From his christening certificate we know that he was born in Alacranes, Matanzas, on February 1st, 1851. His parents were born in the Canary Islands. The boy did not have the opportunity to attend school regularly. He was a reliable and determined young boy, and it was not long before he ran into difficulties with the Spanish authorities. He was sent to prison for a death threat he made against a Mayor who disrespected his wife, Charito Vásquez, and he later injured his stepfather with a machete when he found the man battering his mother. After this, the fear of another incarceration prompted him to take to the woods. Colonel Charles Aguirre from the Ejército Libertador wrote about it: *"I always found an excuse for the damage he caused. He was justified. I don't know of any action by The King of the Cuban Countryside that is not justified. Is there any greater justification than that which forced him to take to the woods and gave his destiny a different turn?"*

Apparently, he joined the gang of a bandit named Lengue Romero and became a public enemy. When Governor Luis Prendergart bent on putting an end to banditry offered to pardon the ringleaders, facilitating their travel abroad and granting them a considerable sum of money, Manuel García left for Key West. The man who had supposedly robbed large sums of money had kept nothing for himself and to make a living he had to apply for a job at the cigar factory of Eduardo Hidalgo Gato, a friend of Martí. According to historians, this played a decisive role in the life of the former bandit since his relations with José Dolores Poyo and Brigade General Fernández Ruz, as well as other Cuban émigrés, channeled his rebelliousness to the struggle for independence. Soon, he became one of the four members of the expedition on the sloop *Dolphin*, which landed in Puerto Escondido, east of Havana, in September 1887. The leader of the group died in combat almost immediately and García took command of the small force to start creating the conditions for the war of liberation.

Search and capture

As from then on he did not rest. In November 1890, the Captain General offered ten thousand pesos in reward for his capture and surrender to the authorities, and five thousand more for each member of his group. It was useless; nobody denounced him and nobody even tried to catch him. A large troop chased him and he was encircled by a ring of spies charged with on checking his every movement. But, García was not an enemy to be taken lightly. He had remarkable natural talents and intuition, while his gift for organization and his absolute familiarity with the area favored his actions. His most bitter adversary, Lieutenant Colonel Tejada, head of the paramilitary group *Escuadras de Guantánamo*, would have to admit to his superiors that García had provided his men with modern weapons, uniforms and discipline. In addition, García removed the so-called "bonus," that is, an additional amount of money given to the gangs' leaders, and distributed whatever he got in equal shares among his men; this earned him their respect and consideration.

García basically operated in the areas of Havana and Matanzas but he also carried on military actions in Las Villas and later deployed to Pinar del Río. He conducted assaults and kidnappings and asked for ransom. The Spaniards were well aware of his ideas and motives, thus the Captain General reported to Madrid that *"Manuel García has never renounced his ideas to seek separation from Spain, and he keeps corresponding with revolutionaries here and in Key West while nearly every person he has kidnapped does not profess such ideas and the money he obtains as ransom he uses only to purchase weapons and ammunitions, and to help the peasants."*

He demanded money –fifteen thousand pesos— from the railway company. The company did not accept his claim and he started shooting at trains and destroying railway stations; then he asked for twenty thousand pesos and when they refused to oblige he derailed the train running between Empalme and Matanzas, and raised the figure to thirty thousand. The end of these exchanges is unknown. Apparently, the company struck a deal because a senior Spanish officer declared that García had accepted to leave Cuba. But, he did not; he just stayed quiet for about three months and then resumed his actions.

A mysterious death

In 1939, Gregorio Ramírez, one of the last survivors of the uprising at Ibarra, said that being López Coloma's "*trusted man*" he had met twice with Manuel García who, on two occasions before the rebellion, had met personally with Coloma at the town of Ibarra. He also said that on the night of February 23 to 24, 1895, he was ordered by his chief to wait at the encampment for García's arrival from the road of Ceiba Mocha. But García did not come and a few hours later they learned through a paper that he would never do. He also said that Juan Gualberto and Coloma were very upset.

In fact, Manuel García was heading for Ibarra in the evening of February 24. After leaving the store known as El *Seborucal* in *Ceiba Mocha*, where he bought supplies, he moved on ahead of his troops with two other men. A few minutes later, his troops caught up with one of the two men who was bleeding to death near their chieftain. The details have never been known. This is as much as can be said about the dark and mysterious death of *The King of the Cuban Countryside*.

October 3, 2004

THE DEATH OF JOSÉ MARTÍ

The first monument to the memory of José Martí was built on the initiative of Máximo Gómez at the height of the War of Independence. On August 9, 1896, the General in Chief of the Ejército Libertador, at the head of over three hundred *mambises* including Major General Calixto García and other senior leaders of the insurrection, visited for the second time the place where the Apostle had found his death, and left a mark of this visit.

The site was well identified. A peasant named José Rosalía Pacheco who lived at the Dos Ríos farm, and had met Martí shortly before his death, went to the area in the company of his son Antonio and looked carefully into the place where the hero's body had laid, found the trace of clotted blood on the ground, and marked it with a stick from the tree known as heart suit.

A few months later, exactly on October 10, 1895, Enrique Loynaz del Castillo visited the area. He had been instructed by the Marquis of Santa Lucía, President of the Republic in Arms, to determine with as much precision as possible the exact place of the event in order to rise there some day the deserving monument. Seemingly, neither the Marquis nor Loynaz were aware of the gesture of José Rosalía but it was no other than this farmer who took the government's envoy to the exact place and said, *"I collected Martí's blood right from this place. You can still see the mark left by the knife I used to cut around the earth drenched in his blood which I've kept in a bottle."* Many years later, José Rosalía's son said: *"He must have lost much blood because the ground was soaked in it."*

Loynaz, deeply moved, kissed the piece of land the farmer showed him, drafted a document registering the fulfillment of his mission and put it in a bottle, which he buried under the wood cross that José Rosalía prepared and hammered in the site.

The *Contramaestre* and *Cauto* rivers converge in *Dos Ríos*. That August 9, 1896, on the road leading to the place, Máximo Gómez ordered every man in his force, from soldiers to officers, to pick up a stone from the river. Then, the troops resumed their march in silence. Only Gómez spoke. Finally, they came to the place which was covered with buffalo grass. He ordered it cleaned up and once this was done, the Generalísimo followed by Calixto García dropped their respective stones at the place. Then, the senior officers did likewise, followed by their subordinates and on to the last soldier.

And so it was that a rustic pyramid was formed and a wood cross set up *"facing the sun,"* as Máximo Gómez timely recalled that Martí wanted to die. The Chief of the Ejército Libertador evoked the combat at Dos Ríos on May 19, 1895, the extremely compromised situation, the unexpected news of Martí's disappearance, the uncertainty about his death and the impossibility of his rescue...the General in Chief did establish in unequivocal terms that the Delegate of the Cuban Revolutionary Party went to his death *"with all the energy and courage of a man of indomitable will and integrity."* He also set a precedent: *"Every Cuban who loves his country and respects Martí's memory should leave a stone at this monument every time they come here."*

And so it was done until the end of the War of Independence in 1898. In their book *Piedras Imperecederas: La Ruta Funeraria de José Martí*[14] *(1999)*, Omar López and Aida Morales wrote that *"Many passed by the place and left there a stone as an homage and tribute..."*

The goal and the path to it

Military experts have agreed that the action at *Dos Ríos*, which became significant because of Martí's death, was really unimportant from a strictly military viewpoint. There are several versions about the circumstances of that combat that differ in certain aspects but generally coincide in the basics, mostly in the way the Apostle died.

Historian Rolando Rodríguez who found and studied documents on the subject in the military archives of Madrid that *"are real treasures for the history of Cuba"* states in his book *Dos Ríos: A Caballo y con el Sol en la Frente*[15] *(2002)* that from the days of the tragedy *"and contrary to all historic evidence, the authors of various types of fantasies and fiction have tried to distort the facts and seized inexact stories or documents full of gaps and, without further examination, forcing a particular and completely wrong narrative of the event."*

Did Martí deliberately run to his death at Dos Ríos? Did the enemy catch him by surprise as he headed for the coast with the purpose of leaving the country? Had the discrepancies among the military chiefs of the war become untenable? Was it the spirit of his horse *Baconao* what unwillingly led him to clash with the Spanish forces?

Second Lieutenant Angel de la Guardia who accompanied Martí at the time of the tragedy told his wife one version of that event which was later repeated by his son. After crossing the *Contramaestre River* alongside Gómez, a hollow altered the course of Martí's horse and his own forcing them to move diagonally

[14] Everlasting Stones: José Martí 's Funeral Path.
[15] Dos Ríos: Horse Riding Toward the Sun

with respect to the position of the troops commanded by the General in Chief until they came across the enemy advanced party. But this account, says Rolando Rodríguez, shows such inexactitudes as to make it impossible to believe it to the letter.

Another rather unreliable version relates that Martí had joined a small group of *mambises* that he had accidentally met, charged with their machetes on a Spanish advanced party and chased the survivors to the house of José Rosalía, where they sought refuge. That there the farmer's wife, hiding with her children under the bed, heard as the Apostle ordered De la Guardia to go on ahead with him, the two alone, and that's how he clashed with the Spanish force that killed him. If this were true, at least a member of that Spanish advanced party had witnessed the event, but nobody did, and none of the protagonists of the action at *Dos Ríos* ever said anything like that.

On the other hand, many have offered testimony to the spirit and uncontrollable nature of the horse that used to scare easily and bolt. But Rodríguez indicates that although Martí was not an experienced horse rider he was not without skills. By the way, in the action *Baconao* was hit on the abdomen by a bullet that exited through its hindquarters. The animal survived the wound and Gómez ordered its release at the Sabanilla farm with instructions of never letting anyone ride it, out of respect for Martí.

At the time of the tragedy, Martí was marching through the center of the province and far from the coast; therefore, it could not be his intention to leave Cuba, at least not immediately. Five days before, he wrote in his diary that he was reflecting on what would be the right thing to do, that is, whether to stay in the woods or leave the country as Gómez and Maceo wanted. Those who speak of a suicide, points out Rodríguez, ignore his character and forget that if that had been the case he would not have urged his young assistant to ride with him. A man of his ethics would have found it unacceptable to risk someone else's life in a destiny that was his own.

"It would mean ignoring that Martí was a seasoned politician well acquainted with feuds, unfair attacks and even humiliations that never led him to a depression, simply because he could not

allow himself such weakness," writes the author of *Dos Ríos: A Caballo y con el Sol en la Frente. "He was trained to swallow bitter aloe, bile. How can anyone forget his words, still fresh when he died: 'There is no pain, humiliation, mortification, setback or cruelty that I am not willing to take in the service of my Homeland.' On the contrary, in the face of rough storms, terrible squalls and cloudy skies he always responded proudly, firmly and with bravery. The fact is that his strong will never failed him and he always recovered from the worst setbacks because he was a combatant who fought adversity with courage and spirit and who knew, when he decided to bring independence to Cuba, that his path would be fraught with thorns rather than flowers. To that man, the goal was more important than the path leading to it."*

"You step back, Martí..."

On May 19, 1895, as he returns to the encampment in *Vuelta Grande* from which he had departed on the 17th with about thirty men to harass the convoy led by Colonel Ximénez de Sandoval, Máximo Gómez finds that Major General Bartolomé Masó, at the head of three hundred men, is accompanying Martí. The three Generals review the troops and Gómez and Masó harangue them. Then comes Martí's turn to address the fighters and he says that for Cuba he is willing to die on the cross. Perhaps without fully understanding his words the troops start applauding and shouting, "*Long live the President!*"

They all have lunch. The attendants lay the hammocks for the chiefs to take a nap and it is said, although it seems unlikely, that Martí stays up working on the draft of the Constitution of the Republic in Arms. Suddenly, a lieutenant comes into the encampment running and breaks the news: shots are heard in the direction of *Dos Ríos*. The General in Chief orders his men to ride with him. The Delegate will not stay behind as some versions would have it.

Gómez wants to fight the enemy further away from *Dos Ríos*, where his horsemen have more space to maneuver, but he can't make it and so he must start fighting at this place, about 2.5

miles from *Vega Grande*. The rebels cross the *Contramaestre River* and once in the savanna a Spanish party tries to stop them. The *mambises* annihilate it but the column headed by Ximénez Sandoval, aligned in combat formation, opens fire on the Cubans. The General in Chief tries to protect the Delegate and orders him: "*You step back, Martí, this is not your place now.*"

Martí holds his horse for a second and Gómez loses sight of him for he is focused on the enemy. Rodríguez states that probably Martí wandered along the field trying to get closer to the immediate scene of the fight until accompanied by De la Guardia he gallops ahead toward the Spanish troops approximately 150 feet to the right and ahead of the General in Chief, where the two combatants make a perfect target for the enemy advanced party hiding in the high grass. The Delegate and his assistant ride between a dry lemonwood and a fallen smoke tree and the bullets mercilessly hit the body of the Apostle who collapses to the ground.

Is he still alive? Is it true that a Cuban guide with the Spanish troops, *Oliva, the Mulatto*, finished him off with his shotgun?

Baconao, soaked in blood

Martí was hit by three bullets. One bullet entered his body through the chest, at the basis of the breastbone, which it fractured; another one broke into his neck and exited through his left upper lip which is torn; and the other, hit him on a thigh. His assistant, Second Lieutenant Angel de la Guardia, who fell under his own wounded horse, managed to escape the weight of the beast and hid behind the fallen smoke tree to fight the enemy from that position in the scrubland but could not rescue the body of the Delegate of the Cuban Revolutionary Party. Slowly, for his wounded horse could barely walk, De la Guardia returned to his comrades almost at the same time that Martí's horse, *Baconao*, showed up soaked in blood. The Generalísimo Máximo Gómez, in desperation over the sad news, left practically alone for the place of the tragedy to rescue Martí, dead or alive. The leader of the Ejército Libertador took such risk that in a first report on the combat Colonel Ximénez de Sandoval, head of the Spanish Column, included his name in the list of dead enemies.

Máximo Gómez would later say to Tomás Estrada Palma, *"When I learned of his fall, I did all I could do riding alone to try recovering his body. It was impossible, and I can assure you that I have never been in such peril. So, the news from a Spanish source that I was wounded made sense."*

Actually, a volley of bullets prevents Gómez from reaching Martí's body. The Spaniards find it and Antonio Oliva, a Cuban known as *El Mulatto* serving them as a guide, boasts that he finished him off with his shotgun. He also boasts of having shot the Apostle from the scrubland. Is it true or mere boasting? A Spanish officer named Enrique Ubieta considered Oliva's alleged shot point blank on a dying Martí plain fiction. To Cuban historian Rolando Rodríguez it is evident that *El Mulatto* was bragging of something he had not done because he wanted the Spanish Army to reward him with a pension. If it is true that he shot on the Apostle from the scrubland as he said, he was not the only one since according to the testimony of Angel de la Guardia both combatants were the target of a volley of shots. On the other hand, insists Rolando Rodríguez, it is impossible to impact three times on a horseman with a shotgun or even a Mauser before he falls down.

Anyway, Ximénez de Sandoval registered Antonio Oliva among the soldiers who distinguished themselves that day in the action of *Dos Ríos.* Later, the man was granted the Cruz del Mérito Militar de Cuba, with a red distinction, but no pension.

Identification and desecration of his body

At the time of his death, Martí was wearing light color pants and a black jacket, a felt hat and black leather boots. His clothing must have attracted the enemy's attention and from the documents found on him, the Spaniards immediately suspected this was the body of the 'alleged' President of the Republic or of the Parliament in Arms, Martí, 'the ringleader'; his watch and handkerchief carried the letters JM. A Captain Satué, who had met him in Santo Domingo, confirmed the identification and a Cuban named Chacón, captured a few hours before, corroborated it, too.

The Apostle was carrying official documents and some personal papers such as the unfinished letter to his friend Manuel Mercado, dated the previous day May 18. From Gómez's letter to Ximénez de Sandoval asking for news about Martí (*"If he is in your custody, injured...or if dead, where have his remains been deposited...?"* he writes) we have learned that the Delegate also had on him over five-hundred American gold pesos.

Subsequently, Ximénez de Sandoval related to Gonzalo de Quesada what Satué had said about Martí's belongings: *"The iron ring he is said to have carried... must have been taken from him along with his revolver, watch, belt, legwarmer, shoes and papers, since when I found his body and identified it, I ordered him searched without dismounting my horse, and the only thing on him was an American five duros*[16] *coin, three silver duros, a rosette, a letter from Máximo Gómez's daughter with a ribbon and his wallet."*

He did not mention the five-hundred pesos. Perhaps he did not know about them because somebody else took them. However, some time later he said that the money taken from Martí and Chacón was used to pay for the eau-de-vie and cigars bought for the troops at the town of *Remanganaguas*.

Part of that war booty remained with the Spanish Colonel: the blue ribbon sent to Martí by Clemencia Gómez, the penknife and the rosette, which is said to have belonged to Carlos Manuel de Céspedes. The letters and documents the Spanish officer surrendered to the military archives while the watch he gave as a present to Marcelo Azcárraga, the Spanish Minister of War, and the revolver to Captain General Arsenio Martínez Campos.

The letters JM on the watch and the handkerchief, the documents seized and Satué's and Chacón's confirmation of the identity of the deceased persuaded Ximénez de Sandoval that he had dealt a fatal blow to the burgeoning revolution. He

[16] Duro, a five-peseta coin in 18th Century Spain.

then decided not to wait any longer and ordered his troops to pull out of the field. The *Dos Ríos* combat had lasted one-and-a-half hour. The Apostle was killed in the second half hour, after 1:00 pm but before 1:30, which was when the Generalísimo received the appalling news.

On the way to Remanganaguas

Initially, Gómez thinks that Martí is neither injured nor dead but only lost in the woods, and that if the Delegate has been captured, whether wounded or dead, he can be rescued during the counterattack he is expecting. But the counterattack never happens and the *mambises* from the exploration party detect that the adversary is withdrawing. Ximénez de Sandoval is moving towards *Remanganaguas* carrying Martí's body bent and tied on the horse of the prisoner named Chacón. Gómez weighs up the possibility of intercepting the Spanish column but his troops are delayed; the heavy rains have turned the road into mud and when he finally reaches the main road, the adversary has passed. He orders some riflemen to harass them but he is disappointed. His old warrior self tells him that he cannot beat this enemy now.

It takes Ximénez de Sandoval longer than planned to reach his destination. He stops at Modesta Oliva's convenience store and later, at sunset, the rainfall forces him to make another stop at the *Demajagual* farm. He decides to stop for the night with his troops on the side of the road. Martí's body is untied and dropped under a tree. At 3:30 am the Spanish troops resume their march and arrive in *Remanganaguas* at 8:00 am. From here, the Colonel sends a telegram to his superiors reporting on the combat.

It is precisely in this town where the remains of the Apostle are buried for the first time; directly in the ground and almost naked, carrying only his pants. On top of his body, they place the remains of a Spanish soldier and a sergeant killed at *Dos Ríos*, too. It's 3:00 pm of May 20.

Although disappointed, the Generalísimo does not give up. He gets to Modesta Oliva's convenience store. The woman says that Martí is dead and hands over a piece of paper left by the Spanish chief. The names of Martí and Ximénez de Sandoval are written between Masonic symbols –both were Masons. It says that the Apostle is wounded, that if he lives, he will be returned to the Cubans and if he dies, he'll have a dignified burial. The mystery of that paper has never been resolved, if it truly existed, although Rolando Rodríguez believes it was definitely not from Ximénez. This historian thinks it was a ruse to mislead Gómez into slowing down or desisting from the pursuit. Later, a physician with the Spanish column, also a Mason, claimed authorship of the note where he said he wrote that Martí was alive but would be killed if his rescue was attempted. However, Rodríguez does not believe this was what the note said.

It is at this moment that the General in Chief of the Ejército Libertador addresses the abovementioned letter to the enemy chief inquiring into the destination of the Delegate. The General's envoy, his own assistant Manuel Garriga, carries the warning to Ximénez de Sandoval that *"if this combatant does not return to us because you prevent it, in whatever way you decide to do so, even with his death, the young officer will not dither as the spirit moving those of us who stay alive will not change in any way."*

The last chance

The Spaniards rejoice over the death of the Delegate of the Cuban Revolutionary Party. Messages cross the ocean back and forth. *"The so-called President José Martí is dead,"* they claim. In Madrid, after a Council of Ministers meeting, the Secretaries of War and Overseas, respectively, assure the journalists in an exultant tone that *"the death of the ringleader José Martí, who was the soul of the insurrection, will make it easier for our troops to fight and dismantle the enemy whose forces are now disheartened and demoralized."* The government and the Regent Queen send a telegram to Captain General Martínez Campos congratulating the army operating in Cuba and Colonel Sandoval over their victory. The newspapers run the news in their ordinary editions and in additional supplements.

But, Spain wants to have the certainty that the dead man is really the President of the Parliament in Arms. They know that such news will be the subject of intensive discussions and they need to remove any doubt. That's why General Salcedo, the military chief of Santiago City and the entire province, orders Ximénez de Sandoval to send to that city the body of José Martí, embalmed, because *"this must have a great moral impact and contribute to the enhancement of the great service paid by you and your troops."* He also states that Martí will be buried in Santiago *"with the respect due to any dead person."*

On his way from Palma Soriano to San Luis, Sandoval comes across Cuban doctor Pablo Valencia instructed by Salcedo to corroborate the identity of Martí's remains and proceed to his embalmment. Once in *Remanganaguas*, Valencia cannot undertake his task without Sandoval's permission, so he sends his assistant to San Luis for the authorization, which he obtains and on the 23rd he starts on his way back with the document hidden in one of his shoes. The man is afraid, despite his precautions, because the horse he is riding belongs to the Spanish Army, something the rebels would know from the animal's branding and short tail if he happens to encounter them. He is, in fact, halted by a *mambises* party that recognizes the horse, but they only change it for a weaker animal and let him go, because after all, the man is only a doctor's assistant.

Those rebels could not know that they were missing the last chance to rescue the remains of the Apostle.

A missing testicle

Upon his assistant's return with the permission issued by Colonel Ximénez de Sandoval, Doctor Pablo de Valencia had the body exhumed. Before that, a local carpenter was asked to build a coffin –that cost eight pesos— where the remains would be deposited to be transferred to Santiago de Cuba. It was 5:30 pm, on May 23, when the Cuban doctor started to work. The body of Martí, who had died on the 19th, at noon, was in an advanced stage of decomposition which prevented a complete embalmment.

Valencia proceeded to identify the cadaver. The physical examination had to agree with the information supplied by people who had known the deceased and who said it was a man about forty-eight years old, of medium height and built, and in good shape although thin. He had dark brown curly hair and a badly receding hairline that gave the impression of a high forehead. According to the description received by Dr. Valencia, his eyebrows were the color of his hair and he had a thin and light mustache, aquiline nose, thick lips, small ears and slightly blue eyes.

In his report, Valencia confirms many of these details. He writes that the teeth of the body he examines *"match the data provided, as well as those related to his head and face."* In his opinion, the man had good teeth although the second upper incisor was missing. He repeats the information about the thin and light mustache and adds that the right leg showed a depression in the skin signaling that the man had dragged shackles. The doctor's certificate also remarks a missing testicle.

Still, some descriptions in Valencia's report seem contradictory; Martí's dentist would say years later that the Apostle was missing the central upper left incisor and that the lateral from the same side was so compromised that it required treating the root in order to insert an artificial tooth on a spike. But the procedure was never completed. Those were the days of the setback of the *Fernandina Plan* and Martí refused to have the treatment completed by the specialist. According to this doctor, he said: *"Leave it now, what's one tooth when my Cuba's freedom is at stake?" "He would not allow me to complete the procedure of provisionally sealing the root,"* the dentist recalled, adding that the two upper lateral teeth of the Apostle were also fatally compromised.

The same applies to the slightly blue eyes since numerous testimonies belie this assertion. According to some, his eyes were black while others claim they were brownish-gray or simply brown, and there are still some who describe them as chestnut brown. There are also doubts about a 'thin and light' mustache, although it is likely that he had it shaved along with the goatee to confuse the Spanish espionage in the days prior to his arrival in the Island. In his diary, he noted two visits to the barber in three days.

Several details were omitted every time the report on the necropsy practiced by Valencia was published, perhaps because they were considered indecent or disrespectful. It was historian Rolando Rodríguez who found the original document in the Spanish archives and the only one who has reproduced it with accuracy. Martí had suffered from sarcocele, that is, a solid tumor of the testicle caused by the shackles that required three surgeries, the last of these in Spain; but they were all unsuccessful. His ordeal continued until 1876, when Doctor Francisco Montes de Oca subjected him to a surgical procedure that, as Martí himself put it, *"the outstanding Spanish doctors had failed to perform but the Mexican doctor did with amazing precision, extreme care and happy results."*

Valencia worked on the embalmment. He extracted the viscera from the cadaver and refilled it with aseptic cotton. He injected a solution of bichloride and then covered the body with a solution of alum and salicylic acid prepared in boiling water. It was past 7:00 pm when the doctor completed the procedure. At about the same time, a Spanish column of more than six-hundred men entered *Remanganaguas*; its mission was to carry the coffin to Santiago.

On its way to *Remanganaguas*, this column was attacked three times by troops commanded by General Quintín Bandera. The Spanish chief, Lieutenant Colonel Michelena, had thought that as soon as he departed for San Luis carrying the coffin the *mambises* would start the harassment. And, this was exactly what happened. General Quintín tried to recover the body at all costs but he could not beat the superiority of the Spanish forces that reached Palma Soriano to stop for the night before marching again at dawn. Still, General Quintín Bandera resumed the attacks, since he had also left early with that purpose.

In his book *Dos Ríos; a caballo y con el sol en la frente*, that we have mentioned before, Rolando Rodríguez writes that *"General Bandera and his troops had already attacked the column when the arrival of enemy reinforcements from the rearguard impacted adversely on the situation. After one hour of fight, the tenacious general who had fought in three wars was unable to recover the body...of that man he had met hardly three weeks before, but that with immediate admiration he had called Apostle."*

No doubt it's Martí

In a freight car attached to the train and under the protection of eighty-one Spanish soldiers, Martí's remains were transferred from San Luis to Santiago de Cuba. He was taken to the Santa Ifigenia cemetery and a battalion kept custody of the necropolis to prevent any action by the rebels. Subsequently, General Garrich, the military governor of the town, took the necessary measures for the burial scheduled for 8:00 am on the 27th and decided that Colonel Ximénez de Sandoval should be present at the ceremony. Spanish Captain Enrique Ubieta, who called himself a friend of Martí, wrote a letter to the Mayor of the city to inform him that Generals Garrich and Salcedo, Commander of the First Division of the Army operating in the province, "*acting with the noble sentiments and gallantry that characterize the Spanish gentlemen had determined that the body of Don José Martí be buried in a niche of the Catholic cemetery since they did not perceive him as the rebel who had died fighting the defenders of the national integrity but rather as a human being deserving a Christian burial.*"

And Ubieta added that if the Mayor's Office was unwilling to issue a five-year exemption from payment for the niche, he and the abovementioned officers would provide the necessary funds. There was no need for this since the City Council decided to grant it free for the period of time requested.

Two Cubans, Antonio Bravo Correoso and Joaquín Castillo Duany, asked some friendly Spanish officers to allow them to identify the body; Captain Ubieta accompanied them to the *Santa Ifigenia* cemetery and facilitated the arrangements with the Spanish officer who headed the battalion in charge of protecting the necropolis. The commander gave his permission making no objections and accompanied the group to the coffin. The cadaver of the greatest of all Cubans lay in a rustic wooden box, adjusted with a metal band. Ubieta asked a soldier from the guarding party to raise the lid. He lay on his back, with the mouth open and his hair combed back, decomposed despite the embalmment. The unbuttoned pants let his abdomen show. Castillo Duany said to those present: "It's Martí, no doubt." Other Cubans also recognized the mortal remains and photographer Higinio Martínez took a picture of the body devastated by death. In the picture, the body does not seem to be inside a coffin.

It was time for the interment. Colonel Ximénez de Sandoval asked twice if among those present there was any friend, relative or acquaintance of Martí who wanted to pay the last respects. As no one accepted, the Spanish officer assumed the mission. He only said a few words. He begged those present not to see in Martí an enemy but rather the mortal remains *"of the man whom the political struggles had placed in front of the Spanish soldiers."*

Much has been said of the words pronounced by the Spanish officer that morning in *Santa Ifigenia*, which contradict his communication to General Azcárraga after Martí's burial in *Remanganaguas* where he rejoiced because *"thanks God"* your troops killed in *Dos Ríos "the restless agitator and propagandist Don José Martí."* In the opinion of Rolando Rodríguez, the fact that he was a Mason, like Martí, must have influenced his attitude. He was also very respectful in the letter he addressed to Ubieta in 1911, as he wrote that *"the action at Dos Ríos is a part of my own military history where that genius found a glorious death...his courage and bravery as well as the enthusiasm of his ideals placed him in front of my soldiers and closer to their bayonets than his high position would advise. He should have never exposed his life in such way for he was very important to the Cuban cause and to others who depended on him, and because of his significance and his senior place as the head of state of a people fighting for its independence."*

Destinies

The mortal remains of José Martí remained in niche No. 134 of the south gallery of the necropolis in Santiago until 1907 when they were transferred to a small mausoleum of Ionic style built at the same place where the niche used to be. The mausoleum where his remains are kept until this day was dedicated by midyear 1951.

The Spanish government distributed many decorations among the soldiers and officers who took part in the action of *Dos Ríos*. Colonel Sandoval was rewarded with the María Cristina Cross third class. As time passed, he was promoted to Brigadier General and it is fair to say that he declined the title of Marquis of Dos Ríos because, he said, *"Dos Ríos was not really a victory, since the greatest genius born in the Americas died there."* He passed away in 1924.

General Salcedo felt that due to the death of the Apostle he deserved a promotion to lieutenant general, but Martínez Campos refused to grant it and he left the Army.

The details about the end of Antonio Oliva, the Cuban who boasted of finishing off Martí, are unknown. Some say that he was assaulted with a machete and killed at a café in *San Luis* or a bar in *Palmarito*. His family insisted that he had left for Spain.

As to Martí's death, there are still unanswered questions. But, in the opinion of Rolando Rodríguez, not as many mysteries are left about those hours as some pretend.

February 28 and March 7 and 14, 2010

II

ELECTORAL BROUHAHA

There is a colloquial term in Cuba to describe that which is forcibly imposed on others: '*brava*'. Someone gives somebody else a *brava* when the other is forced to do something he does not like or that goes against his own criteria, that is, when the other person is forced to accept or to act against their own will.

The term *brava* cropped up early in the Cuban electoral vocabulary. Let's say that a Party refused to accept the results of the elections and somehow managed to get away with 'vote stealing' at the polling station leaving the opposing candidate like the bride at the altar without a groom; that party was giving a *brava*. The looser could protest but it was useless; at the end of the day, the best the loosing Party could do was waiting for the next elections.

Don Fernando Ortiz, includes the term '*brava*' in his *Nuevo catauro de cubanismos*[1], with the meaning of 'imposition'. Other authors go further and explain that such term came into use on the Island during the general elections of 1906, four years after the establishment of the Republic. But the term would not go away

[1]*New Box of Cuban Words*

easily since the last *brava* occurred on November 3, 1958, when Carlos Márquez Sterling became the victim of the 'vote stealing' that gave victory to Batista's candidate Andrés Rivero Agüero. In the so-called 'Home of Salazar', at the Columbia Barracks, Batista ordered the 'fixing' of the ballots that secured the victory of the ruling party. That much is said in the book *Batista; últimos días en el poder*[2], authored by José Luis Padrón and Luis Adrián Betancourt, and confirmed with more details by Batista's ex General 'Silito' Tabernilla in his recent book *Palabras esperadas*[3].

Combat Cabinet

In 1906, the Liberal Party was the victim of an electoral *brava* orchestrated by the Moderate Party bent on giving Tomás Estrada Palma one more term in office. Actually, there was nothing moderate about that political party and the so-called Combat Cabinet, established by Don Tomás in his senile obduracy to stay in power, resorted to painful and even bloody actions to secure the president's re-election. All sorts of things happened in those days, from the detention of leaders of the Liberal Party and the removal of Mayors opposed to the government, to the murder of the young Member of Parliament and national leader of liberalism Enrique Villuendas, by the Chief of Police in Cienfuegos.

As of this moment, the procedure was often repeated during the period known as the republican Cuba. In 1916, the Liberals were again the victims of another *brava* when President Menocal and his closest assistants refused to acknowledge the victory of Dr. Alfredo Zayas and went ahead with a 'vote stealing' operation that would ensure their president's re-election.

On the two occasions, the Liberals responded to the *brava* with an armed protest. In 1906, they were the protagonists of the so-called *'August Little War'*. The government was unable to control the protest. President Estrada Palma turned down an

[2] Batista, His Last Days in Power
[3] Long-Expected Words

offer to negotiate with his opponents and instead invoked the Platt Amendment and called for a US military intervention.

The 'vote stealing' in 1916 would lead to an uprising the following year headed by former President José Miguel Gómez. The common people called this revolt *La Chambelona* after a popular song of the time. The fact is that José Miguel Gómez, a chieftain from the area of Sancti Spiritus, had more than a few followers in the budding National Army which managed to bring under control, rather smoothly, the province of Camagüey and the territory of Santiago while José Miguel carried on to the west. It was clear that if he made it to Las Villas, which was then a Liberal stronghold, there would be no force capable of preventing his victorious entrance to Havana. However, a shrewd military chief, an unknown lieutenant, without receiving any orders or asking for them, decided to destroy the Jatibonico Bridge thus changing the course of the insurrection. Soon, José Miguel and his bodyguards were arrested and sent to the Castillo del Príncipe, a prison where they would all spend more than a year.

"We'll be back"

Not every candidate subjected to *bravas* and 'vote stealing' reacted like that. Zayas ate dirt, he did not shoot a shot, but José Miguel fought to defend the votes he had received. Others kept their countenance and philosophically said: *"We'll be back."* This was the laconic comment made by Dr. Ramón Grau San Martín after learning that he had lost to fraud in the 1940 elections.

Grau knew that he was a long shot. He was facing Batista, who from 1933 was the true master of a nation that he controlled from the Columbia Barracks, a man who would do anything to be elected, even use weapons if it came to that. Also the electoral law gave the advantage to the candidate representing a party alliance. Grau's name was written only in the ballot of the Authentic Party whereas the name of Colonel Batista was included in the ballots of the six parties making up the Socialist Democratic Coalition for which he was running. This gave him an edge since he would reap the votes obtained by any of the provincial candidates of the six parties. On the other hand, during the election campaign the members of the Authentic Party were under pressure from the Army while Batista, with the support of the government machinery, proceeded to purchase votes. Still, Grau played down these inconveniences for he thought that the new Constitution soon to be enforced would not be besmirched with an action against the right to vote.

He was wrong. Batista resorted to the use of force to steal the ballot boxes and alter the vote count to claim his own victory, and almost immediately a piece of legislation was issued preventing any legal challenge to the election results.

Nevertheless, Grau proceeded as promised and ran for president again in the 1944 elections. The Constitution of 1940 provided that the President of the Republic must remain out of office for two consecutive four-year terms before he could run again. Thus, Batista could not be re-elected this time, unless he imposed himself by force. The innocuous Carlos Saladrigas running for the government coalition was supposed to ensure the continuation of Batista's ways. Saladrigas would be President and Batista, by now a Major General despite his distance from active duty, would return to Columbia as Chief of the Army and handle the real power. But, such plans failed; 1944 was not 1940, the circumstances had changed and Grau won the elections by a landslide.

The few

It was common for a President who could not immediately run to choose a candidate from his own party to ensure continuity. Grau came up with the concept of the programmatic re-election and chose Carlos Prío as his successor. But, the latter would soon distance from his predecessor. Actually, funny things happened in Cuba at the time. For example, liberal President José Miguel Gómez refused to have another liberal, his own Vice-President Alfredo Zayas, as his successor to the executive position or to *Doña Pilar's Chair* as the highest office was popularly called at the time.

The divisions among liberals, already split up between Zayistas and Miguelistas, (Zayas' and Miguel's loyalists) continued and many of them joined the conservatives in a movement known as Patriotic Convergence, the same that with José Miguel's support gave the victory to General Menocal in 1913.

Come the general elections of 1920 and again José Miguel runs for president with the Liberal Party. Zayas, who never ceased running and who had expected to be the liberal candidate, left the ranks of liberalism and founded the Popular Party with such a trifling membership that the people gave it the nickname of 'The Few'. These were not the few who took him to power. He won with the support of the conservatives, with whom he allied in a National League, and above all with the boost of President Menocal, his former enemy that had given him the *brava* in 1916, and who pledged his support on the condition that Zayas help him to win the election of 1924.

But Zayas decided not to honor this promise and Menocal, already convinced of his betrayal, paid him a visit on No.1Refugio Street, the seat of the nation's executive; *"You have given me the brava,"* Menocal said. And, Zayas, without mentioning the 'vote stealing' that had left him out of the game in 1916, responded: *"And, it hurts, right?"*

In fact, Zayas had decided to pave the way to power for the liberal Gerardo Machado. He was persuaded to do so by the five million *pesos*[4] that Faya Gutiérrez, the wealthiest man in Cuba at the time, offered him. He didn't think it twice. For his phlegmatic and parsimonious ways, Zayas was nicknamed *El Chino,* but he was also nicknamed *El Pesetero* (the money-grubber).

By this time, Machado had won the Liberal Party's Convention over Colonel Carlos Mendieta, the liberals' natural chieftain. The truth is he had bought the convention before buying its chairman.

Machado also gave a *brava* in his own way when with the backing of the three parties represented in Congress he managed to amend the Constitution of 1901 to remain six more years in

[4] *Peso*, one Cuban peso equaled one US dollar from 1902 until the 1960s.

office, without a vicepresident, and run as the only candidate in the elections of November 1, 1928. That alliance of the Liberal Party –in office— with the opposition parties –the Conservative and the Popular parties— was known as cooperativism. Its architect was Senator Wilfredo Fernández, the same incorrigible sycophant who whispered in the dictator's ear: *"Gerardo, your millennium has begun!"*

Perhaps Machado believed him. The fact is that after this President was ousted on August 12, 1933, the Island never again had a liberal executive. Mendieta, a *de facto* President, was a member of the Nationalist Union, and Miguel Mariano Gómez, despite his origins, came to power as a member of the Republican Action Party, albeit with the support of liberals and nationalists, and above all with the support of Fulgencio Batista, who imposed him and then toppled him seven months later. It was not until 1948 that a liberal candidate ran for President. This was Ricardo Núñez Portuondo, an outstanding surgeon whom the students expelled from his position as university professor because of his association with Machado's actions and for being the dictator's personal doctor. He would have made it possible for Machado's loyalists to return to power after fifteen years.

During his first government, Grau used legislative decree No. 19 of September 1933 to break up the three political organizations that supported Machado, and subsequently prevented their reorganization. Then, journalist Ramón Vasconcelos launched an intensive press campaign which rehabilitated the Liberal Party. But, the tyranny had given liberalism the evil eye and it would never again be what it had once been in Cuba.

April 4, 2010

THE LIVES OF CUBAN PRESIDENTS

Did you know that the former province of Las Villas, in the center of the Island, was the area that contributed the highest number of Presidents to the Republic of Cuba from 1902 to 1959? Did you know that no one from the province of Camagüey ever reached the highest office and that the three who did were born abroad? Did you know that six Presidents of Cuba were lawyers and two were physicians, two others were engineers and one was a Bachelor in Arts? Did you know that those of most humble origins were the ones who amassed the largest fortunes while in office?

I will next deal with these and other stories related to the heads of state prior to 1959.

Short and very short terms in office

We had in Cuba constitutional presidents and *de facto* presidents, and we also had those who were only provisional heads the state. Among the first, Carlos Prío could not serve his four-year term, for which he was elected in 1948, because Batista dealt him a coup d'état on March 1952. Miguel Mariano Gómez could not complete his term because he was impeached by the Senate seven months after his inauguration in 1936, tried in court and dismissed from office. On the other hand, Estrada Palma, García Menocal and Gerardo Machado each forced their re-election with terrible consequences: Estrada Palma was obligated to resign; Menocal clung to power until the end but in so doing he gave rise to the revolt known as *La Chambelona*; and, Machado was overthrown by a revolution.

Among the provisional heads of government, Carlos Manuel de Céspedes was in office for twenty three days; Grau San Martín's first term (1933-34) lasted a little over one-hundred days and his replacement, Carlos Hevia, was President from January 14 through 18, 1934, followed by Carlos Mendieta who stayed in office from January 18, 1934 to December 12 the next year when he stepped down to make space for José Agripino Barnet who remained in office until May 20, 1936. The next president, under Batista's protection, was Andrés Domingo y Morales del Castillo from August 1954 to February 1955. President Federico Laredo Bru took office following Miguel Mariano's removal from that position, thus he did not serve a full term.

Some presidents served even shorter terms in office. This was the case of General Alberto Herrera and journalist Manuel Márquez Sterling. The former had replaced Machado on August 11, 1933 but he could hardly take a liking to that office because following instructions from the US embassy he transferred it to Céspedes the next day. But Márquez Sterling lasted less. He took the oath of office in a room at the Hotel Nacional de Cuba, under a candle light, at six o'clock in the morning of January 18, 1934 and relinquished it at noon that same day. As provided by the Constitution, the Republic, headless due to Hevia's resignation, would be led by its Secretary of State, Don Manuel, until Mendieta assumed office on orders of then Colonel Batista.

Origin and background

Las Villas was the birth province of José Miguel Gómez and his son Miguel Mariano (Sancti Spiritus), of Machado (Santa Clara), Herrera and Mendieta (San Antonio de las Vueltas), and of Laredo Bru (Remedios). Oddly enough, Manuel Urrutia Lleó (Remedios) and Osvaldo Dorticós Torrado (Cienfuegos), both of them lawyers, were also born in Las Villas province, albeit they have not been included in the list because they were both presidents after 1959. Dorticós was the last one to hold that position that ceased to exist upon the approval of the Constitution of 1976, which created the position of President of the State Council.

On the other hand, Matanzas was the birth province of Menocal (Jagüey Grande), while Grau (La Palma) and Prío (Bahía Honda) were born in Pinar del Río. Then, Hevia and Alfredo Zayas were born in Havana, the latter in the neighborhood of El Cerro. Oriente was the birthplace of Estrada Palma (Bayamo), Batista (Banes) and Andrés Domingo (Santiago de Cuba), while Céspedes was born in New York, Márquez Sterling in Lima and Barnet in Barcelona.

Of these seventeen personalities –let's not forget that Grau and Batista were in office on two different occasions— six were lawyers: Zayas, Céspedes, Miguel Mariano, Andrés Domingo, Laredo Bru and Prío Socarrás. Menocal and Hevia were both engineers graduated in the United States, the former in Cornell University and the latter in Annapolis. Estrada Palma graduated in Arts in Havana and went on to study Law in Spain but he quit at the death of his father and returned to Cuba to take over the family businesses which would be confiscated during the War of Independence [also known as The Ten Years War]. Grau and Mendieta were physicians; the former was an excellent clinician and a specialist in tuberculosis as well as a Physiology Professor at the Havana University. When he took office for the second time, in 1944, he asked for an audit which showed that his personal fortune amounted to seventy two thousand pesos; then, before abandoning his position, in 1948, he requested another audit proving his personal assets had decreased to twenty two thousand pesos. He said that being away from medical practice for four years had impoverished him.

José Miguel Gómez was a senior high school graduate who did not pursue university studies because he enlisted with the Ejército Libertador to fight in the War of Independence. He fought in the three wars launched against Spain. Machado and Batista failed to complete grammar school. Herrera had fought in the war. According to their biographies, Barnet and Sterling did not pursue higher studies. The former spent his entire life working abroad as a diplomat for the Republic and the latter was a journalist by the age of fifteen; in fact, he is considered one of the great Cuban journalists of all times.

From the abovementioned personalities, Barnet was the oldest at the time he took office (71) and Carlos Hevia (34) was the youngest. Batista took on this position for the first time at the age of 39 and forced his way to it at 51. Estrada Palma became President at the age of 70, Céspedes and Márquez Sterling at 62, Zayas at 60 and Mendieta and Laredo Bru at 61. Others were in their fifties when they assumed the highest office, like Machado (54) and José Miguel (51). Grau was 51 at the time of his first term and 62 the second time around. Menocal and Miguel Mariano were 47, Prío 45, Urrutia 58 and Dorticós 40.

Nicknames, marriages and other trivia

Unlike José Miguel, Miguel Mariano, Grau, Mendieta...who were born to rich families, Machado was a man of humble origins and at a certain point in his life he was even a farm worker. Batista joined the army, something poor people often did, and it is known that Prío used to wear darned trousers to the university... the three would grow rich through stealing from the public coffers.

Machado's nickname was *El Mocho*, the One-Arm, because he lost the forefinger in his left hand working as a butcher in his hometown; José Miguel was nicknamed *El Tiburón*, the Shark, because of the perks he got from his job; and Menocal was called *El Mayoral*, the Foreman, for he had been a manager at the Chaparra sugar mill owned by an American company. Zayas was known as *El Pesetero*, the Money-grubber, since he accepted low perks provided they never ceased falling in his pockets. At the last minute, he agreed with Machado to help him get the presidency in exchange for the moderate figure of $5 million pesos that he would receive in installments from the incomes produced by the National Lottery. By the way, in 1913 Zayas accepted a request to write a *History of Cuba* and the government paid him up to his death a monthly allowance of 500 pesos for that assignment, although he never wrote a single line.

But, going back to nicknames, Grau was called *El Viejo*, the Old Man, due to his age, while for his convoluted and repetitious rhetoric he was also nicknamed *El Divino Galimatías*, the Divine Gibberish; Mendieta was called *El Solitario*, the Loner from Cunagua; and Batista, craving to be popular –which he never was— must have enjoyed the nickname of *El Guajirito de Banes*, the Little Peasant from Banes.

These seventeen presidents were married, all but Grau, a confirmed bachelor, whose platonic love and exchange of letters with an American nurse extended from 1932 through 1965. Two presidents married foreign women: Céspedes married Laura Bertini, an Italian; and Estrada Palma married Genoveva Guardiola, a Honduran President's daughter, whom he met when he was postmaster in that country.

Among First Ladies, the most beautiful was undoubtedly Mary Tarrero, married to Carlos Prío; América Arias, known as Doña América, married José Miguel and Miguel Mariano was their son; she was a widely respected lady and an experienced messenger of the Ejército Libertador during the War of Independence. Mariana Seba de Menocal bought in Paris such necklaces as Victoria Eugenia, wife of Alfonso 13th, King of Spain, could not afford; the most humble was Genoveva Guardiola who sat at the balcony of the Palace to mend her husband's socks and who only had three dresses. Estrada Palma was the stingiest of all Cuban Presidents while Menocal was the most spendthrift of them all. In 1969, the British press claimed that Batista was the wealthiest man in Spain whereas in Miami, Prío solemnly stated that he was poor, not for having lost his fortune but because he had transferred every penny to his wife. In Havana, Grau spent the rest of his life enjoying a 500 pesos monthly pension assigned to him by the Revolutionary Government.

Márquez Sterling passed away in Washington in 1934, during a diplomatic mission and Machado in Miami, in 1939. In the 1940s, the Congress of the Republic decided that Machado's remains could never be brought to Cuba. Others died in exile, also in the United States: Carlos Hevia and Carlos Prío. The latter took his life in 1977. Mendieta died in Havana in 1960 and so did Grau in 1969. Batista died in Spain in 1973 and Urrutia in the United States. The others died in Cuba before the triumph of the Revolution. Mendieta's passion for fine game roosters was such that one breed of such animals was named after him.

April 11, 2004

LIFE AFTER THE PRESIDENCY

A young professor from Las Villas Central University who has kept in touch from his days as a student asked me to write about the Cuban Presidents. He is not interested in their lives in office but in what became of them after that, and I'll oblige but avoiding, as much as I can, to assess the results of their work and their efforts to win the first office.

We must say first that some like Tomás Estrada Palma, Mario García Menocal and Gerardo Machado served two terms but only Menocal completed the second one. Although the Constitution of 1901 permitted one re-election, Estrada Palma's continuation in office was opposed by the liberals headed by José Miguel Gómez opening the way to the so-called '*August Little War*' of 1906. In 1917, in order to stay in office, Menocal gave a *brava* to Alfredo Zayas that motivated the liberal revolt called *La Chambelona*. Machado's re-election was opposed by the entire people that would finally overthrow him in 1933.

The Constitution of 1940 removed the right to re-election and established that a head of state had to wait a minimum of eight years to be re-elected. Still, some would give it a try, like Grau San Martín, who failed and then started talking about 'programmatic re-election' in favor of another member of the Authentic Party, in this case Carlos Prío.

The phlegmatic Zayas also nicknamed *El Chino,* the Chinese, for his countenance, wanted to do the same in 1924. He had spent his life running for office. In 1908, José Miguel Gómez won the nomination and Zayas had to accept being number two in the ticket. Four years later he ran against Menocal and lost; he had to endure the *brava* in order to get the office in 1921 with the support of no other than Menocal himself. To that end, he struck a pact with the ex-foreman of the Chaparra sugar mill to whom he would hand down the presidency in 1925, but when the time came to deliver he betrayed Menocal and sold the highest office to Machado for five million pesos.

Only two Cuban politicians were heads of state twice. Grau was a *de facto* President from 1933 to 1934 and a constitutional President from 1944 to 1948. Batista was a constitutional President between 1940 and 1944 and then returned to the top office through a coup d'état he dealt on March 10, 1952. But he could not take the title of President because Prío had left the country but not resigned the position, therefore, Batista assumed the title of Prime Minister. In 1953, he called for elections, as the sole candidate, and seized the presidency.

A curiosity about politics in Cuba is that the name of Carlos carries a negative aura. It brings bad luck; it's like losing your rabbit's foot. No one with that name ever completed his term in office and they all had to run away from the Presidential Palace at full speed. This happened to Carlos Manuel de Céspedes, a son of The Father of the Homeland; Carlos Hevia, Carlos Mendieta and Carlos Prío. Others with identical names never made it; this was the case of Carlos M. de la Cruz in 1936; Carlos Saladrigas in 1944; Carlos Márquez Sterling in 1958; and, Carlos M. Piedra y Piedra who, after Batista left, considered himself a President, signed decrees and called for harmony and concord until the Supreme Court of Justice brought him back to reality with the information delivered to him at noon of January 1, 1959, that it would not take his oath. This is the President who never was.

Proud and stubborn

Estrada Palma stayed at the Palace four days after his resignation. He wanted to settle in the province of Matanzas. Actually, acting American Governor George Taft offered one of his country's battleships for the journey but Don Tomás declined the offer. He and his family boarded a tugboat at the Caballería dock and left for the town of Regla where they took a train to the city of Matanzas located in the Yumurí Valley. There, General Pedro Betancourt provided accommodation. With his entire fortune amounting to one thousand pesos, he settled with modesty, but as he wanted to play the role of ex President his savings diminished by the day. Despite his compromised financial situation, he returned a gold watch he never wore presented to him by the Speyer Bank of New York after an agreement reached on a 35 million dollars loan to pay the Ejército Libertador.

Former President Tomás Estrada Palma spent several months in Matanzas until he decided to settle down at *La Punta*, a farm near Bayamo inherited from his family. The once prosperous farm was in ruins after forty years of abandonment, most of these years foreclosed by the Spanish government, and occupied by farmers who had divided the land into lots to exploit it as the rightful owners. The former President inhabited a wooden house with thatched roof until he managed to build a small house with Arab-tiles roofing on a hilltop. He wanted to make the land produce and breed cattle, but to do that he first had to sell his property in Central Valley, New York. He did it but then decided against investing all of the money and saved two thousand pesos for contingencies.

Estrada Palma's situation was really distressing. A man who had always been a teacher did not do well as a cattle breeder. Those were challenging times for the country and he had to sell his cattle at low prices and in installments which were not always paid. His two sons helped him to tend to the farm while the two daughters helped their mother with the house chores. The publisher of *The New York Herald* offered to raise funds for him in the United States and somebody else volunteered to obtain from Governor Charles Magoon a more comfortable destination for the ex President. Someone else wanted to have a whip-round in Cuba among the ex President rich friends. But, Don Tomás was proud and stubborn, and he refused all assistance. He said that he would take nothing from the officials involved in the intervention; nothing, he insisted. As to friends, he admitted to have no wealthy friends. The truth is he had no friends at all.

He pledged to never again take part in public life. He would not speak about it or allow anyone to discuss politics in his presence. However, he made no effort at concealing his annoyance upon learning of the American decision to return the government to the Cubans. The case of Estrada Palma was really contradictory. It would be unfair to say that he was not an enemy of Spain, but he never thought Cubans had the capacity to rule themselves. He thought that he was the only leader capable of directing the destinies of the Island. This is why he favored a policy of dependence instead of a sovereign republic, annexation or at least endless occupation of the country by the United States; and these criteria he held until his death.

By 1908, Don Tomás, then 73 years old, was very ill and weak. He was taken to Manzanillo and later to Santiago de Cuba, to the residence of Francisco Antúnez, in No. 17 Segarra Street, where he was accommodated at the coach house. The doctors managed to save the ex President from his serious medical condition but there was nothing they could do to save him from his depression. He seldom left his bed and pneumonia struck. He passed away on November 4. It was his expressed wish to be buried in the Santa Ifigenia cemetery, near the tomb of José Martí who admired him and loved him so much.

Doña Pilar's chair

It is said that Major General José Miguel Gómez never gave a thought to re-election while he was President. The best about him is that he was not intoxicated with the nectar of power. He chaired an election that his party lost. The local aristocracy, the major sugar interests and the bourgeoisie never concealed their apprehension over the ascent of the masses that they pejoratively called *'la chancleta'* (the scum) during José Miguel's administration. The political class felt that this peasant from Sancti Spiritus, who pretended not to see what was going on and behaved too openhanded with the masses, had to be replaced with a right-wing man known as an energetic organizer: General Menocal.

But, the fact is that since José Miguel left office on May 20, 1913, he did nothing else but trying to get back to the Palace. His inauguration as President had taken place on January 28, 1909. It was then that Doña Pilar Samorano, owner of the Telégrafo Hotel where the politician had set up his campaign headquarters, presented him with a chair he would use during his term in office. As of this moment, it was said that the Cuban Presidents sat on *Doña Pilar's Chair*, even after the chair was no longer used.

In 1917, José Miguel took arms against Menocal and victory seemed to be within his reach as the liberals brought the territories of Camagüey and Santiago the Cuba city under control. It was said at the moment that if José Miguel and his troops entered Las

Villas, an area dominated by the liberals, nobody would be able to stop the progress of his triumphant march on Havana. But the chieftain lost too much time –he even danced to the tune of *La Chambelona* at the Majagua Park— and the army moved faster and more efficiently than its opponents while President Menocal received the US support: Washington would not recognize any government resulting from the insurrection. Thus, José Miguel was arrested in Caicaje, along with his son Miguel Mariano and their bodyguards, and taken to the Castillo del Príncipe prison. During his eleven-month incarceration, the former President was cheered up by María Calvo Nodarse, a woman still remembered today by her nickname of *La Macorina*. She was his intimate friend from better times and her loyalty to him never faltered, not even in those dark days.

José Miguel and his loyalists had the benefit of an amnesty. He ran for President again in 1920 but lost to Zayas. Then, disappointed in Cuban political life he traveled to the United States where he died of pneumonia on July 13, 1921, at the Plaza Hotel in New York. His funeral ceremony was held at the Saint Patrick Cathedral, and the US Army accorded him the honors befitting his rank of Major General and ex President.

His remains arrived in Havana in a brass coffin. Those waiting on the quayside wanted to carry his coffin on their shoulders and his son Miguel Mariano had to calm down the crowd to preserve order. His wake was held in his house at Prado and Trocadero streets. So many wreaths were received that they had to be displayed on the sidewalk. His funeral was one of the largest demonstrations of mourning remembered in Havana.

Like a maharajah

Menocal left the Palace on May 20, 1921 and went straight to the port to take a ship to Europe. The journalist Loló de la Torriente, who saw him then for the first time, remembers that there were lots of people at the Harbormaster's to see him off. Loló wrote: *"Standing up in an open car Menocal waved his hand to the people. He was neither tall nor hefty. His main attraction was his enigmatic mysterious face with a sparse beard and gleaming eyes. After eight years of imposition, he was leaving the Republic exhausted and helpless but he had saved his fortunes and passed on power. Now, he was ready to arouse in Paris the admiration and excitement of the French people already used to generous and lavish tycoons. In this sense, the Cuban General and former President of an agricultural republic would emulate the most amazing munificence of the great maharajahs."*

But Menocal would return to Cuba and embark on the promotion of sugar companies like his own Santa María sugar mill. Of course, he also remained active in politics, and in the 1924 general elections he ran as a conservative only to be defeated by General Machado. Then, when the construction of the Central Highway started he was appointed Inspector General of the works, a position he occupied until 1930, when he made some statements diametrically opposed to Machado's tyranny.

He revolted against Machado in August 1931 but was arrested a few days later and sent to La Cabaña military prison, and subsequently to the Model Prison in Isla de Pinos. After his release from jail, he again became the target of persecution and was forced into exile. When Machado was ousted he returned to the country and became involved in national politics. Again, he ran for President and was defeated; this time by Miguel Mariano Gómez, the son of his old nemesis.

He led the opposition to Colonel Batista's military regime but struck an agreement with him during the Constitutive Assembly of 1940 and immediately afterwards launched the reorganization of the dispersed conservatives into one party. He was working on this when death caught up with him on September 8, 1941. He passed away in the house located in Línea and G streets, which is today Casa de las Américas' periodicals library. His wake was held at the Capitolio.

Zayas: smart and shrewd

What kind of life did the Cuban Presidents lead after leaving office? We have talked about Estrada Palma, José Miguel Gómez and Mario García Menocal. We shall continue now with those who followed them up until Miguel Mariano.

In 1921, attorney Alfredo Zayas Alfonso replaced Menocal in office thanks to his endless patience. His government operated in a permanent state of crisis that he was able to overcome because he was smart and shrewd. He had to put up a balancing act to avoid being swept away by the increasingly high wave of popular discontent. He suppressed the insurrection of the Movement of Veterans and Patriots without a shot; of course, he visited the enemies' camp carrying a checkbook in his pocket. He had the insight of having a statue built in his honor when he was still alive that he unveiled himself before leaving office.

He then retired to private life and died in his Vedado house on April 11, 1934. He never wrote the *History of Cuba* for which the republic had paid him five hundred pesos a month for 21 years. Eventually though, his widow María Jaén, donated to the National Archive valuable documents that the ex President had accumulated as an official historian.

Not a minute earlier

On August 11, 1933, General Gerardo Machado appealed to the Congress of the republic for a license and the following day he took a plane to Nassau. His luggage was rather strange: eight small but heavy canvas bags where he carried his money, in gold. Well, the money he could take with him because he had to leave a lot behind in Cuba. The safety box that his wife Elvira had in a bank in Havana was sealed and confiscated on orders of President Grau: it contained jewelry and one million pesos in cash.

"This is a holdup!" the ex President remarked when he heard the news. He then proceeded to bribe a commission of incorruptible gentlemen with one-hundred and fifty thousand pesos to recover half a million he still kept in another bank under his own name. While his huge fortune was discussed in the Cuban press, Machado –just like Batista would do later—didn't stop claiming poverty. Once he received a closed envelope and

ordered it open. Inside, there was one cent and a note that read: *"Since you're so poor, please accept our modest aid."*

Machado would not stay long in Nassau. By early September, he was in Toronto, Canada, from where he traveled on to the United States where many of his loyalists had already found sanctuary. The Cuban government requested their extradition, and although Washington did not return them in the end, at the beginning it seemed that a favorable response was forthcoming and so the dossiers were prepared for the extradition of Machado and ex General Alberto Herrera, the Army Chief from 1922 to 1933, and Machado's intended replacement in the highest office.

A bunch of police agents showed up at Machado's residence in New York to carry out his detention, but the former dictator persuaded them that the person they were looking for was not home and escaped right under their noses, as a vulgar petty thief. He ended up at the harbor where he rented a little boat that took him to Santo Domingo under Trujillo's protection.

Orestes Ferrara, who had been his ambassador to Washington and later his Secretary of State, and who had close connections with large US monopolies the likes of ITT, insisted that Machado appear in court for an immigration trial. Ferrara, in a sudden attack of anti-imperialism, wanted to use the legal process to denounce American interference in the internal affairs of Cuba. Machado disagreed and said: *"I don't speak English, I don't know anything about laws, I'm not an orator and I'm not familiar with these international issues."*

During his stay in Cuba, the tyrant had repeatedly claimed that he would not abandon the presidency until noon May 20, 1935, and *"Not a minute earlier."* Accidentally, that day caught up with him in Paris. Early in the morning he made statements to the press. The journalists were interested in his assessment of the situation in Cuba but Machado refused to answer. He had been in exile for almost two years but it was not noon yet and he considered himself President of the Republic of Cuba.

He passed away in Miami on March 29, 1939, under the knife. His personal physician, Dr. Ricardo Núñez Portuondo was operating on him.

A fleeting moment

General Herrera, who replaced Machado, could not get a taste of the presidency. He was a bargaining chip but the military didn't want him. He spent less than 24 hours in the highest office, barely enough time to appoint Carlos Manuel de Céspedes Secretary of State, turning Céspedes into his replacement, in accordance with the Constitutional amendment of 1928 abolishing the position of vicepresident. Once out of office, he hid in the Hotel Nacional and with the support of the US Ambassador managed to leave the country by boat, alongside his family. In the United States, he accepted an immigration trial and won. A few years later, he returned to Cuba and passed away in Havana in 1954.

Carlos Manuel de Céspedes occupied the highest office for only twenty-three days. On September 4, 1933, he was ousted by a military coup d'état and left the Palace but did not submit his resignation. An envoy of the rebel officers, who had entrenched at the Hotel Nacional to put up a fight against Grau's government, went looking for him in his house on M and 23rd streets. He was asked to take on the presidency in that hotel and to issue his decrees by radio. It was all a maneuver by Horacio Ferrer, an ophthalmologist, to give the impression that there were two governments in Cuba and pressure Washington into a military intervention on the Island. Carlos Manuel, who decided not to play along with them, said: *"I will not be the cause of bloodshed or of a foreign intervention in Cuba."*

By January 1924, President Carlos Mendieta appointed Céspedes ambassador to Madrid and that same year he assumed Cuba's representation to the Special Session of the League of Nations meeting in Geneva. In 1935, he was back in Havana ready to run for the presidency as the candidate of a weak Centrist Party. In view of his limited popular support, he gave up his intent and returned to diplomatic life. On May 1937, he resigned his ambassadorship but was appointed, with the same title, a technical advisor to the Secretary of State and shortly after he became a judge in the Arbitration Court.

He was a member of the Academy of History and published some interesting books like the biographies of his father and uncle, Major General Manuel de Quesada. He left unpublished a book he wrote on his fleeting moment at the presidency. Céspedes passed away in Havana on March 27, 1939.

Very short terms in office

I should now refer to Ramón Grau San Martín, whose first term as President lasted from September 1933 to January 1934, at which time Grau said, *"We are leaving, but we'll be back."* And he did return to office in 1944. But, I'll go into that later.

Grau's government was followed by a brief stint in office of engineer Carlos Hevia –January 14 to 18, 1934. Colonel Batista, who had forced Grau's resignation, didn't want Hevia either. The graduate of Annapolis resigned and abandoned the executive mansion before his replacement came in. The Republic was left without a leader. It was necessary to take Manuel Márquez Sterling out of bed as he slept like a log at the Hotel Nacional, so that in his capacity as Secretary of State he accepted the highest office. At this moment, there was a blackout in Havana and in room 412 of the hotel Don Manuel, one of the great Cuban journalists of all times, took the oath under a candle light and went back to sleep. His was the shortest term of any President in Cuba; it lasted only six hours, from six in the morning to twelve noon of January 18, barely the time required to pass the position on to Carlos Mendieta, who had Batista's blessing. Márquez Sterling died during an asthma episode in Washington, where he was an ambassador, a few months after his brief tenure as President.

Hevia was one of the founders of the Authentic Party. He left Cuba due to police persecution. In the days of World War II, his former persecutor –and now President— Batista assigned him the organization and leadership of the Price Regulation and Supplies Bureau (ORPA). He left the ORPA when he realized that his honest efforts could not prevent speculation and black marketing, and he was unwilling to compromise. Thus, he returned to private life. He became CEO of the Modelo (Hatuey) brewery until Carlos Prío appointed him minister of State in 1948. Later on, his honesty was again put to the test as chairman of the Promotion Commission and Secretary of Public Works, and he acquitted himself gracefully.

Hevia should have run in the general elections of June 1, 1952, as a presidential candidate for a coalition made up by Authentics, Republicans, Liberals and Democrats, in addition to the Cuban Identity Party headed by ex President Grau.

But Batista prevented the celebration of these elections by dealing a coup d'état, and Hevia left the country again. He returned in 1959 and stayed for a short time. In Miami, he became a member of counterrevolutionary groups.

General Menocal made trouble for Colonel Mendieta when he said that as the leader of the Nationalist Party, Mendieta was openly biased in favor of that political organization and unable to ensure the transparency of the elections, if he was asked to chair them. Batista listened to Menocal's complaint and Mendieta resigned, or was forced to, on December 11, 1935, and relinquished power the following day to his successor, José Agripino Barnet y Vianajeras.

As a leader of the opposition to Grau's government, Colonel Mendieta was pushed by Batista to take on the presidency. He had to face tough calls during his term in office. In June 1934, he was the target of an assassination attempt in the town of Casa Blanca but escaped with a light injury. It was during his government that a large strike was convened in March 1935; and Antonio Guiteras' death also happened under his watch.

On October 4, 1940, Batista signed up Mendieta as his delegate to the Institute for Sugar Stabilization, a position he resigned on December 15, 1943. He then tried to restructure the Nationalist Union Party but failed and chose to move on to private life. His great passions were cockfighting and breeding roosters. He passed away in 1959, at his house on 12 and 3rd streets in Miramar.

José Agripino Barnet was an Assistant Secretary of State in Grau's government and a Secretary of State under Mendieta.

Of all Cuban Presidents, he was the oldest, 61 years old, at the time of his access to that position. He was also one of the three presidents born outside Cuba, along with Céspedes and Márquez Sterling. Barnet, who was a diplomat his entire life, spent his six months at the Palace in an endless succession of banquettes, cocktails and receptions. After leaving the highest office, on May 20, 1936, he went on to live modestly in apartment 44 at the Chibás building, on 25 and G streets, in the Vedado area.

On October 11 that same year, his successor, President Miguel Mariano Gómez, appointed him technical adviser to the Secretary of State with the rank of ambassador, a job he kept until his death on September 19, 1945. During the following governments his wife, Marcela Cleard, would undertake the commendable effort of imposing etiquette at the Palace.

Dismissed from office

Miguel Mariano was President for seven months. His differences with Colonel Batista surfaced early and the Senate, acting as a Court of Justice, dismissed him. He traveled overseas and returned in 1939 when he was granted a credential to be a delegate to the Assembly in charge of drafting the Constitution of 1940. Then, he ran for Mayor of Havana and lost to Raúl Menocal, the son of his father's adversary. He would soon take the country by surprise with the announcement of his retirement from political life when he was still in his prime as a politician. He agreed to chair the Association of Cattle Breeders that he soon renounced for he refused to play along with the speculation practiced by some members during World War II. He then fell seriously ill and traveled to the United States seeking for a cure. But it was useless. He died in Havana, at his house on Línea and L streets on October 26, 1950.

That same year, Congress passed a legislation vindicating the dismissed head of state. President Prío invited the family of the deceased and in a solemn ceremony he presented Josefina Diago, Gómez's widow, with a scroll reproducing the legislation.

A bronze plaque, describing his vindication by Congress, was placed at Miguel Mariano's tomb.

A fortuitous president

Laredo Bru was a fortuitous President and the last combatant of the Ejército Libertador to have lived in the Palace. He won the vice-presidency of the Republic in 1936 with the ticket of the Tripartite Alliance that took Miguel Mariano Gómez to the highest office. Due to pressures from Army Chief Colonel Batista, the House of Representatives accused President Miguel Mariano before the Senate of restricting the free operation of that legislative body. The Senate accepted the denunciation and, acting as a Court of Justice under the Chief Magistrate of the Supreme Court, tried and dismissed the President from office on December 24, 1936. Then, Laredo Bru became President until October 10, 1940, albeit the real power remained all along in the Columbia Barracks. After leaving his responsibility, Laredo Bru returned to private life but his successor, President Batista, brought him back as Secretary of Justice, a position he held until the end of Batista's term on October 10, 1944. He then retired for good. On July 7, 1946, he died unexpectedly at his house on I and 21 streets, in Vedado. With the family savings his widow, Leonor Montes, had an apartment building constructed on 23rd and N streets, at a time when La Rampa was emerging as the most popular and coveted avenue in Havana.

...A long winter

In the general elections of June 1, 1944, rather than *for* Grau San Martín the Cuban people voted *against* Batista, represented by his candidate Carlos Saladrigas who would have certainly reinstated him at the head of the army. During the general elections of 1940, Colonel Batista had managed to trick his adversary, and he intended to do likewise this time over but he had second thoughts and eventually relinquished power and left the country. To his closest staffers he said: *"We must prepare for a long winter."*

Then, ex President Batista went on to turn his personal life around. He divorced Elisa Godínez, whom he had met at Wajay where she was a washerwoman and he was a private guard in the farm of President Zayas; they had three children. Subsequently, he married Martha Fernández with whom he had a relationship while still married. No one knows how this poor girl, Martha, from the area of Buenavista in Marianao, got involved with the President. It is said that they met for the first time when the presidential car struck her as she was riding a bicycle. Batista covered the girl's hospital bill, visited her and fell in love with her. This is certainly a good story, but it's not true.

In his book *Mis relaciones con el General Batista*[5], Martha's brother does not even mention the beginning of the relationship. Some say that it was Andrés Domingo y Morales del Castillo, a straw man and intimate of the dictator, who introduced them. Another version relates that Martha was one of the girls around Galitzian poet and writer Mary Morandeyra who lived in Havana for some time. The author of *Plenilunios* and *El hombre visto a través del corazón de una mujer* introduced Martha to some powerful figures, Batista included, and being much younger than him and very pretty she picked him up. Batista's divorce from Elisa forced him to give her half of his declared fortune of 22 million pesos.

The former President traveled extensively through Latin America and wrote (or somebody did for him) a book with his impressions of that trip. For a short time he settled in Mexico and New York, and later in Florida at his property in Daytona Beach. He was eager to return to power and so, one way or another, he was behind every conspiracy against Grau. In 1948, a coalition of Liberals and Democrats managed to have him elected *in absentia* a Senator for Las Villas province, and President Prío offered him all guarantees for his return to the country; he even offered Batista the possibility to chose the military for his security detail, the same with whom he would start plotting. The long winter was almost over now and he organized Unitary Action, a small political party

[5] *My Relations with General Batista*

designed to take him to the general elections of June 1952. These elections would not take place; a few weeks before Election Day Batista dealt a coup d'état and took over the Republic.

His second trip to the Presidential Palace left Batista a very rich man. In 1958, he was either the owner or one of the shareholders of nine sugar mills, one bank, three airlines, several radio stations, one TV channel, newspapers, magazines, printing shops, a tourist resort, several construction and ground transportation companies as well as numerous buildings, among other interests. It has not been possible to determine exactly how much money he took out of Cuba, but in 1969 he was considered the wealthiest man in Spain.

It is not true, as some would have us believe, that he was not involved with the counterrevolution. As a matter of fact, as early as January1959 he organized and paid for a thwarted attempt on the life of the leader of the Revolution; the first one in a long list of over six hundred of them. He lived in the Dominican Republic until Washington put pressure on the Brazilian foreign ministry to find him accommodation in Portugal. No one wanted him, and so the government of Lisbon confined him to the Madeiras Islands until many years later when he was given access to the rest of the country.

While in Spain, the members of the security detail that he had taken from Cuba asked him for a pay raise. Martha refused to oblige and pressured Batista to fire them and hire new bodyguards, despite the fact that some had been with him before the coup d'état of March 10, 1952, and even entered Columbia with him. Only Colonel Hernández Volta, his lifelong assistant remained with him. Sometimes he sent for some of his old pals who joined him in remembering the good old times, but they were soon returned to Miami. Washington never allowed Batista again into the US territory although he applied for a visa several times and even made a juicy contribution to Nixon's presidential campaign.

He published some books, like *Respuesta*[6], telling his side of the story about his days as President and the insurrection that

[6] *Response*

ousted him, and left unpublished his autobiography and at least two novels. He died in Marbella, Spain, on August 6, 1973, and was buried in Madrid.

New winds

Now, we shall go back to January 16, 1934, two days after Batista forced the resignation of Grau who left the Island and went to Mexico. President Grau's demise marked the end of the so-called 'one-hundred day's government', that actually lasted one-hundred and twenty-seven days. More than a hundred thousand people saw him off at the Havana harbor. It was the first time in our history that a Cuban President challenged Washington, –which never recognized him— respected the public coffers, and attended to usually neglected popular demands. And with this aura he would return to power.

On February 8, 1934, at the headquarters of the *Alma Mater* magazine, his followers headed by Félix Lancís organize the Authentic Party. Grau returns to Cuba but there is no guarantee that his life will be respected and the party orders him to leave the country again. He goes back to Mexico. In Panama, he lectures about the revolutionary process of 1930. He then settles in Miami until Batista agrees to one of the main demands raised by the opposition, that is, to convene a Constitutive Assembly. Grau, who wins his delegate credential in five of the six provinces, is elected to chair the convention in charge of drafting the Constitution of 1940, a position he renounces when the Batista-Menocal Pact leads to the dismantling of the opposition majority that supports him.

After leaving the highest office on October 10, 1948, Grau carried on with his political life. It was not long before he broke with his successor and disciple Carlos Prío, for he was bent on a 'new winds' kind of politics. He abandoned the Authentic Party and organized the Cuban Identity Party, which he would later disband, and registered the Authentic Party as his own. He was the only personality who accepted to run for President in the 1954 elections convened by Batista with the intention of legitimizing the regime he had established through the coup d'état of

March 10, 1952. However, the absence of guarantees forced him to back off on the eve of Election Day. Still, he would also run for the highest office in the election mockery of November 3, 1958. It was an unfortunate step at the sunset of his life.

Grau remained in Cuba after the victory of the Revolution. Although he was not personally involved in actions against the new social process, his house on 5th avenue and 14 Street, in Miramar, was used to hatch counterrevolutionary plans, particularly attempts on the life of Commander in Chief Fidel Castro, with the active participation of his nephew and niece Ramón and Leopoldina. His residence was the place where a significant part of the sinister Operation Peter Pan was set up.

Grau's sister in law Paulina Alsina died in March 1964 and the following year his nephew and niece were arrested, tried and sentenced. The ex President did not have any other close relatives or source of income. The Cuban Presidents were not given pensions and although he had owned a number of houses before the enforcement of the Urban Reform Law, he had not filed the corresponding demand for compensation. He fell ill and was diagnosed with mouth cancer. His meals were limited to three glasses of milk a day, and perhaps a boiled egg. He quickly deteriorated. Grau seldom left the house and when he did it was to visit Paulina's tomb or the women's penitentiary in Guanabacoa where his niece was doing time. He constantly complained of being broke and insisted on begging for alms in the streets of Galiano and San Rafael with a hat in his hand. But, actually his friends never abandoned him and the Revolutionary Government assigned him a 500 pesos monthly pension. However, after his death, when his house was given to the ministry of Education, fifty thousand dollars were found concealed in a hidden compartment inside his safety box. Eventually, he lost control of the sphincters. He cried and refused to leave his room. The end was near. At the Oncology Hospital, Dr. Zoilo Marinello cared for him with dedication knowing he was tending to a man who had been twice President of the country, and also an outstanding doctor and a professor of Medicine. Ramón Grau San Martín passed away in that hospital at 10:23 pm on July 28, 1969.

The suicidal president

After his ousting, Carlos Prío leaves for Mexico, and later travels to the United States. In 1956, he returns to Cuba where he is harassed by Batista's police, and the Military Intelligence Services detain him after the attack on the Goicuría Barracks in the province of Matanzas. He is released but remains in house arrest at *La Chata*, his recreation farm in Arroyo Naranjo, where police agents from the 14th Precinct prevent him from going out or receiving visitors. This situation does not change until the decision is made to take him outside the country. In Miami, immigration officials exhibit him handcuffed.

Prío contributed to various undertakings against Batista, including the purchase of the *Granma* yacht, for which he donated a significant amount of money. In January 1959, he mixed with the crowd waiting for the arrival of the Caravan of Freedom bringing Fidel from Oriente. *"I don't have personal aspirations,"* he then said. He distanced from everything and lived in his farm until he decided to leave the country. By then, the flow of hard currency was strictly controlled and a special permission was required to carry dollars outside the nation. At the Presidential Palace, Prío received the money needed for his trip. Outside of Cuba, he was right up to his neck in the actions of the counterrevolution.

Later, on April 5, 1977, he took his own life in Miami. In a letter addressed to his wife and daughters he asked that his remains be kept in the United States for five years and then be brought to Cuba to be buried in the Colon necropolis near his mother, Doña Regla Socarrás, a Captain with the Ejército Libertador. His relatives have not honored his last wish. Recently, there were comments that his suicide was somehow related to Kennedy's assassination, since he was afraid that the Mafia might take reprisals against his family if it ever learned what he knew about the US President assassination in Dallas.

July 12, 19 and 26, 2009

SAVING A PRESIDENT'S LIFE

In February 1913, Cuban ambassador to Mexico Manuel Márquez Sterling uselessly tried to safe the life of President Francisco I. Madero and his Vicepresident José Pino Suárez, both detained in the National Palace. The noble and humanitarian efforts undertaken by the Cuban diplomat on his own initiative were backed by President José Miguel Gómez and the government of the Island nation that would also provide sanctuary to the family of the martyred President of Mexico. Cuban Foreign Minister Manuel Sanguily let Washington know that his country considered it repugnant that the US government recognize General Victoriano Huerta, the protagonist of the coup against Madero. Immediately, Havana worked out a strategy: it would not sever relations with Mexico but it would neither recognize the new government nor approve the encroachment on the rights of the fraternal people of that country. A similar line would be pursued by the foreign ministries of Brazil, Chile and Argentina.

Madero's parents, sheltered at the Japanese mission in Mexico City, begged Márquez Sterling to appeal on their behalf to the diplomatic corps to intercede for the lives of their sons Francisco and Gustavo, the latter a deputy to the Union Congress, and also in favor of Vicepresident Pino Suárez. Aware of the fact that none of his colleagues could be more influential than the American ambassador, Márquez Sterling, who was the Dean of the diplomatic corps, had already addressed a note to this official asking him to endorse this initiative and offering the cruise ship *Cuba*, anchored in the port of Veracruz, to take the ousted President out of the country.

It was Márquez Sterling who made possible for Madero's wife to be received by the American ambassador. *"Your husband could not govern and he never asked for my advice nor listened to me,"* he claimed. The ambassador also said that he did not believe the President's life was in danger, and that it would suffice to commit him to an institution. *"That would be enough,"* he asserted. The curt dialogue was long and still the diplomat never used a gentle word or provided comfort to the troubled woman.

"How could I ask for the release of Mr. Madero or intercede for him? I'd never do such thing! Huerta will do as it pleases him." She then retorted: *"Other ministers and ambassador are making efforts to avoid a catastrophe: those of Chile, Brazil, Cuba..."*

The ambassador responded with a cruel smile and hammering on every word: *"Those gentlemen lack any influence."*

Madero is doomed

Madero had been inaugurated as President of Mexico fifteen months back, after leading a movement that put an end to the three decades of General Porfirio Díaz's dictatorship. Then, one nephew of the dictator, General Félix Díaz rebelled against Madero and bombed the capital from the Citadel. But the General stood no chance in that mousetrap where hunger and the government forces could prove insuperable enemies, or so the President thought, as his military chiefs assured him that the enemy's resistance would not last under the pressure of forces loyal to the government.

The President was unaware that treason dwelled under his own roof. General Huerta, the Chief of the Army, was negotiating with Félix Díaz, while General Blanchet, who had just come in from Toluca with two thousand troops and sworn allegiance to the legitimate government, was actually waiting for the right moment to strike. The majority of the diplomatic corps was hostile to Madero and the US ambassador had it in for him. This diplomat had links with both Díaz and Huerta, and was encouraging the two to act. He was also aware of Blanchet's role in the affair, so he knew that at the moment of truth, 'the lunatic' would only have the support of the insignificant battery of General Angeles. The American ambassador moved as if a military intervention was forthcoming and went on to make a sinister threat to the President: *"Resignation is your only chance,"* was the message that the Spanish ambassador had the unworthy mission to convey to the president.

Madero writes a letter to US President Taft appealing to *"the sentiments of the great American people"* to help prevent *"a conflict whose consequences would be much more damaging than what they were trying to remedy."* Actually, the US ambassador is toying with the ghost of intervention without consulting his government. Taft, who would soon be leaving office, is not interested in such a small matter. Meanwhile, the ambassador insists on his provocative attitude and his awful threat. His embassy is full of people at all times. He moves among the different groups and talks with the visitors in whispers, as if he had secrets to tell to everyone of them.

In one of such diplomatic gabfests he is amazed at the presence of Márquez Sterling. *"Order will be soon restored,"* he says to the Cuban ambassador adding that he has no time to personally talk with him and that his personal secretary shall feed him the details. They enter an adjacent room where the secretary –a chatty and unpleasant fellow whom Márquez Sterling dislikes— ceases to act like a subordinate official and for a moment behaves as a senior representative. *"Madero is doomed,"* the man says with an air of solemnity. The Cuban ambassador realizes that Huerta and Félix Díaz have struck an agreement. Later on he would write: *"The struggle became a travesty soaked in blood. The cat had reached an agreement with the mouse. Huerta had all the cards and he played them calmly and coldly on the political table, in a tragic and solitary game of cards."*

"I will never resign"

In the early morning hours of February 18, the machineguns of General Angeles interrupt the silence and the Citadel cannons boom. The international problem seems to clear up with Taft's reassuring response to Madero's message. The military chiefs assure the President that they will throw the enemy out of its position that same evening. Huerta knows that will not happen and he tells the eleven Senators he has summoned that it is impossible to take over the Citadel with an attack and that the government lacks the indispensable elements to crush the rebellion. The Senators appeal to the War Secretary urging him to either persuade Madero to resign or to force him to do so in order to prevent a foreign intervention. Then and there, in front of Huerta and Blanchet, the Secretary accuses them of corrupting the army, and the Senators tune down their demands. Now they only want to meet with the President and the Secretary volunteers to make the arrangements, but Huerta moves faster. He rushes to President Madero who says: *"I have just learned that some Senators, enemies of mine, were inviting you to force my resignation,"* and Huerta responds, *"Yes, Mr. President, but pay no attention to those bandits. The troops have just seized a building that is crucial to the assault on the Citadel."*

The Senators arrive in the presence of Madero and on behalf of the group one of them asks the President to resign as the only way to thwart all dangers. Madero has one answer only: *"I'll never resign. I've been elected by the people and I'll die, if need be, loyal to my duty; and this is here."*

But his destiny is sealed. General Huerta is about to wrap up his slow and tragic cards game leaving the President practically helpless. The troops that unconditionally supported Madero and that had been with him since 1910 are decimated in an unfair combat since they are ordered to go fight in the open against the heavy artillery set up at the Citadel, and the Palace guard is no longer in the hands of those that Madero called *'my brave carabineers,'* his compatriots, but of soldiers commandeered by General Blanchet.

"Calm down, boys, don't shoot"

When the opposition Senators leave everything goes back to normal in the President's office. He is analyzing with his closest assistants the way to provide food to the poorer segments of the population if the conflict carries on for long, when Lieutenant Colonel Jiménez Riveroll, one of Blanchet's men, breaks into the room. The officer says that he is carrying a message from Huerta: the Governor of Oaxaca has rebelled against the government and is advancing on the city, thus the President must abandon the Palace. President Madero and the Lieutenant Colonel walk outside to a corridor to talk. Madero knows the unwavering loyalty of the Governor and doubts Riveroll's words so he tells the officer to go ask Huerta to come himself to report to him. At this point, the officer grabs the President's arm and tries to drag him. Madero, a strong and agile man, gets rid of him and enters one of the rooms followed by ministers and assistants while Riveroll and some twenty strange soldiers chase them.

"Where are these troops going?" shouts with authority an officer loyal to the President and orders the soldiers to leave. The soldiers obey automatically and Riveroll, pale and shaken, orders them to return to him and ready their weapons. He cannot finish the phrase for he is shot by a Captain loyal to Madero. A Major rushing in from the back door tries to take command of the soldiers but he is shot, too. At this point, the soldiers shoot simultaneously on Madero but one of the President's men covers him with his own body. The soldiers shoot again while Madero walks up to them with his arms stretched out to the sides. *"Calm down, boys, don't shoot,"* he says and the group disbands. The ministers run downstairs looking for General Huerta whom they believe has nothing to do with these developments while Madero looks down the balcony listening to the people shouting their support for him on the streets of Acequia and the Plaza de la Constitución; this returns his confidence.

President Madero walks down to the patio. The officers of the honor guard present arms as the rules provide. It's not an illusion. He has recovered his authority. Then, he walks to the troops. These are soldiers from the 27th Battalion that take orders only from General Blanchet, but Madero doesn't know it. He addresses the men: *"Soldiers, some people are trying to apprehend the President of the Republic, but you will defend me because it is the will of the Mexican people that I am here..."*

He can't say another word. Blanchet puts a gun to his chest and cuts off his speech. *"Sir, you are my prisoner now. Surrender!"* he contends.

President Madero understands that at this point it's useless to resist so he lets the men take him to the headquarters of the Palace Guard where he is placed in custody. His ministers who preceded him downstairs looking for Huerta are already detained and crammed in a sentry box, except for the minister of Treasury who could escape. The District Governor and General Angeles are also arrested. And, deputy Gustavo, the President's brother, is arrested on Huerta's orders after the two had lunch together and the General ate with a good appetite in a restaurant near the Palace. The leader of the coup d'état counts his prisoners and orders to release the ministers and to lock up Vicepresident Pino Suárez in the Palace Quartermasters where Angeles and the President have already been taken. "*Where is Gustavo?*" Madero insists. The night before his brother had sent him a laconic and prophetic message: "*We'll all die.*"

Treason is sealed

As soon as President Madero is arrested, the US ambassador who has waited three days for this development summons the diplomatic corps to report on it. His colleague, Cuban ambassador Márquez Sterling, does not think highly of him: "*He is one of those people who say what they should silence and silence what should be said; it's the most indiscreet man alive.*" At this moment, the American diplomat is overjoyed: "*Mexico is now safe. There will be peace, progress and wealth,*" he asserts and explains that he has already informed Félix Díaz –the seditious general entrenched in the Citadel— of the developments and that he did so before Huerta, the putschist general, even asked. He then adds the names of those who will be the ministers of the new government, which he already knows, even when Huerta has yet to take on the presidency.

Cuban Ambassador Márquez Sterling leaves the meeting but about 10:00 pm returns to the US embassy for news. There, he finds the Brazilian and Chilean ambassadors waiting for news, too, for they are concerned over the fate of the toppled president. The American ambassador walks outside to meet them and says that he will soon ask them to come in. At this very moment, in an adjacent room, Huerta and Díaz, allegedly enemies the day before are sealing their treason with a hug.

"Don Pancho will be shot"

The night of February 18 was a sad one for the Cuban ambassador. The following morning someone came up to him as he was buying cigars at a kiosk and said: *"Don Pancho will be executed; they are capable of anything."* Márquez Sterling found such possibility unbelievable, but his interlocutor convinced him with the argument that the President's brother had been shot after terrible tortures and his only healthy eye emptied out with the point of a sword. *"Unfortunately, the opposite would be unbelievable here,"* the man argued. The ambassador wanted to respond but the words died in his throat. The man added: *"Don't waste a second, Ambassador, take the initiative."*

Ambassador Márquez Sterling went back home and wrote a private note addressed to his American colleague. At the Japanese embassy, Madero's parents asked the Cuban ambassador to appeal to the diplomatic corps on their behalf to use their good offices to save the lives of Francisco and Gustavo, who they thought was still alive. The Cuban ambassador called on the American embassy again. The head of the US mission could barely keep his indignation in check; he categorically opposed any such action by the diplomatic corps. *"You go to the Palace and you talk to Huerta on your own behalf but not on behalf of the diplomatic corps,"* he said and asked the Spanish ambassador, always willing to oblige, to accompany the Cuban diplomat.

On arriving at the Palace, an officer showed both diplomats to the room where the Chilean ambassador was talking to the General who had detained Madero. When the officer heard the reason of the visit he gave them assurances that the life of the detainee was in no danger whatsoever. The President had refused to submit his resignation and that complicated matters, but he had now caved in...then he informed the visitors on the conditions of the resignation. Madero, his brother Gustavo, Vicepresident Pino Suárez and General Angeles, with their respective families, the necessary protection and the guarantee of foreign diplomats would travel that same night of February 19 to Veracruz by train and from there leave the country. The accompanying diplomats would be the custodians of his resignation and of a letter in which Huerta committed to abide by the pact. The resignation would not be sent to Congress until Madero had left the national territory which meant that he was leaving the country as President of the Republic. Madero had also asked that the state governors remained in their positions and that none of his friends were bothered for political reasons.

The Cuban and Spanish ambassadors could not meet with Huerta; they were told that the General was sleeping. They requested to visit with Madero and were authorized. In his confinement at the National Palace Quartermasters, alongside Pino Suárez and General Angeles, the President welcomed them gladly. He was unaware of his brother's death. He accepted the offer of the *Cuba* cruise ship to leave the country as well as the company of the Cuban ambassador up to Veracruz, and said that they would depart about 10:00 that same night but asked that Márquez Sterling arrive earlier for his presence could smooth things out.

The candid atmosphere dispelled any thought of an eventual tragedy. Only General Angeles suspected a horrible outcome. He took the Cuban ambassador aside and said: *"Don Pancho will be shot."*

"My fine and hospitable friend..."

At 9:00 pm that same night Márquez Sterling returns to the National Palace. President Madero is talking with his uncle Ernesto and another visitor. He realizes that General Huerta's safe-conduct has not been received. Uncle Ernesto goes to fetch the document and comes back with strange news. Madero's foreign minister is heading for Congress carrying Madero's resignation and that of his Vice-President. Madero asks his uncle to catch up with the minister and bring him to the Quartermasters. The uncle returns with still worse news. The resignation has been submitted. *"Then go and tell him that he should not resign, that he should hold the position of acting President until we leave the country."*

It's too late. The Foreign Minister retained the position of acting President for only forty-five minutes, just the time needed to resign after appointing General Victoriano Huerta Minister of the Interior and Secretary of Relations with the States. At this point, Madero realizes that he is in a trap and that Huerta will not honor his word. However, Uncle Ernesto believes it is still possible to travel to Veracruz, perhaps at 5:00 in the morning, the same hour at which Huerta had taken the ousted dictator Porfirio Díaz out of Mexico City.

Vice-President Pino Suárez fears an attempt on their lives if the Cuban ambassador is not with them and General Angeles thinks that they will not survive this predicament. Cuban Ambassador Márquez Sterling gladly volunteers to keep them company. Madero opposes putting the Cuban ambassador through such trouble since they cannot even offer him a bed there. Márquez Sterling insists. He would later write about it: *"Taking my hat, saying good-by and forsaking them to the sentry's bayonet would have been unworthy of my position, my condition as a Cuban and my chivalrous race. Protecting with my homeland's flag the President to whom a month before I had solemnly presented my credentials was tantamount to honoring our coat of arms and interpreting in its full magnitude the mission of concord that the circumstances had imposed on me."*

The ambassador receives a message from Huerta. He can go home to rest, if he so wishes, for there will be no train that night. Márquez Sterling inquires if the trip might be possible in the morning but the messenger knows nothing, so he asks for permission to leave and goes back to his friends.

Madero, who has listened to the exchange, says resignedly: *"There will be no train"* Then he takes a picture of himself from the centre table and writes: *"To my fine and hospitable friend Manuel Márquez Sterling as proof of my appreciation and gratitude."* He then gives the present to the ambassador and says: *"You may keep it in memory of this sorrowful night."*

Breakout law

President Madero takes three chairs and fixes a bed for the Cuban Ambassador. At 10:00 am Márquez Sterling is still with the detainees. Madero finds it inconceivable that General Huerta may want to kill him or that Félix Díaz might consent to it, for the latter owns his life to the President. But a few hours later, President Madero and Vice-President Pino Suárez are killed. About 10:00 pm, they are taken out supposedly to be transferred to the penitentiary but never get there. In vicious concert, co-conspirators Huerta and Díaz have decided to eliminate them. A group of guards are waiting near the penitentiary for the two cars carrying the detainees. As these approach the main entrance to the building, the officer in charge of their custody orders the vehicles to go for the back door, then he sees those ambushed and orders the cars to stop. Step out, he says to Madero, and shoots him on the head, while Pino Suárez faces an identical fate. The guards shoot repeatedly on the two cars to justify with those bodies still beating the enforcement of the 'breakout law'.

The Madero family must leave Mexico. Cuban President José Miguel Gómez summons Márquez Sterling to Havana for consultations. The ambassador is troubled by many doubts. Is the Cuban government displeased with his actions? Will relations be severed with Mexico? Can this call be related to his old mother who's very ill? He reviews every one of his actions in favor of Madero and finds no reason for regret. His endeavors in support of the murdered President are known beyond diplomatic and government circles. One day, as he is leaving the US embassy a group of people cheer for him and somebody shouts: *"Ambassador, you have won for Cuba the heart of honest men."*

He is wanted in Havana hastily. At the railway station Márquez Sterling anxiously looks for the wife, mother and sisters of the martyred President. These are now under protection of the Chilean ambassador but without documents to allow their departure. He can't see them but somebody brings the message that they are already in one of the wagons, hiding in the drawing-room. On his arrival aboard the cruise ship *Cuba*, the soldiers present arms to the ambassador who receives the honors corresponding to his position. He is followed by the Madero ladies, dressed in black and mourning; on the ship, the father and uncle of the murdered President are waiting for them.

In Havana

The Mexican tragedy was a world event with an extraordinary repercussion in Cuba. That Madero was betrayed came as a shock to Cubans, but his martyrdom aroused indignation. Many rallies and demonstrations were organized in solidarity with the Mexican people and a huge crowd waited at the docks and the approaching streets for the Madero family to get off the ship about 10:00 in the night of March 1, 1913. Foreign Minister Sanguily accompanied by other officials and by José Miguel's daughters welcomed them at the Harbormaster's Office. The cars that carried the newly arrived to the Telégrafo Hotel, in Prado and Neptuno, were surrounded by an impressive human wave that made it necessary for the police to clear the access to the building for the deeply touched travelers to get there.

Contrary to the wish of the public opinion, José Miguel did not sever relations with Mexico but refused to recognize General Huerta's government. President Taft had just a few more days before the end of his term in office and his successor soon dismissed the US ambassador to Mexico who tried to destroy the Mexican Revolution right from its birth. It was, however, a simple change of men for Washington insisted on its invasive attitude. Márquez Sterling, one of our great journalists, knew perfectly well the source of interventionism, that was way beyond the actions of an insensitive and incompetent ambassador and that threatened both México and Cuba just the same.

(Source: *Los últimos días de Manuel Márquez Sterling*[7])
May 12 and 18, 2008

LA CHAMBELONA: A UNIQUE REVOLUTION

In February 1917, a fraudulent election and the certainty that the next round would bring more of the same paved the way in Cuba to a unique revolt known as *La Chambelona Revolution.*

[7] The Last Days of Márquez Sterling

This happened when the Liberals led by José Miguel Gómez took arms against the Conservative's government of Mario García Menocal.

Despite the fact that the right to re-election of the President of the Republic was endorsed by the Constitution of 1901, its precedent had been disastrous. President Estrada Palma's stubborn decision to remain in office four more years had led to a conflict known as the *August Little War* of 1906 and resulted in the second direct US military intervention in Cuba. It is said that initially Menocal, who had been President since 1913, was not interested in his own re-election but that he caved in to the pressures of the court clique and that his party's national convention nominated him with ninety-two votes against sixty-one. The conservatives felt that with the resources that power made available to them, he would be a safe shot against a fragmented Liberal Party that, nevertheless agreed to nominate Alfredo Zayas.

As of this moment, a day would not go by without press reports on more or less violent clashes and sometimes fatal encounters between Liberals and Conservatives, and the struggle aggravated when after its approval by the House and Senate, Menocal vetoed the law providing that if the President was nominated for an elective position he must cease his functions seventy-five days prior to Election Day. This legislation had been introduced by a conservative, no less. That presidential veto consolidated the Liberals' unity while the catchy and defying music and lyrics of *La Chambelona*, composed in Camajuaní by Rigoberto Leyva, reached every corner of the Island stirring the passions of the opposition.

And so came Election Day on November 1, 1916. The situation grew violent and at numerous polling stations the Liberals had the resolute support of the Army and the Rural Guard which sympathized with José Miguel despite his government purges of these institutions. At a polling station in the municipal area of Vueltas, in Las Villas, its chairman expelled the conservative delegate to the Electoral College and directed the soldiers there to prevent the members of that Party from casting their votes.

That's why when the time came for vote counting one ballot box contained 200 votes for the Liberals and only one for the Conservatives.

Hey, hey, hey La Chambelona!

The Liberals won the elections in Havana with an overwhelming majority and the government conceded right away, but it assured that the votes from the provinces would bring victory to the Conservatives; wishful thinking. The Liberals would also win in Camagüey and Oriente, Las Villas and Pinar del Río, and only Matanzas would remain in question. On November 2, the Minister of the Interior stated: *"The Liberals did not win more provinces because this is all there is."* Even President Menocal himself was wiling to graciously admit his defeat.

But, his advisers thought otherwise. On the very same day, November 2, the Minister of the Interior started to replace the reports sent by telegraph to the Election Central Board. Every possible ballot was replaced and the government apparatus launched an all out offensive to deny the adversary's victory already recognized by official spokesmen. But even these actions failed to reverse the government failure. The most it could do was to annul the ballots in a number of polling stations. The scandal then grew exponentially, to the point that representatives of both parties decided to hold a meeting where they agreed to review the outcome of the elections at the Election Board, which confirmed the Liberals' victory in three of the six provinces.

The Conservatives appealed to the Supreme Court and although that judicial body certified the victory of the opposing party in Oriente, Las Villas, Camagüey and Havana, it conditioned it to a second round in the first two provinces mentioned that would surely ratify the supremacy of the Liberals. The Menocal loyalists armed their followers, accused the Supreme Court of bias and characterized their opponents as Germanophiles –these were the days of World War I. Then, they said that Menocal would never relinquish the office to Zayas.

Washington in sight

Liberals and Conservatives appealed to the American ambassador in Havana for support. On February 10, four days before the date scheduled for the elections, Liberals Orestes Ferrara and Raimundo Cabrera left for Washington, surreptitiously. They asked the US Administration to send witnesses –they are now called observers— to each and every one of the polling stations involved in the second round, for example, in Las Villas the Liberals needed only 276 votes to consolidate their victory. But Wilson's Administration, totally absorbed in its declaration of war to Germany, simply ignored the request.

Then the Liberals felt their only choice was violence and José Miguel received the support of senior military chiefs in Oriente and Camagüey. The action burst out sooner than planned in this province when the chiefs of the military district and the Cavalry Regiment revolted and arrested over one-hundred local government representatives, including the Governor of the province and the City Mayor.

José Miguel's followers also took over the regiment in Santiago de Cuba. In Havana, Matanzas and Pinar del Río there were several unrelated uprisings and in Las Villas –the Liberals bulwark— Brigadier Gerardo Machado led the insurrection. José Miguel headed the rebel troops in their march from the center of the Island to Havana.

The rebels from Camagüey converged with José Miguel in Ciego de Avila. They planned to take a train to Havana but made an inexplicable tactical mistake. A group from the light cavalry should have explored the grounds near the railway to be used by the train which was four times faster than the horses. They also lost time in street celebrations, including José Miguel who danced at the Majagua Park to the tune of *La Chambelona*.

On the other hand, the government wasted no time. As of November 3, the chief of the Army General Staff had taken on the leadership of the military barracks in Santa Clara and started to act. He knew that if José Miguel made it to the city the entire province would join him. He thwarted sedition in the troops and calmly and shrewdly subdued the soldiers. An unknown lieutenant, acting on his own, burned the bridge over the Jatibonico River thus halting the successful march of the Liberals.

A failed insurrection

The rebels achieved some military victories but the government had the upper hand. In the political arena, they did not receive the support they expected from Washington. The US Administration declared that it would not back any insurrection or recognize any government resulting from it, and sent four battleships to reassure Menocal. In Santiago, a unit from the US Navy induced the rebels to evacuate the plaza. Ferrara and Cabrera, who had requested a direct military intervention, were 'invited' to leave the US territory.

The insurrection faded out. Zayas was captured in Cambute, close to Guanabacoa where he is said to have dodged, and Machado surrendered to the authorities in Santa Clara. José Miguel was arrested in Caicaje alongside his son Miguel Mariano and all of their bodyguards; the General of the War of Independence Gustavo Caballero was assassinated. A telegram from the Presidential Palace read in a coded line: "Take Caballero's body to Camagüey."

The second round of the elections took place under intimidation; it was a fraud. At the polling stations of Las Villas more voters supposedly showed up than were registered in the census and in other areas the putsch was complete. Next, Congress was convened on May 8, 1917 to proclaim Mario Menocal President of the Republic. This occurred with forty Liberal lawmakers in attendance to meet the quorum.

January 30, 2005

A BLOOD STORM

A bad omen weighed heavily on Doctor Carlos Manuel de la Cruz. Lately, he had only been retained to defend people implicated in actions against President Gerardo Machado's government and he felt that at some point that would backfire. He was already working in the case of the so-called "sherbet bomb" –an explosive device set up on a sherbet-making machine that was to be detonated on the Fifth Avenue as the tyrant's car was passing by— when he had to take on the defense of one of those implicated in an attempt on the life of Lieutenant Diez Díaz, chief of a military barracks in Artemisa, who had been killed as he opened an explosive package, similar to those received by Commander Arsenio Ortiz, known as the *Jackal of Oriente*, and Colonel Federico Rasco from La Punta Castle neither of which had exploded.

In both cases the defendants were the same men being tried in war councils, and so were the defense attorneys. In both cases De la Cruz shared the stand with Ricardo Dolz, Pedro Cué and Gonzalo Freyre de Andrade.

Hatred grows

This is getting nasty, De la Cruz thought as his fear grew of the increasingly strained situation surrounding these councils. The military prosecutors' hatred towards the defense attorneys kept growing and in one of the hearings in Artemisa the prosecutor had even tried to punch him, an action prevented by Sergeant Fulgencio Batista, the stenographer in this trial, who stood between them. The sergeant himself had accompanied De la Cruz twice in his trips back to Havana to prevent a fateful encounter with the army.

It was precisely from Artemisa that Dr. Carlos Manuel de la Cruz was returning when before reaching his office he stopped at Old Havana to buy a newspaper. That day's edition of the *Heraldo de Cuba*, the government's paper, reported a fateful attempt on the life of Clemente Vázquez Bello, President of the Senate and leader of the Liberal Party, shot to death by a revolutionary commando at the Country Club Great Boulevard (today 146th Avenue) as the man was driving home in that suburb.

According to the report, Ricardo Dolz, House Representative Miguel Angel Aguiar, the brothers Gonzalo, Guillermo and

Leopoldo Freyre Andrade and others had also been killed...at this point, a bewildered De la Cruz cut short his reading to go back to the first lines of the paragraph; either the drafting was wrong or he was missing something. He re-read the article holding the paper with shaky hands and suddenly realized what was coming on to him because his name was mentioned among those killed by unknown assassins. Apparently, being outside Havana, in Artemisa, had saved his life, at least for the time being.

De la Cruz entered his office on O'Reilly Street and wasting no time called Ricardo Dolz who had just found out that the government's newspaper had reported him dead. He had barely hung up the phone when it rang; it was his wife calling to warn him that some strange heavy-set nasty-looking men were standing outside their house. The lawyer decided not to wait. He left the office through the back door and did not stop until he reached the Uruguayan Embassy, at the apartment 245 in the Manzana de Gómez. Attorney Dolz did likewise taking refuge in the Brazilian Embassy then located on 17 and A streets, in Vedado.

The warnings went from phone to phone and from mouth to mouth. Pedro Cué phoned the house of communist Juan Marinello whose name was in the list, too, alongside that of Mayito García Menocal, son of the former President, who would be killed "*to teach his father a lesson.*" At the same time, Joaquín Llaverías, a Captain with the Ejército Libertador and director of the National Archives, was arriving at the house of author Renée Méndez Capote, with a personal message from Army Chief General Alberto Herrera. She should try to take her brother Eugenio out of Cuba right away or else he might be murdered, something that not even Herrera himself could stop despite his senior military position and his friendship with General Méndez Capote for whom he had worked as an assistant during the War of Independence.

'My pal'

Vázquez Bello was neither a murderer nor a thief, but he was very close to Machado who called him 'my pal'. He was responsible for Machado becoming President of the nation when in 1924 he deployed all his skills to impose the man as a candidate to the highest office during the Liberal Party nominating convention, opposing Carlos Mendieta, the liberals' natural chieftain. Such a proposal was also advocated by the no less resourceful Orestes Ferrara.

Both, Vázquez Bello and Machado were originally from Santa Clara. It is said that the tyrant considered him almost like a son and even contemplated the idea of making him his successor when he left power in 1935. Hitting Vázquez Bello was like hitting Machado. In fact, Vázquez Bello had escaped a first attempt on his life but the second time, on November 27, 1932, he was not so lucky.

His death would become the first dramatic scene of an inconclusive play. Machado was expected at the funeral of his pal, and given the hierarchy of the deceased as Senate leader and chairman of the Liberal Party, the entire government and Parliament were supposed to attend alongside senior police and army officers, sycophants and snitches. Since Vázquez Bello did not have his own pantheon in Havana, it was assumed that he would be buried in that of his father-in-law Regino Truffin, the owner of the area where the Tropicana nightclub seats today. Thus, the necropolis drainage system was used to set up loads of dynamite in that tomb and its surroundings. Over sixty kilograms of dynamite were set to explode when Machado arrived in the place.

Then, something unexpected happened: The widow decided to take Bello's remains to Santa Clara to bury in his home city. This changed the course of events. It was only the following day that the police force found the explosive charges and the tyrant realized that he had narrowly escaped the same fate as his pal.

Different narratives

Of course, the news of Vázquez Bello's death quickly reached the Presidential Palace. Once confirmed, Machado was notified in his room. Historian Newton Briones Montoto has affirmed that a little later the executive mansion received Police Commissioner Brigadier Antonio Ainciart and Interior Minister Octavio Zubizarreta for a brief talk with the President on the serious development. According to Briones, it was Zubizarreta who called the *Heraldo de Cuba* before leaving the Palace to communicate the death of Vázquez Bello and announce that of Dolz, De la Cruz, Aguiar and the Freyre Andrade brothers "*at the hands of unknown individuals.*"

Another narrative of the events was offered in his memoirs by Orestes Ferrara, State Secretary in Machado's cabinet. He said that he was having lunch as usual at the house of his brother in law when he heard the news. He rushed to the Military Hospital in Columbia but Vázquez Bello had already passed away. Everyone there spoke of revenge and some even wetted their hands in the dead man's blood before it dried up. From there he went to the Palace only to find the tyrant in bed, depressed and dumbfounded over the developments. They were talking when the phone rang. An assistant got the call and said: "*Mr. President, they want to give you important news.*" But, Machado refused to take the call and said: "*I already know it. Some unknown people have killed the three Freyre Andrade brothers and Dr. Miguel Angel Aguiar.*"

How had the tyrant known? Or is it perhaps that he didn't need to hear the news because he had issued the order or the decision had been made in his presence? Ferrara would not say it in his book. He says, with his characteristic cynicism, that for a long time he had doubts about who were the authors of that criminal revenge but that he had always thought that the police had been unable to prevent the crime. Many years later, as he wrote his memoirs published in 1975 under the title *Una mirada sobre tres siglos*[8], he concluded that the police had been responsible for those murders. He tries to save his image for posterity saying that he begged with Machado to order the military occupation of Havana to avoid greater evil and advised him to take advantage

[8] A Look at Three Centuries

of the situation to make an appeal for harmony and declare that he had little interest in ruling a country divided by so much hatred but the dictator responded: *"It is my duty to also listen to the sound of other bells."* In the case of Ainciart, Ferrara was more categorical when he said that he had told Machado's Police Commissioner: *"You are causing more damage to Cuba than all the revolutionaries combined."*

The events

About 2:30 in the afternoon of that September 27 the bell rang at No. 13 on B Street, almost at the corner of Calzada Avenue, in Vedado, the residence of the Freyre de Andrade family. The housekeeper attended. The men asked if Gonzalo was at home and when the man answered affirmatively they pushed him aside and went in. Briones Montoto affirmed that the murders happened in the living room. Other sources have said that they were killed in the upper floor. Only one of the brothers was involved with the opposition but as the assassins could not identify him they chose to kill the three young men.

At 3:00 pm it was Dr. Aguiar's turn to die in his house on 19 and 10 streets, also in Vedado. Several men called from the house garden and the parliamentarian, a Menocal loyalist, walked out to the porch. The murderers talked but Aguiar, who was hard of ear, had to lean forward to listen. At this point, they riddled him with bullets.

After accomplishing their feat, the assassins returned to their convertible car and drove around the block of 17, 19, 8 and 10 streets still carrying in their hands the smoking guns. They carried their hats pushed back and insulting smiles on their repulsive faces.

The neighbors, who ran to the street as they heard the first shots, could see the assassins leaving and felt shocked by such felony.

A blood storm had hit Havana.

October 18, 2009

RUNNING AWAY

Many years ago, back in the 1970s, a friend told me that for decades he had kept a couple of neckties which had belonged to a politician: Machado's loyalist Orestes Ferrara. It was war booty. On August 12, 1933, several students, including my already deceased friend, tried to capture in the Havana harbor the man who had been Secretary of State in the government of the tyrant Machado. They failed. The shrewd Italian that during the War of Independence had received the rank of Colonel from the hands of the Generalísimo Máximo Gómez made it safely to the hydroplane that would leave the Arsenal quay at three in the afternoon, as it ordinarily did. His wife soon followed him, but in her haste she left their luggage which was seized like a trophy by their persecutors.

Aware that Ferrara, historian Ramiro Guerra and journalist Alberto Lamar were the last three officials to abandon the Presidential Palace a few minutes before the people crashed it and plundered it I had always assumed that he had left straight for the harbor. But he did not. That day, Ferrara would take a last look at Havana, walking and driving around the city.

We shall soon enjoy that juicy scene of days long past.

Open rebellion

Ferrera returned to Cuba on Wednesday August 9, 1933, three days before the collapse of the regime. A pompous and useless international conference had kept him in London for a few weeks, and once in Washington, where he had expected to meet with President Roosevelt, he received a compelling call from Machado urging his swift return to Cuba. *"Come as soon as you can,"* the tyrant ordered in his message. There was an open rebellion in the country and the role of broker between the government and the opposition assumed by US Ambassador Benjamin Summer Welles had only embittered those involved while the tyranny lost support and hope.

For two days, August 10 and 11, Ferrara works tirelessly. He meets with Machado, who gives assurance of his resignation although the President was never fully determined. He also meets with Ambassador Summer Welles whom he rebukes for his mediation. Ferrara also talks with traditional politicians who oppose the tyranny. He knows that the die is cast; the days of the tyranny are numbered. That's why he seldom goes to the ministry. He stays home working feverishly with the help of Ramiro Guerra, the president's chief of staff, in the documents that will avow the transfer of power: the resignation of ministers, the request for a license –tantamount to his resignation— that Machado will file with Congress, the decrees that will blow life into the new government...a complete skeleton that he wants to orderly submit to General Alberto Herrera, the man Machado has chosen to be his replacement.

On Saturday 12, he heads for the Presidential Palace. It is 8:00 in the morning and on the way from his house in San Miguel and Ronda, near the University, he realizes that the people have taken to the streets but they are not aggressive. At the Palace, he comes across Machado. They talk. He tells the tyrant that he will be traveling with his wife to Miami on the hydroplane scheduled flight at three in the afternoon, and that from there they'll go to New York. Machado admits that he doesn't know exactly what he'll do but that he might probably go to Las Villas and set up camp on the Escambray Mountains with about a hundred loyalists. That same morning he had said to others that he would set up camp at Rancho Boyeros.

Ferrara insists with the President that he should forget about going to the Escambray Mountains and travel abroad instead. Meanwhile, Machado walks along the halls of the Palace in a sort of limbo like he doesn't know whether staying or leaving. Eventually, he decides to leave with his bodyguards for his farm *Nenita*, on the road from Santiago de las Vegas to Managua. Meanwhile, at the President's private office, on the third floor of the mansion, Ferrara, alongside historian Guerra and journalist Lamar, goes over the documents that must be ready before he runs away. The Palace, so lively with people a few days before, is now empty. The mansion servants leave when they realize that the presidential family is gone, including the old servants who impervious to politics go from one President to another. Only one maid remains at the President's private chamber. No one has asked her to do so but she continues to clean up for love of tidiness.

For rent

A crowd starts gathering outside the Palace. The documents are finally ready and Ferrara and the others prepare to leave the building. But the door they intend to use is closed and a sign has been hanged on the outside that reads 'For rent'. The main door is closed, too, and so is the gate used by the staff. The policeman on duty, who has been a porter from the days of Estrada Palma, walks nervously back and forth as he jokes about the crowd. Ferrara and his colleagues find him and the man opens the padlock. Ferrara asks to be allowed out first and once outside he raises his hands waving a bundle of papers as if announcing the resignation of the head of state. The crowd shouts in excitement and the ex officials of the government reach for the car of the ex Secretary of State which is waiting. The impatient crowd breaks into the Presidential Palace.

Guerra comes down first and goes toward the police station on San Lázaro Street. A little later, Lamar gets off the car on Infanta Street. Ferrara is heading for General Herrera's home, on L and 21st streets, in front across the Reina Mercedes Hospital (where Coppelia ice-cream parlor seats today) to deliver a bundle of documents nobody cares about any more. He is welcomed by Ambassador Welles, but he can't meet with Herrera. The Army refuses to accept the General as a replacement for Machado and at this point, by the grace of the American ambassador, Carlos Manuel de Céspedes, a son of the Father of the Homeland, is already the new President.

Ferrara must walk his way back home alone. He can see his old friend, the new President, passing by in his car and turning his face to avoid saying hello. As he walks home, some friends join him offering protection. Then, as he talks with the Spanish ambassador in front of his residence a shot aimed at him kills a trusted friend; a shootout ensues and the ambassador insists that Ferrara and his wife take refuge in his embassy. The couple declines the offer. The ambassador insists but the answer is still the same. They must find a way out of this predicament. Ferrara asks his wife to go to her sister's house but pack their luggage first. He would go to a friend's house where she should join him later. But first they sit at the table and enjoy some good spaghetti Napolitano.

No disguise

Looting, lynching, arsons and detentions follow...the radio broadcasts alarming news. A friend of the family has booked two tickets for the hydroplane flight at three in the afternoon. The difficulty lies in reaching the Arsenal quay. Ferrara decides against wearing a disguise and drives in an open car. As his chauffeur refuses to drive, a nephew offers to take him to the quay and his sister in law joins them. Another nephew comes with the group as a bodyguard. Ferrara also carries a weapon. After some last minute arrangements his wife follows in another car carrying two small suitcases with their indispensable belongings.

They reach the harbor without further complications. Of course, they avoid the crammed streets. The car takes G Avenue, turns left and reaches Carlos III Street. They drive at normal speed to avoid drawing attention. Many recognize the official of the toppled government; some salute him while others insult him, but nobody stops him. As they approach Belascoaín Street, they can see a brawl two blocks further, on Reina and Escobar streets. The house of Senator Wilfredo Fernández is under assault. The car quickly turns right then left and escapes along the Estrella Street.

There is no one at the Arsenal quay. Ferrara pays for the travel tickets and although there is still time before take off they are allowed to board the hydroplane. The nephew who has been acting as bodyguard stays outside, armed and watchful. The former minister's wife arrives and sits by her husband.

By now the crew is on board and the Captain, a '*white Russian*'[9], decides to separate the vessel from the quay and tie it to the buoy. The quay is no longer empty. A large number of students, sailors and soldiers have been gathering here. From the hydroplane they can see the others excited making gestures although their words can't be heard. However, the sound of the machinegun shooting is perfectly audible. They start shooting on the hydroplane. No less than 50 shots hit it. As a bullet goes through Mrs. Ferrara's hat the waiter freaks out, close to a nervous breakdown.

"*The engine, the engine!*" shouts the skipper and the aircraft starts moving. Once in flight, the pilot makes an unexpected decision. He is afraid that the Cuban Army planes might chase him and attack in midair so he changes direction and only rectifies it when he is convinced there is no danger.

At the Miami airport, a group of Cubans shouts angrily at the ex minister of the tyranny. Ferrara responds the verbal aggressions and jumps on one of them but at that moment four police agents in plain clothes hold him and carry him to a car. The couple books rooms at the Columbus Hotel and from there both are picked up by the Immigration authorities determined to open them a file.

They need to buy some clothes. Ferrara, dressed in white, is really a mess; he looks haggard to the point that a journalist writes that he seems to have escaped a public brawl. He has been severely punished by the scorching sun of August, and one thing leading to another, he has been unable to change in two days. Actually, he can't change since their two small suitcases are back at the Arsenal quay, in Havana, at the mercy of their persecutors that decades later still showed them as trophies and as a memento of the day when the people were forced to take justice in their own hands, and given Ferrara's complicity with the tyranny, and

[9] *White Russian*, said of those who supported the monarchy in Russia in the early 20th century.

Machado in particular, it can be expected that he would have been lynched if the people had laid hands on him that August 12.

October 29, 2006

THE COUP OF 1933

These are rough times. There is chaos after Machado is toppled on August 12, 1933. Céspedes is President of the government but he can't rule and the American ambassador is growing afraid of the people's fighting spirit. Hunger, unemployment and strikes are rampant. The popular fire is burning throughout the Island and workers and students prepare to fight. At the Havana harbor, two American battleships stand by with their cannons exposed and the marines ready to land.

In the Army, the atmosphere of indiscipline and insubordination keeps mounting. The officers are no longer in command and the conspiracy of the sergeants –now organized in the so-called Junta de Defensa o de los Ocho (Defense Junta)— is winning support among the troops all over the country. The leaders of the Junta are Juan Pablo Rodríguez, José Eleuterio Pedraza, Manuel López Migoya and Fulgencio Batista, among others. They demand benefits for soldiers and noncommissioned officers. They do not accept having their wages cut down and instead demand them to be raised as much as possible, the same as the pensions; they want peaked caps and two more buttons on the army jackets. But, soon the sergeants' movement will show its political hues: they don't need to demand what they can get by themselves.

The coup d'état is scheduled for September 8, 1933. On the 4th of the month, Batista assumes he has been found out and decides to bring the coup forward to that very night. At 8:00 pm he is practically in charge. At 9:00 pm, journalist Sergio Carbó urges him to invite the Directorio Estudiantil Universitario, DEU, (University Students Directorate) to join him. At 10:00 pm, Columbia, the major military fortress in the country, is already booming with civilians. At 2:00 am on the 5th, every military district has signed up with the sedition and Céspedes government is no more. Thus emerges the Agrupación Revolucionaria de Cuba (Cuba Revolutionary Association) and the new regime adopts the Directorate's political program.

Almost every sergeant involved in the plot had some 'dirt' to conceal. Pedraza was a loan shark. Batista had been a member of Machado's Secret Service and Pablo Rodríguez had organized a soldier's homage to the tyrant in 1930. Batista had not even been a member of the Defense Junta. He was asked to join because he was the only sergeant to own a car and the conspirators needed a vehicle. But, to be truthful he was the most daring of all; he appropriated the movement leaving the others out. He then went on to become the protagonist of the revolt at the Columbia Barracks while the others moved to the regiments in the provinces. In the absence of Rodríguez, Batista issued an order designating himself the main leader and spokesman for the movement. Additionally, he appointed Rodríguez Chief of Columbia with López Migoya as his assistant, but did not sign the document; Migoya did, as assistant to Rodríguez who was completely unaware of what was going on.

It is said that the soldiers at the camp protested Batista's decision and demanded that Rodríguez be the main leader, but when this officer returned from Matanzas he chose to let things stand this way.

Coming of age

Soon, the Revolutionary Association issues its first proclamation addressed to the people stating that it will undertake the economic reconstruction of the country and hold a constitutive assembly; it promises a quick return to normality and the punishment of the culprits of what happened under Machado's government; it states that the lives and properties of Cubans and foreigners will be protected and that it will take responsibility for the debts and obligations of the Republic. *"Considering that the current government (Céspedes') does not respond to the pressing needs of the revolution, the Revolutionary Association of Cuba now takes charge,"* reads the proclamation signed by Ramón Grau San Martín, Carlos Prío Socarrás, José M. Irisarri, Carlos Hevia, Ramiro Valdés Daussá and Sergio Carbó, among others. It is also signed by Fulgencio Batista as Sergeant- Chief of the Armed Forces.

At Columbia, the idea prevails of a collective government that shall adopt decisions by simple majority. Thus is established the Comisión Ejecutiva or Pentarquía (Executive Commission or Five-Men Government) made up by Guillermo Portela, Porfirio Franca, Irisarri, Grau and Carbó.

And so they move from Columbia to the Presidential Palace. The Association wants to inform Céspedes that he has been toppled. The members of the Association wait at the garage of the executive mansion before they are received by Céspedes. Eventually, the five leaders of the organization are led into the mansion. They are accompanied by Batista, who still carries his sergeant insignia, and by Prío, who is initially denied entrance because he is wearing a short-sleeved shirt but then somebody lends him a jacket.

Céspedes waits in his office standing in pontifical solemnity. No one talks. Batista hides behind Carbó. *"Well, gentlemen, what do you have to say?"* Céspedes asks. Grau takes a step forward and says: *"We have come to inform you that we are now in charge of the government and that it is an honor to receive it from a patriot like you..."* At his point, Céspedes interrupts him to ask about the members of that Revolutionary Junta that is toppling him and Grau answers that it is made up by the Student's Directorate, the Revolutionary Union, the Radical ABC, and the Pro Law and Justice Organization. Céspedes asks again: *"Do these groups feel strong enough to overthrow the legal government?"* to which Grau responds: *"Every soldier and marine of the nation is with us too."* After hearing this, Céspedes takes a step back and pointing to the picture of his distinguished father hanging in the office of the Cuban Presidents he asks: *"Are you aware of the responsibility you are assuming?"* To which Grau sharply replies: *"Sir, it's been years since we came of age."*

Putting out the fire

The coup de grâce to the Executive Commission was dealt by Pedro Carbó on September 8, 1933 when he promoted Batista to Army Colonel. He did not consult with the other four government leaders although he did share his initiative with members of the Students Directorate loyal to him. This promotion was the pretext used by Irisarri, Franca and Portela to create a crisis just as thirty American battleships moved around the Island and Washington mobilized a considerable part of its marine infantry and reinforced its troops stationed in Guantánamo Naval Base for an intervention in Cuba. *"We are walking on fire!"* Irisarri said, and Grau responded: *"Let's put out the fire."*

Batista chose to ignore the Executive Commission and took to defining the future of the Republic all by himself. Franca decided not to show up at the Palace while Grau and the Directorate insisted on preserving the Five-Men Government. Irisarri was in favor of returning power to the petty politicians, and Portela supported him. They were scared at the possibility of a direct American intervention.

Grau, who sustained the revolutionary tendency of the government, felt that the most important thing was to save the revolution. But the Five-Men Government could not survive because both Irisarri and Portela submitted their resignation. It was necessary to go back to the presidential formula. At this point, the Directorate asked the members of the Executive Commission to appoint a President.

On the 9th, at 8:00 pm, Grau, Carbó, Irisarri and Portela meet on the third floor of the Presidential Palace. On the second floor, the Students Directorate is holding a closed session. The students suspect that Irisarri and Carbó want to hand power over to the politicians and that there is a plot to arrest Batista and bring back to their positions the officers removed on September 4. They agree to withdraw the vote of confidence given to the Commission for appointing a President, and Prío and Padilla put forward Grau's proposal for the highest office.

Prío and two of his comrades go up to the third floor and a violent discussion breaks out, then Portela asks them to leave because *"we have the historic and transcendental mission of electing a President."* Then Prío, his face red with anger, tells Portela to hold his horses. *"No, Mister Portela, that historic and transcendental mission is no longer yours. The Directorate has withdrawn its vote of confidence and elected Doctor Grau San Martín President of the Republic."* Irisarri and Portela are speechless. Carbó stands up and addresses Grau: *"Mr. President, at your service." "Thank you, Carbó,"* he responds adding, *"And now, let's move on!"*

This marked the beginning of *The One-Hundred Days Government.*

(Sources: *Crónica del año 33,* by Enrique de la Osa and texts from José M. Irisarri, Ramón Grau San Martín and Fulgencio Batista)

September 5, 2004

SHOWDOWN AT THE HOTEL NACIONAL

On October 2, 1933, after the coup d'état dealt a month before by a sergeant named Batista, some four hundred officers from the Army and the Navy, concentrated at the Hotel Nacional de Cuba, surrendered to their former subordinates after a bitter resistance. Two dead and twelve wounded officers was the result of the showdown; but this figure would rise dramatically to eleven and twenty-two, respectively, after the end of the confrontation when seventy detainees, already disarmed, were shot at close range. Although the exact figures were never released, it was estimated that the winners sustained no less than one-hundred dead and nearly two-hundred wounded. Here is the story.

Fifteen thousand bayonets

The military coup that toppled President Carlos Manuel de Céspedes, son of the Father of the Homeland, had stripped the officers of their command, which the soldiers and noncommissioned officers assumed, but they had retained their ranks. However, very few of those officers recognized the authority of that unknown stenographer sergeant, –and a mulatto to cap it all— who took over the Army leadership after the military putsch. By September 8, that sergeant was a colonel, and the following days would see the main leaders of the movement and others promoted to the ranks of captain and first lieutenant while the previous officers, depending on the view of the winners were divided into two groups: the "blemished" and the "unblemished". The former would be taken to trial for their crimes and outrages, and their complicity with Machado, while the others could remain in their respective camps or go back to them immediately if they were not there already. Such was the demand of the new government, that is, of the Executive Commission or Five-Men Government, and of Batista himself.

The journalist Sergio Carbó, a member of the Executive Commission in charge of the ministries of Interior, Defense and the Navy, offered the leadership of the Army, or at least he pretended he had, to colonels Perdomo and Quesada, but both declined due to the humiliating conditions in which they were supposed to discharge their duty. *"Look, you must understand that officers cannot take orders from a sergeant,"* said a captain to Batista in the presence of Carbó who emphatically responded: *"the fact of the matter is that you, the officers, have the discipline but he has fifteen thousand bayonets on his side."* It was right at that moment that it occurred to Carbó to promote Batista to General, but the sergeant only accepted to be a colonel and Carbó promoted him without consulting his colleagues in the government. With such promotion decree, Carbó was inadvertently dismantling the Executive Commission established only four days before, and opening the way to the government of Ramón Grau San Martín.

Ferrer's plan

On September 6, General Julio Sanguily, ousted from his position of Army Chief only four days after his appointment, booked a room at the Hotel Nacional. Still convalescing from a surgery, he wanted peace and quiet, something he could not find in his house located near the Columbia Barracks since Sergeant Belisario Hernández, an assistant to Batista, constantly harassed his family and everyone who visited his home. Soon other displaced officers who refused to submit to the soldiers also sought accommodation at the Hotel Nacional. They recognized Sanguily as their one and only chief. It is no accident that they sought refuge there, since US Ambassador Benjamin Summer Welles had set up his official residence in that hotel after the end of his diplomatic mission to the Island was announced and he had to leave his house at the Barandilla suburbs.

Since the days of Machado's fall, the hotel had enjoyed a certain extraterritorial status; it was being managed by an American company while the Platt Amendment and other bilateral treaties obligated the Cuban government to ensure its integrity, just like all US properties and lives in Cuba or else…a direct American military intervention could be expected. After the collapse of Machado's government on August 12, when the people were carried away by passion, many of Machado's loyalists sought refuge at the Hotel Nacional where Ambassador Welles provided a *de facto* extraterritorial protection. The most notorious case was that of ex Army Chief General Alberto Herrera, since the ambassador threatened to disembark the marines to guard the hotel if at any point he felt the life of the general was in jeopardy.

Those military men and their chief were not precisely on vacation there, nor were they enjoying the amenities offered by the luxurious hotel. On September 4, they had failed to defend their positions with as much as a gesture; however, they did not abandon their hopes to get them back. To that end, Doctor Horacio Ferrer, an outstanding ophthalmologist and veteran of the War of Independence, retired army colonel and, for a short time, Secretary of Defense and the Navy in the Céspedes government, was moving swiftly but conscientiously. He went from his house on Línea and L streets to the hotel and from there to the US embassy in No. 5 Misiones Street and back to the hotel.

He was contacting the old political chieftains and calling on the connections he still had in the armed institutions.

He also visited ex President Céspedes in his residence on 23rd and M streets...What did he want? In his book entitled *Con el rifle al hombro*[10], 1950, he answered this question without even flushing; acting as a spokesman of the dismissed officers he was trying to attract people to what Welles called Ferrer's Plan with the purpose of inviting an American military intervention of the Island. The plan consisted in returning Céspedes to the presidency with the support of the marines and reinstating the officers. Then, these would dismiss the newly appointed officers, disarm the troops and the civilians, and recruit and train a new army.

Ambassador Welles, who had initially supported Ferrer's project, was forced to explicitly withdraw his support when Washington refused to go along with the plan. At that time, President Roosevelt was fostering his *Good Neighbor* policy and the upcoming 7th American International Conference in Montevideo advocated the principle of non-intervention enthusiastically sponsored by the governments of Mexico and Argentina. Given the circumstances, Grau's dismissal had to be the result of an operation that short of a military intervention could facilitate both political and military domestic actions against him.

According to this plan, Céspedes should go to the Hotel Nacional and from there inform the diplomatic corps that he was reassuming his presidential duties, which he had not officially renounced on September 4. Subsequently, he should issue his decrees by radio. The situation, according to Ferrer, would become untenable for there would be two governments in Cuba and this would force the hand of the US administration which up to this time had not recognized Grau's government. But Céspedes declined the proposal. He said: *"I will not be the instrument of bloodshed or of a foreign intervention in Cuba."* After his death, a plaque with this phrase was placed on the

[10] *With the Rifle on My Shoulder*

wall of the mausoleum where his remains were laid to rest at the Colon necropolis; a plaque that some vandals recently destroyed with a hammer.

"Give them a hug!"

Despite all efforts to find some accommodation, the officers refused to abandon the Hotel Nacional and submit to the troops' classification of '*blemished*' and '*unblemished*'. But, they sent new envoys to Ambassador Summer Welles. These told the American diplomat that they were willing to return to the barracks if that helped avoid the eclipse of sovereignty. The ambassador, who always played with two sets of cards, replied that he was in no position to teach dignity to the officers but that nothing could change the course of events. That is, his intransigence was closing the door to a possible Cuban solution while the intervention hung on the country like the Sword of Damocles and he insisted with Washington on a restricted or limited intervention because the mutineers could not prevail without US assistance.

Meanwhile, Dr. Ferrer, who did not stop waging the ghost of intervention from the car of interference, visited President Grau at least twice. He asked for Céspedes to be reinstated in his position and even offered Grau a ministry in that government; of course, provided he first resigned from office. Ferrer wanted to take the President's resignation to the officers. *"My resignation?"* said Grau –who was not yet 'the Old Man'— giving a hint of the sly politician he would become later, during his days as the Messiah of the Cuban Identity: *"No, Dr. Ferrer, I can't give you my resignation for your friends, the officers, but look there is something you can give them. Give them a hug, an affectionate hug, from me. Don't forget to tell them."*

By then, Welles had decided to keep his distance so he checked out of the Hotel Nacional and moved to the Hotel Presidente. On the other hand, as the government threatened to cut off water and electricity to the Nacional, its employees abandoned their jobs to avoid serving the officers. They were starting to suffer what a subordinate must stand when they had to clean the officers' rooms, polish their shoes, operate the elevators, wash the dishes and cook the meals while the provisions lasted at the hotel.

No, no, but yes

When after September 6, 1933, the officers dismissed from their positions by the coup d'état of September 4 began showing up at the lobby of the Hotel Nacional de Cuba, the first reaction of hotel manager Robert P. Taylor was to deny them accommodation under the pretext that he had no rooms available. But, in the end, he caved in to the insistence of the officers when these offered guarantees of payment for which they received money from the most affluent colleagues and from more than a few civilians. The ophthalmologist Horacio Ferrer contributed one hundred pesos while two thousand were donated by someone supposedly named Agapito García but who was never identified. As the grapevine would have it, it was no other than Benjamin Summer Welles, the US Ambassador in Havana.

But, on the 12th, Taylor grew scared again as he realized that his hotel had become a military commanding post. He then phoned his senior, the chairman of the Manhattan Plaza Hotel Co. in New York, who had the Hotel Nacional under a management contract but was told not to worry because Washington had given Grau San Martín 48 hours to reinstate Céspedes in the presidency and then the officers would leave the facility.

The military commanding post had a military guard, an information bureau and a foreign communications office. They produced a daily agenda which was placed on a bulletin board at the lobby where the higher officers were notified when they were on duty as well as those who guarded the hotel main floor, the second floor terraces, the roofs, the storages, the boilers, the dinning room and the kitchen. A specially arranged guard protected the water reserves. The headquarters was headed by Julio Sanguily and made up by two Army colonels, two Navy colonels, an Aviation captain and Horacio Ferrer representing no one but himself . At this point, the ophthalmologist, who yearned for the presidency of the Republic said "*No, no, but yes.*" In fact, the highest office had recently eluded him when the Armed Forces refused to accept General Herrera as a replacement for Machado and proposed to Summer Welles the name of Ferrer, which the diplomat rejected choosing Céspedes instead. The officers designated to leave the hotel had to spend the night at the Ford agency, located where the ministry of Labor stands today, on 23rd St, and move around in its cars. An assault company was also structured.

Twenty-six Springfields

The officers, who had carried their handguns to the hotel, also had twenty-six Springfield rifles, with fifty shots each, which were distributed among the guards based on the rooftops, and six or seven other rifles distributed among the guards in the different floors. The entrance to the lobby and the staff door on P Street were protected by hand machineguns. Lieutenant Adam Silva, one of the officers staying at the Hotel Nacional, wrote in his book *La gran mentira*[11], that they found in the building about forty shotguns "*best fit for chasing kittens than for warfare,*" and a few hunting rifles –he doesn't say how many. Some say that the shotguns were introduced by friends and relatives of the officers during visits when soldiers and militiamen from the Pro Ley y Justicia organization and the Ejército Caribe, based at the University, had not yet laid an extensive and rigorous circle around the hotel. Others believe that these weapons were taken there by US embassy officials who were never denied access, the same as women.

The days went by and the US military intervention anticipated by Ferrer and the officers did not materialize. Off the coast of Havana and Santiago, the *USS Mississippi*, the cruisers *Indianapolis* and *Richmond* and twenty-four American destroyers of various tonnages as well as four gunboats stood by. But, the assistance they expected from the No. 1 Artillery

[11] *The Big Lie*

Battalion of the Tactical Forces in Matanzas and their accomplices in the Columbia Barracks was not forthcoming. They still trusted the support they hoped to receive from the terrorist organization ABC. Meanwhile, the situation in the hotel became distressing due to the lack of supplies. They could only make one meal a day.

It was then that, on Sanguily's orders, a plan was designed to leave the hotel on a warpath, march on the Presidential Palace and make Grau their prisoner. To that end, ABC groups would simultaneously attack the five positions covered by soldiers and militiamen in control of the various ways of access to the hotel so that the officers could outmaneuver, subdue and disarm them. But the plan was soon rejected since the officers distrusted the civilians' capacity to move around the city inadvertently with their weapons and to act simultaneously against the five enemy positions. The hopes then focused on another objective. The ABC would send them two-hundred rifles, of the two thousand it claimed to have, with 200 bullets each. But those weapons were never received because the ABC was preserving them for its own plan that would soon unfold.

The green light

Meanwhile, Grau's government would spare no effort to reach an accommodation with the officers. Journalist Mario Kuchilán, a witness to these events, claimed: *"The truth is that everything possible was done to negotiate an agreement but the officers were adamant...they would only accept the restoration of the command that they had failed to defend before with as much as a word."*

In the meantime, Welles proceeded with his underhand scheming ways alternatively moving between Grau and Batista, speaking ill of one to the other fomenting a showdown between the two men. One day he would find Batista "*reasonable*" and the next Grau would be "*extremely conciliatory.*" But the latter, shrewd and hesitant and with his characteristic gift to avoid those subjects in which he would rather not define himself, ended up puzzling, exasperating and annoying the stuck-up diplomat.

Welles went as far as to assure Grau that his own lack of confidence in him was nothing personal, that it was due to the fact that his presidency was the result of a military coup. On the other hand, Welles was coming to perceive Batista, the mastermind of the mutiny, as a more acceptable choice. This much he wrote in his messages to the State Department, because, as he said, the colonel knew well that *"neither the stubbornness of the Students Directorate nor Grau's could interfere with the solution of the immediate political issues"* and because the colonel expressed *"his adamant opposition to all kind of communist activity or propaganda."* Still, Welles did not cease to encourage Horacio Ferrer and the officers in the Hotel Nacional in their conspiracy, which had the sympathies of Menocal, Mendieta and Miguel Mariano and whose "natural ally", albeit passive, was the ABC.

"The Army is more united than ever in Havana and Batista's position is thus stronger…Grau's only support are the students," wrote the ambassador in his reports to Washington. If he had to choose from Grau and Batista, he would reject the former because the man did not toe the line and slipped away with his hollow or sharp words, depending on the circumstances, while the latter submitted to the ambassador's orders. About these moments Lionel Soto wrote: *"Summer Welles had started to perceive Batista's potential, he had taken the man's measure, but in the end he would have to take sides with the oligarchy because despite Batista's first steps on the path of treason he was no more than an outsider, an ex sergeant, a mulatto, and an absurdly pretentious man with a shady background. Welles was not playing Batista's card yet; therefore, if in need of precision, the man could be sacrificed in favor of the golden reaction."* As a crafty person, maybe Batista was aware of that for he hurriedly assured the ambassador that Cuba would pay back the interests on its foreign debt; that the army would remove from the sugar mills any person the managements considered undesirable; and, that the authorities would expel from the Island every agitator and foreign communist.

On October 1, 1933, the ambassador and the colonel met again at a house in the Kohly suburb. Welles urged him to preserve order and Batista, always his sly self, responded that he would not be able to preserve it *"while the Hotel Nacional remained a hotbed of tension with the officers in a rebellious mood."* Of course, he knew that that hotbed of tension and those officers were under the protective umbrella of the US embassy, but he insisted: *"That order you're demanding depends on the possibility of attacking with our troops the pocket of resistance of those officers at the Hotel Nacional."*

"Do what you have to do," the ambassador said, thus giving the green light for the assault. Batista did not waste a second and ordered the onset of actions the following day.

"Didn't you want groceries?"

In his book *Con el rifle al hombro*, Horacio Ferrer writes that in the morning of Sunday October 1, the officers received a truck that managed to smoothly get around the soldiers guarding the hotel staff gate. *"The truck brought plenty of groceries but since there were four hundred of us that could last for only three more days."* They would not need that many days. On Monday 2, about six in the evening, they surrendered to the soldiers. During the twenty-five days the officers spent at the Hotel Nacional, General Sanguily, the leader of the mutineers, insisted with his men to keep up their courage for their plans had a 75 percent possibility of success. Obviously, the General had not considered the 75-mm cannons Colonel Batista had at his command.

On October 2, at 5:25 in the morning, Commander Américo Lora could see from his window in room 668 that on 23rd Street, in front of the Ford agency building, several soldiers were getting off an armored vehicle and taking positions by the hotel laundry. It struck him that the assault was imminent so he ran to room 620 to inform Captain Carlos Montero, Sanguily's assistant, who at the moment was in charge of the company on duty. A few minutes later, several officers in room 202 watched as the armored vehicle returned via 23rd St. with another group of soldiers. Carrying out their instructions, one of the officers shouted to the new arrivals that they should leave, that nobody in the hotel was interested in a fight, to which one of the soldiers retorted: *"Didn't you want groceries? Now, you'll get them!"* At that point, the senior officer on duty, Commander Emilio Rousseau, advised of the situation, ordered various groups to examine the perimeter of the building. By now, a row of soldiers could be seen crossing the hotel fence on the Malecón. The officers asked them not to fire but the response was a simultaneous discharge of a number of firearms. After this, those who had laid siege to the hotel fired a volley on the facility. Ferrer, who was sleeping in room 735, woke up to the barrage of shots coming through his window.

Journalist Mario Kuchilán has said that what happened at the Nacional during the first hours more than a combat was a "*target shooting*". The mutineers better positioned and with better shots –including members of the Army and Navy shooting teams— were easily getting rid of their adversaries. The assault on the hotel lobby was repelled with a machinegun while the riflemen on the terraces of the second floor swept the reinforcements and silenced the machineguns set up 150 to 200 meters from the building. From 21st and N streets, a 75-mm cannon was shooting grenades into rooms and halls, but the shots of the 37-mm cannon positioned at the School of Physics in the University were falling in the sea, and on the Manhattan Hotel in Belascoaín and San Lázaro streets; the same as the shells from the battery set up on M and Calzada streets. There, several blocks away from the Hotel Nacional and out of sight from it, in an underground garage, Colonel Batista organized his commanding post. According to Kuchilán, the colonel remained inside the armored Lincoln that had been General Herrera's wrapped in a black Napoleonic coat and carrying a huge peaked cap.

Approximately at 8:00 in the morning the assailants reduced the volume of fire and sought more guarded positions. At that point, Batista communicated with Grau over the phone and said: *"Doctor, to seize the hotel, we must destroy it. I'm going to use every cannon available."* The President expressed his consent and instructed the deputy minister of Foreign Affairs to ask the diplomatic corps to evacuate the residences close to the theater of operations.

A truce

Batista ordered to concentrate on the Hotel Nacional the cannons from all of the light batteries available, and also those of large caliber from one of the batteries positioned at La Cabaña Fortress which could target the hotel from its location. A visit was paid to López Ferrer, the Spanish ambassador and dean of the diplomatic corps, who lived at N and 13 streets, to inform him of the upcoming shelling. The diplomat volunteered to act as a broker in the conflict but not before he protested for the violation of International Law since the hotel was not a fortified position and it was surrounded by civilian population that would be exposed to grave risks. At the end, López Ferrer could not exercise his good offices because his daughter would not allow him to leave the house.

At 12:30 pm there was an unexpected calm as the assailants declared a ceasefire to allow a representation of the Red Cross into the hotel. This was carrying a note from Batista to Sanguily urging the officers to lay down arms and leave the building in groups of five, at ten-minute intervals. He offered to respect their lives. The truce, Batista indicated, would last one hour.

The officers then asked to have it extended until 3:00 pm, which was accepted. They wanted to take out their wounded comrades –no one had died until that moment— and some wives like Sanguily's, who were still at the hotel. During that period they would also vote on whether to admit defeat or carry on fighting. As Kuchilán put it, in the hotel they had a strategy for resistance but not for winning; they had discipline but not solidarity and for some days many officers had wanted to leave which they didn't do for fear of retribution. By this time, the ammunition could last them one hour to the most, if they economized it, but it would last barely fifteen minutes if they had to fend off another assault.

General Sanguily personally counted the votes and Horacio Ferrer started to draft the answer to Batista's note. He asked that, under supervision of the diplomatic corps, the surrendered officers were released and their handguns respected, but some asked to be taken to a foreign flag ship in order to leave the country under protection of the US marines. Batista did not receive any proposal since at 3:00 pm the shooting resumed.

Taking advantage of the truce, the army had surrounded the hotel with cannons and machineguns while the Navy gunboats *Patria* and *Libre* also shot the hotel from the sea. The building was filling up with toxic fumes and the officers, realizing that they would receive no help from abroad and refusing to fight sought refuge in the cellar and demanded Sanguily, who opposed it, to order capitulation. Eventually, one of General's staffers ordered the white flag hoisted on the terrace. The combat had lasted nearly twelve hours.

The slaughter

Once detained, Sanguily and Ferrer were taken to the commanding post. Batista was accompanied by Guiteras and when Sanguily who addressed him as 'mister' instead of colonel asked him to discuss the conditions of the capitulation he didn't pay attention and ordered them both transferred to La Cabaña Fortress. That military prison, as well as the ones in Columbia and Castillo del Príncipe received the rebel officers. But not all of them because when the last seventy, already disarmed, had left the hotel and were waiting in the garden to be transferred to the prisons, a shooting burst out and a number of them were killed.

It has never been determined exactly who gave the order or how the shooting started. Some say that it was Batista himself who arrived in the hotel via O Street in his armored Lincoln and asked the soldiers to leave the detainees alone. After this, writes Adam Silva in his book *La gran mentira*, a whistle blew and many civilians came to the garden from the adjacent tennis courts. These were students and members of the group *For Law and Justice* or the *Radical ABC* who opened fire with pistols and revolvers on the helpless officers. Others who were also in the group with Adam Silva have said that they were shot from the second floor of the hotel by civilians who did not respect the orders of the soldiers and sergeants who had them in custody and that somehow tried to protect them.

However, *Time* magazine wrote that as the officers left the hotel with their arms down and ready to surrender, the soldiers opened fire killing ten of them right there. Actually, there were nine dead and ten injured.

The *Bohemia* magazine of October 15, 1933 wrote that the following day officers from the American battleships docked in Havana harbor visited the Hotel Nacional de Cuba where they saw the damages caused to the building and took whatever they wanted as souvenir.

(Sources: Texts by Lionel Soto, Horacio Ferrer and Mario Kuchilán)

October 2, 9 and 16, 2005

THE ATARES CASTLE

President Grau smelled something fishy when he asked the usher to find the assistant on duty and he was told the man was not in the Presidential Palace; he asked for the man's stand-in but he wasn't there either. Then, he asked for Commander Pablo Rodríguez, chief of the Palace's Guard, and was told the man was out. Almost at the same time engineer Gustavo Moreno, Minister of Construction, came into his office with the news that *"something strange"* was going on at the Columbia Barracks. The President understood that he was alone in the Palace, and besieged; it was November 8, 1933.

At this time, shots were heard near the executive mansion. The previous day, an officer with the aviation corps had informed Grau that on orders from his superiors he would be pulling out the two antiaircraft machineguns set up on the rooftop, but the president did not cave in. When Pablo Rodríguez showed up and informed the President that the air force had rebelled, Grau called Batista on the phone and requested troops to reinforce the executive mansion's guard but Batista replied that he could spare none because the forces had failed to respond to the call of general alarm and *"this here looks bad, Mr. President, pretty bad."*

At the Palace the situation was no better, since the guards were giving obvious signs of indiscipline. Grau went down to the patio and harangued the troops. "*Soldiers, you are now the protagonists of a great historic privilege...the reaction wants to bring back the darkness of another tyranny. You will help me save the Republic...!*" he said and his words were met with a resounding applause.

Soon, he organized defense. The bloodiest urban confrontation known in Cuba until then was about to begin.

The conspiracy

Batista who right to the end proclaimed his alleged condition of "*natural leader of the Armed Forces*" was never really convinced of that himself. On September 1933, following the coup d'état that ousted President Céspedes, as Batista gave himself the rank of colonel and Army Chief swearing time and again on the life of his wife and daughter that he had no personal ambitions, he was already unpopular with the troops that wanted to bring back the old '*unblemished*' officers they had chosen to be their leaders. These same old officers dismissed from their positions, including Commander Ciro Leonard, were the ones that in connivance with the American ambassador encouraged the disgruntled troops.

The countercoup was planned for September 12 and then postponed for October 2, when it was not carried out because the rebel officers entrenched at the Hotel Nacional were put down that same day. The new date agreed on was November 8. In the first minutes of that day, the aviation, with pilots Martull, Pepe Barrientos, Agüero and Collazo moving swiftly, the latter as leader of the group, would bomb the Columbia Barracks and if met with resistance, those inside the facility who were committed to the movement would revolt, as well as those from the barracks in Dragones, San Ambrosio and the Atarés Castle. It was thought that the troops in La Cabaña Fortress and the Navy would join the rebels, and –despite the reservations of the military who felt that the incorporation of civilians could create other problems— also many individuals from the ABC under Carlos Saladrigas, leader of the A-2 group of that terrorist organization who decided to take part without informing his chief, Joaquín Martínez Sáenz, leader of the A-1 group, who preferred to toy with the political opposition.

The ABC conspirators set up camp in a house on Concordia and Galiano streets, while the military, which constantly changed places to avoid Batista's Secret Service, were eventually given away by a traitor. On the eve of the rebellion, in the afternoon, Batista ordered the arrest of all of the senior officers who had not been detained during the events of the Hotel Nacional, and phoned Collazo to the aviation headquarters to advise him to be tough if anything was tried against him while offering the man a promotion from lieutenant to commander. Collazo then tried to backpedal and informed his colleagues that he was taking distance from the issue, but they did not believe him. Anyway, it was too late already to contradict the order and the aviation proceeded according to plan. Three *Corsario* aircrafts with ten twenty-five pound bombs, and two fighter planes with two one-hundred pound bombs, were ready for take off.

Resistance

Approximately two thousand members of the ABC reached the aviation corps. Many police stations, including the headquarters of that force located some two hundred meters from the Presidential Palace, were restrained by the government's opposition. The same happened with the Dragones barracks, where there were soldiers but also outstanding members of the so-called Republican Guard led by Guiteras. Commander Leonard took on the San Ambrosio barracks where the army kept its weapons and the reserve of ammunitions. Then, aircrafts piloted by Barrientos, Martull, Agüero and Collazo took off and, after several nose-dive actions on the barracks, dropped a twenty-five pound bomb near Batista's house, but of course by this time the colonel had already taken refuge in the basement of the Military Club, while Agüero flew over Havana but did not drop his bombs and Collazo, an inexperienced pilot, dropped his bombs without removing the save, and the antiaircraft batteries on the rooftops of the Presidential Palace fended off the blows of Martull's aircraft. President Grau remained in the Palace, alongside the soldiers. In the morning, he had ordered the battery of a small cannon to fire on the police station that kept urging him to surrender.

The aviation rebels failed to take advantage of the confusion in Columbia as the revolt broke out and those inside who were committed to the action didn't keep their end of the bargain. In addition, they overlooked the need of taking measures to defend their position and instead called on Leonard to come from San Ambrosio with reinforcements and attack the headquarters. They also called on those entrenched at the Dragones barracks but there was no answer. Meanwhile, Captain Gregorio Querejeta, with a clarity that Batista didn't show, reorganized the troops in Columbia and attacked the aviation field, which he seized after three hours of violent fight.

But this action that took the lives of some twenty men, left forty injured and some four hundred prisoners was not the end of the uprising. At ten in the morning, there was a rumor that Columbia remained loyal to Batista and Grau. Army troops under Belisario Hernández, an assistant to Batista, seized back the police stations although some of them resisted, such as those of Cerro and Almendares, while those in the precinct near the Palace joined by Blas Hernández, the rebel from Las Villas, decided to abandon it and head for San Ambrosio to stick together with Leonard. But prior to this, the members of ABC had hastily left the aviation facilities and sought refuge in Almendares. Still, despite the turn of the events, the radio stations controlled by the mutineers continued broadcasting news on Batista's detention and the proclamation of Leonard as Army Chief.

In the meantime, those gathered in San Ambrosio left the facilities under harassment from the Navy vessel *Cuba*. Then, Blas Hernández advised that they cross Havana to gather force on the Managua hills, and Lieutenant Otero, Leonard's second in command, suggested to head for the hills of Jaruco. Neither of the two advises were accepted by Commander Ciro Leonard who, trusting the arrival of the five thousand men from the center of the Island promised by ex Colonel Emiliano Amiel –that never came— decided to head for the Atarés Castle, a mousetrap that he would not leave alive.

A period of confusion

Today, when so many years have passed, the final months of 1933 still seem one of the most confusing periods of republican Cuba. Grau's government, never recognized by Washington, made all sorts of concessions to win that recognition. The President wanted to dismiss Guiteras, the minister of the Interior, Defense and the Navy, but inexplicably Colonel Batista backed the combative minister. The reason behind this support was Batista's interest in appointing Sergio Carbó to that position, something the US ambassador rejected thinking the candidate might be too radical. The parties of the oligarchy and the bourgeoisie tried to raise Mendieta to the highest office as the man kept saying *"yes, I want but no, I don't, although yes, I do;"* he really wanted to be President, without undermining the predominance of Batista and the Army.

The plan conceived by Fernando Ortiz to keep Grau in the executive mansion with a renovated cabinet falls through. At the University, the students blame the Directorate for the disasters of the government. In a meeting where the Directorate speakers are booed by the crowd, Chibás stands up to support *"the only government in Cuba that has defended the Cuban interests from the voracity of the American companies."* This calms down the participants but the Directorate is already a dead political force. With its historic mission fulfilled, the organization is dissolved since the students won't appear supporting a President who hesitates and caves in to Batista's insolence and his repression of the workers movement.

Grapevine

The press echoes the most incredible grapevine. On November 1, for example, the newspapers take for granted Grau's resignation, the ascent of Mendieta and the return of ousted President

Céspedes as well as Batista's continuation as Army Chief and the US recognition of any government that replaces the current one. Amidst these rumors, *El País Libre* runs large headlines announcing that Washington has ordered a military intervention in Cuba. This was untrue but it seemed real on November 3 when the battleship *Wyoming*, with two thousand marines on board, entered the Havana harbor.

Although the *Wyoming*, a flagship commanded by Admiral Freeman who was the head of a fleet of thirty naval war units threatening Cuba for months, was really coming to replace the battleship *Richmond* the confusion was capitalized by the government and its loyalists who claimed –and this was not far from the truth— that an occupation would reinstate in their positions the officers displaced on September 4, and lead to the creation of a new army, among other things.

In the interim, Batista ordered the restructuring of the armed institutions with the suppression of the military rank of General and a reduction in the number of officers. As of this moment, the top rank in the Cuban Army would be that of Commander, although a colonel –no other than Batista himself— would be Chief of the General Staff, assisted by several officers with the provisional rank of lieutenant colonels, while they remained in that position. One of the sergeants of the September 4 coup promoted to Commander on October 12, José Eleuterio Pedraza, would be a lieutenant colonel and the army General Supervisor, that is, the second man in the military hierarchy. At the Navy, fifteen students of the Naval Academy were promoted to ensigns. The decision was also made to raise the pensions of soldiers and noncommissioned officers.

In that month of November 1933, the government headed by Grau San Martín, attacked from left and right by Tiryans and Trojans –students, communists, the petty bourgeoisie, the oligarchy and Washington, and Batista from within its own ranks— seemed to have its hours numbered. Still, on the 7th, on the eve of the uprising against him, Grau, who had already signed a legislation limiting the number of working hours to eight and providing the paid weekend holiday, also signed the law nationalizing labor thus ensuring every Cuban the right to work as every work center must have 50% of their payrolls covered with Cuban nationals. None of his ministers, not even Batista, agreed with this piece of legislation. At the cabinet meeting where it was discussed Guiteras had opposed it on the grounds that it was an assault on the solidarity of the working class. *"However,"* he said, *"if the President approves it I shall defend it."*

The uprising

Come November 8, ex officers, active officers and soldiers, and members of the terrorist organization ABC take over the barracks of Dragones and San Ambrosio, the Atarés Castle and numerous police stations, including the headquarters of this force. They also seize the headquarters of the judicial police and the site of the provincial government along with the ministries of Public Instruction, Healthcare and Communications. They take over radio stations, too, and rather easily dominate the Aviation Corps where a mutiny has started while in the Columbia Barracks the soldiers, apathetic and disconcerted, don't know at the beginning whether to take sides with Batista or his opponents.

At dawn, on the 8th, Havana was practically in the hands of the rebels. Still loyal to the government were La Cabaña and La Fuerza fortresses and the 1st Artillery Battalion as well as the Navy whose leader invited Grau to move to the seat of his General Staff at La Punta Castle but the President declined the offer because he was determined to stay in the Palace come what may. Another offer, this time of Uruguayan Ambassador Benjamín Fernández Medina, to receive the presidential family in that country's diplomatic mission was also declined by Paulina Alsina, Grau's sister in law, who responded that the President's family would share his fate.

In the morning of that same day, Captain Gregorio Querejeta at the head of army troops managed to take over the aviation field, and the Palace Guard commanded by Grau himself put to flight some 1500 to 2000 people who were advancing from the police station on the executive office with the aim of occupying it and arresting the President. The same guard, alongside marines and civilians under Guiteras and army troops commanded by Batista's assistant Captain Belisario Hernández fought the opponents concentrated at the already mentioned precinct and in the course of the day recovered the other police stations.

As to the thwarted effort to occupy the Presidential Palace, Grau would write some years later that "*...a crowd armed with every tool they found fit for the assault geared for action. Somebody told me they were coming to take over the Palace. I ordered the antiaircraft on the rooftop to be ready to shoot up to the air while the soldiers positioned behind the windows would shoot forward. I wanted to avoid an unnecessary bloodshed. When the crowd was about to cross the street I ordered the troops to fire. There was a terrible noise and the reaction was what we expected, a disorderly and tumultuous escape leaving behind hats, sticks, rifles and old junk spread all over the plaza in front of the Palace, like trophies of that battle we had won...*"

State of siege

The barracks of Dragones –Fifth Military District to which the Rural Guard operating in the countryside of Havana province subordinated— and San Ambrosio, seat of the Army Management Department, would not resist for long. In the early hours of November 9, the occupants of the Dragones barracks, much decimated by defections, realized they could not win and started pulling out slowly and moving toward the Atarés Castle. Those in San Ambrosio did likewise after enduring three hours of shelling from the cruiser *Cuba* anchored in the bay, and before the army troops, again under Captain Querejeta, seized the facility.

Very little happened outside the capital of the country; a few groups unsuccessfully revolted in support of their comrades in Havana. This was the case in Matanzas, Las Villas, Camagüey and Oriente, while in Batabanó and Bejucal there were some outbursts of violence but they were quickly suffocated. The swift response to the mutiny in Havana had a paralyzing effect on its sympathizers in other regions.

On November 8, the government proclaimed a state of war for the entire country and let the rebels know that once captured they would be court-martialed. The next day Havana woke up to a state of siege.

On the Soto Hill

The construction of the Atarés Castle on the Soto Hill, at the depth of the Havana Bay, took place in the aftermath of the British occupation of Havana (1762) which evidenced the necessity to safeguard and defend the roads leading from the city to the neighboring rural areas. Thus, after some other works were completed, the construction of this fortress was undertaken some 1500 yards south of the old city wall. During President Machado's term in office, this facility was under command of a notorious Captain Manuel Crespo Moreno. At that time, it was the seat of the 5th Squad of the Rural Guard, a very well trained unit that also provided security to the President of the country. During the uprising of November 8 to 9, 1933, some 1000 to 1500 civilians, ex officers and active members of the army opposed to Grau San Martín's government, took refuge there.

These people were under command of Ciro Leonard, an academy officer who after the coup d'état of September 4 had kept a low profile and moved carefully among army cadres but that as from October 2, when the government drove the officers out of the Hotel Nacional, had remained in hiding at a house on the Malecón.

The Atarés Castle was the last pocket of resistance of rebels in the capital. Leonard had rejected every suggestion and kept his ground. He really thought that the US marines would land and take him out of that mousetrap.

The slaughter

The army moved swiftly to position itself in the surroundings of the fortress that it needed to recover. Infantry troops, again commanded by Captain Gregorio Querejeta, were deployed in the area and the shelling began at 9:00 am. A mortar under command of Corporal René L. Scott, kept shooting on the castle from the intersection of Concha and Cristina streets while one 37-mm cannon and four Schneider cannons shot from the Mercado Unico and Loma del Burro, respectively. These were supported by the artillery and the Navy cruisers *Patria* and *Cuba* shooting with their three and four inches batteries while Querejeta's men kept harassing the position with rifles and 30- and 50-mm machineguns.

The men under siege in Atarés responded with heavy fire but the effects of the mortar shots were devastating. The grenades, with their 260 pellets and metal pieces from the cover, accurately fell in the patio of the building and the place was so packed that the ammunitions caused numerous victims. It is said that one of these grenades had killed twenty soldiers and injured scores of others.

At 2:00 in the afternoon, the situation of the besieged was desperate. Lieutenant Gener, who had been in command of Atarés until the arrival of Leonard, was gravely injured and Blas Hernández, wounded and captured the day before at the police station from which he was transferred to Casuso's Clinic, in Jesús del Monte, from where he escaped, had been injured again. It is said that at this point Commander Leonard gave a friend officer the mission of communicating by phone with the US Embassy to inquire when the marines would be landing and when he was told there would be no landing, he took his own life with a shot to the head.

At this time, inside the castle many were claiming for surrender, most emphatically the members of the ABC. At 3:00 pm, a number of them left the fortress and carrying white handkerchiefs in their hands slid down the hill; it was fatal, for they were caught between the fire of the assailants and of those inside the fortress, therefore, many were killed or wounded. After this incident, the besieged claimed for negotiations, and at 4:00 pm the army recovered Atarés.

A situation similar to that experienced at the Hotel Nacional had unfolded here as civilian and military men shot on those who had already surrendered. Mario Alfonso Hernández, a soldier who was part of the Junta that orchestrated the coup d'état in Columbia on September 4 and who was now a Captain and assistant to Batista walked toward a group of prisoners and asked for Blas Hernández. The wounded man who was lying on the floor tried to rise on his elbow to respond, but the captain put a pistol to his head and said: *"This was your last rebellion,"* and pulled the trigger.

Antonio Guiteras, who was just arriving in Atarés, was immediately told of the execution. *"I think that killing Blas was not a correct decision, but Mario Alfonso is one of the few revolutionaries of the September 4 Movement,"* he said. Soon, Batista would give Mario Alfonso a dosage of his own medicine.

It happened when in August 1934, Alfonso, who by this time was lieutenant colonel and chief of the Juan Rius Rivera Regiment in Pinar del Río, demanded from the Army Chief to honor the pact establishing that the leadership of the Armed Forces would rotate among members of the Junta. Batista did not respond immediately but said he would soon do.

Mario Alfonso had a big mouth. The fact is that on September 4, when Sergeant Batista hesitated before aviation Captain Mario Torres Menier and tried to persuade him that the only purpose of the movement of soldiers and noncommissioned officers was to claim for some material advantages, Alfonso fired back in public: *"Hey, Batista, cut off that crap...what we really want here is a change of government."*

Faced with the possibility of losing his position at the head of the Armed Forces due to that agreement, Batista accused Mario Alfonso and two other officers of being drunkards and drug-addicts, and said they were responsible for organizing an alleged coup d'état. The senior officers were immediately arrested and summarily court-martialed. The document making the announcement and saying that the Army Chief loved Mario Alfonso not as a subordinate or a comrade but as family was read in every military barrack at reveille and after the sound of the retreat. But, by then Mario Alfonso was dead. In the early hours of morning someone had knocked on his door; he asked who it was and after hearing the response he confidently opened up. At this point, he was machine-gunned in the presence of his wife. This was Colonel Batista's response to his demand.

Promotions

Like in the Hotel Nacional, the number of victims in the combat of Atarés was never known. After walking around the place, Guiteras spoke of 150 to 200 dead, but the people have always suspected there were many more. The press reported some 500 dead and over 1,000 injured from both sides in addition to the victims of other actions that took place in the capital. The number of detainees exceeded eight-hundred.

During the events of November 1933, Ambassador Summer Welles stayed in touch with the rebels. In his reports to the State Department, he mentioned the ABC calls to destroy US properties with the purpose of attracting a US intervention, and aware that President Roosevelt was opposed he made the request surreptitiously as an alleged appeal from the foreigners' community in Cuba. He also touched on the humanitarian issue: the lives of the members of said organization would be in danger if the uprising was crushed. He was wrong. President Grau refused to sign the death sentences dictated by the military courts.

Both Batista and Grau, the same as Guiteras, understood that if the uprising had succeeded the three would have been removed, that's why after these events Batista's position consolidated and the government strengthened. On November 9, following the developments in the Atarés Castle, Batista made statements in support of Grau and the President did the same for him. That same day, the executive office issued a decree for the *post mortem* promotion of officers and sergeants killed in the actions of the Hotel Nacional and the Atarés Castle and the granting of the Order of Military or Naval Merit with a red sign to those wounded in both actions.

That night, on his return from Columbia, Batista received Captain Querejeta and said to him: *"Tell me the rank you want and it's yours."* Querejeta, a black career officer who had joined the sergeants on September 4 and years later obtained the rank of Brigade General, answered solemnly: *"Only the one that corresponds, the immediately higher of Commander."*

(Sources: Texts from Lionel Soto, Mario Kuchilán. Hernández Bauzá, Briones Montoto and Tabares del Real)

October 23 and 30, and November 6, 2005

STORIES OF THE CAPITTOL

When Carlos Manuel de Céspedes, provisional President of the Republic, dissolved Congress on August 24, 1933, twelve days after Machado's collapse, the only employee left at the Capitol was a warehouse custodian by the name of Manuel Parra Hernández.

He had come to the building in 1925 as an employee of the construction company *Purduy & Henderson*. It was there that a member of Machado's cabinet, Secretary of Public Works Carlos Miguel de Céspedes (not to be mistaken with the President), found him and for unknown reasons decided to keep him when the construction company transferred that palace of palaces to the State and the Secretary received it on behalf of the Executive. The fact is that on February 24, 1928, Manuel Parra Hernández was registered in the Congress payroll as 'warehouse custodian' with a monthly salary of thirty six pesos.

The Capitol was exquisitely cared for until 1933. Its employees, mostly black people, who had previously worked at the old parliamentary offices, took great care in the cleaning and maintenance of the building. They were deeply motivated to keep shining that glamorous edifice whose construction had cost the Republic 18 million pesos.

The situation changed radically after the dissolution of Congress when these workers were massively laid off. To make things worse, during President Grau's term the courts and the recently created Department of Labor were both installed in the Capitol, and under President Mendieta, the Council of State and other public and even private offices set up shop there, too.

Everything was upside down. It was no longer possible to keep the place shining or to provide the proper maintenance to the facility. And the same happened with the gardens. The furniture upholstery deteriorated, and soon there were in the living rooms only eight easy chairs instead of the original twelve, while the book shelves –specially made for certain spaces— were simply moved somewhere else. The marble benches of the Salón de los Pasos Perdidos (Hall of the Missing Steps) were indiscriminately transferred to other rooms and the beautiful hall was subdivided giving it the appearance of slave quarters while the luxurious restrooms were dismantled to make more space for offices. To cap it all, a bookie's facility was established on the fourth floor to sell tickets for la *bolita* and la *charada*, that is, two popular games similar to lottery played by betting on certain numbers.

The situation did not show much improvement when in 1936 Congress was reinstated and both the Senate and the House of Representatives returned to the Palace of Law. This time, typewriters and fans disappeared from the offices along with rare and valuable books from the library, and the bronze covers of the lamps were cut off in the night. Also the lights outside the building were taken away to illuminate somebody's private party. The robberies reached a climax when the thieves, who were all inside the building, took to stealing the bronze hinges of the large inside doors and the chief of maintenance ordered to hammer the adjusting screws to prevent their extraction with screwdrivers.

Meanwhile, Manuel Parra Hernández zealously looked after the warehouse. Even when he was fired and his salary suspended for three months he continued going to work everyday. He felt that he was the only one capable of guarding that deposit where the valuable chinaware of the Capitol was kept among other valuables. However, when Fulgencio Batista acceded to the highest office in 1940, Parra Hernández could not prevent the transfer of half of the pieces of the Capitol's china to the Presidential Palace. In 1944, the poor man was still in his job earning eighty-six pesos a month.

On the other hand, the bookmaker on the fourth floor hit the roof when he was notified that his business had to move out of the building and angrily demanded the return of the 400 pesos he had paid for the space. The reply, which is not the product of this scribbler's imagination, was that he should go ask the Statue of the Republic.

The Reign of the Magnificent

Machado kept a tight rein on Congress. He behaved as a school principal. The President went as far as checking the senators' and representatives' attendance to the sessions on a daily basis and following the congressional vote through an office on the ground floor of the Presidential Palace. The story goes that fear of the dictator was such that on one occasion a seriously ill House member was carried to the Capitol on a stretcher to meet the required quorum.

The submission showed by Congress under President Machado has no precedent in our parliamentary life. The conservatives that could have monitored the actions of the government from the opposition struck an agreement with the liberals under the so-called 'cooperationist formula' and submitted to all excesses. Members of Parliament of all political shades showed up at the Palace to present their respects to the Magnificent who really despised them, and when someone gave away any sign of rebellion Machado simply had him killed or exiled. This was the case of Congressman Bartolomé Sagaró beaten to death in 1927. And five years later two other congressmen were murdered in their respective homes, in broad daylight: Miguel Anger Aguiar and Gonzalo Freyre de Andrade. But, no one in the Capitol inquired into their deaths, none of their colleagues in Congress uttered as much as a word of protest. The Parliament remained quiet like a cemetery.

President Machado would never compensate them adequately for so much cowardice and silence. Under the *Reign of the Magnificent*, the lawmakers accepted their monthly salaries of some 3000 pesos and about ten working posts with the State and the provincial governments–to distribute among their loyalists. That was it; the dictator denied them any involvement in dirty businesses that would allow them to make money on the side. In addition, during the last eleven months of Machado's reign, the government could not pay the salaries of the public workers, ministers included. Then, Senators and Representatives had to sell their own pay checks for 60% of their nominal value to vulgar loan-sharks and moneylenders. However, in the long run, the loan-sharks got their fingers burned because the tyranny collapsed before they could catch the checks.

During Machado's government, the largest benefits were reaped by those directly connected to the Public Works projects or the lawmakers that the tyrant touched with his magic wand. Clemente Vázquez Bello, the Senate Speaker and intimate friend of President Machado –who thought of making the legislator his successor— had no 'perks' because Carlos Miguel that disliked him profoundly was always watchful, perhaps out of jealousy of the tyrant's special sympathy and affection for Vázquez Bello.

The chameleon

It is the year 1936; Miguel Mariano Gómez sits at the executive office and Congress is reinstated. A new legislature is in session and after a lavish banquet served at the *Hall of the Missing Steps*, Senators and Representatives drive to the Columbia Barracks for a meeting with Colonel Batista, the Army Chief who ruled from the military quarters.

Always a chameleon, Colonel Batista is the personification of modesty and simplicity. He congratulates the new legislators, praises them and elaborates on the probity that must guide their every action. He then offers to be sincere with them and confesses that is preparing to enter politics and that he humbly asks them to just listen to him once in a while to be appraised of his projects and to advise him, correct him, enlighten him...

The lawmakers are very pleased with the colonel's words. Of course, he is happily welcomed; the colonel only needs to let them know and they will be all ears. Visibly moved Batista thanks them for that gesture and says that he will communicate with them sometime in the future, either through telephone messages or telegrams but always with the respect a soldier owes the Legislative Power.

When the first messages from Batista reach the legislators, they observe that the colonel couldn't be more respectful and they grow suspicious of how far he might go. A typical message reads: *"On orders from Colonel Fulgencio Batista you are invited to his offices in the Columbia Barracks at 4:00 this afternoon."*

Soon, the differences between Batista and Miguel Mariano become evident. The man 'advising' from Columbia is not of the same mind as the one supposedly ruling from the Palace. Their discrepancies come to a critical point when Miguel Mariano uses his constitutional power to veto a law promoted by Batista's loyalists in Congress establishing a nine-cents tax on every bag of sugar produced. Allegedly, this money is to be used by the army in the construction of three thousand rural schools. The President, pretending to defend the civilian power –although he owes his position to Batista— explains his veto saying that the Department of Education and not the Armed Forces is responsible for children's instruction and schools construction.

Miguel Mariano has sealed his fate. On December 23, 1936, seven months after his inauguration, the President is impeached by the House of Representatives for limiting the freedom of action of the legislative body, and the Senate, acting as a Court of Justice and chaired by the First Judge of the Supreme Court, submits him to trial the following day, December 24, 1936.

Las Villas Senator Antonio Martínez Fraga, originally from the city of Sancti Spiritus like Miguel Mariano, accuses the President while Dr. José Manuel Gutiérrez, a senator for the province of Matanzas, makes a well-documented speech in his defense. Among other things, he says: *"The false accusation brought against the President of the Republic is not an spontaneous expression of the free determination of the legislators that make up this body but the result of the appearance of legality that pretends to mask a coup d'état hatched in the barracks..."* Of thirty four attending Senators, twenty two cast their votes against

Miguel Mariano while the others save their honor resisting the pressure of officers and soldiers positioned in the halls of the Capitol.

Once the session is adjourned and Miguel Mariano is dismissed from office, two senators comment that a third one had visited the President the night before in the Palace to offer him the votes of several legislators in exchange for a certain amount of money and that Miguel Mariano had obliged unsuspecting that even this legislator would cast his vote against him. A journalist who has followed the trial reminds one of the attending senators a phrase by Wagner: *"How miserable is art without freedom!"* to which the other quickly responds: *"But, there is art in slicing the cake!"*

October 11, 2009

MAYORS AND ALDERMEN

Before 1959, the second highest office in Cuba was not the Vice-President's but that of Mayor of Havana. While the Vice-President of the country had his offices in the Capitol where he had to wait for the President's absence, illness or death to replace him in the Palace, the mayor of the capital channeled taxes, fees and donations to his own pockets without asking for anyone's permission; he was extremely autonomous and influential.

Life at the municipality as a local entity went on undisturbed regardless of whatever happened with the government. This precept, although applicable to every municipality in the country, was not always respected. In 1906, President Estrada Palma was determined to remove from office all those mayors who did not support his re-election, and in 1952, Batista left out of the game all those who refused to swear allegiance to the Statutes he wanted to enforce to legalize his coup d'état of March 10. But President Gerardo Machado went a step further when in 1931 he signed a decree abolishing the Havana municipality and the election of its Mayor by suffrage. As of this moment, and up to the collapse of his tyranny in 1933, there was a so-called Central District whose manager was appointed by the President himself.

Of course, the municipality didn't take it easy. In the days of Havana's occupation by the British (1762-1763) the Havana City Hall had given good proof of vigor assuming the genuine representation of the people, whose support it had, in defense of its freedoms and powers and demanding the occupant force to respect the people and their properties. The British Governor, Count of Albermarle, had no choice but to accept the claim because when the Havana City Council decided to hold its ground it was capable of refusing to take orders even from the King of Spain, like in 1551 when it challenged the monarch's provisions on the value of the *real* and declined to submit to them until the Crown took note of the reasons and motives it had to refuse complying.

In the old times, the neighbors of Havana gathered at the public plaza every January 1st to choose their Mayor and aldermen, a system that sustained a number of changes in colonial days. Actually, every year they elected two Mayors who worked in parallel and with identical powers. It has not been possible to determine who the first Mayor of Havana was because the minutes of the town hall prior to 1550, which could offer a daily account of life in the town from its foundation, were destroyed. That's why the names of Juan Rojas and Pedro Blasco, elected in 1550, are the first recorded. The last Mayor elected or appointed under Spanish sovereignty was the Marquis de Esteban, who took up his post on June 19, 1898 and kept that position until the first day of the following year when the American military administrator appointed Perfecto Lacoste.

Ali Baba with glasses

The first Mayor of Havana elected by universal suffrage on June 16, 1900 was Alejandro Rodríguez, a Major General of the Ejército Libertador during the War of Independence born in Sancti Spiritus. But Rodríguez, who had a splendid monument raised in his honor on Paseo and Línea streets, in Vedado, didn't sit for long in the mayor's chair for he returned to the Armed Forces to become the first Commissioner of the Rural

Guard, an armed institution that preceded the creation of the army in 1909.

From then, and until the Revolution, all kinds of people occupied the Havana Mayor's office, from a wise natural scientist like Carlos de la Torre to a notorious thief like Antonio Fernández Macho, who save for the nails of the town hall table stole everything else he could lay his hands on, including the wood of the coffins sold to the poor, which he used to manufacture his election posters. There were, of course, honest men, like the politician from Sancti Spiritus Miguel Mariano Gómez who built the Children's Hospital on G Street and the Maternity Hospital on Línea Street, an institution that still carries his mother's name, América Arias. This Mayor left over four million pesos in the municipal coffers. Another Mayor who deserves to be remembered for his decency is Manuel Fernández Supervielle who took his own life with a gun shot when he realized the impossibility of delivering on his promise of building the new aqueduct to solve the water supply problem in Havana.

Havana Mayor Justo Luis del Pozo, born in Pinar del Río, was the last one in that position. He was a member of the Nationalist Union Party who later founded the Social Democratic Party, which fell into oblivion without living as much as a mark. In 1936, under the protection of Colonel Batista, del Pozo became president of the Senate and from then on he was Batista's unconditional buddy. Batista made him a Mayor in 1952 and although del Pozo made a point of always wearing a blue necktie, the color of probity, he was really a sort of Ali Baba with glasses while his sons Rolando and Luisito did as they saw fit in the municipal administrations of Healthcare and Education.

A piece of gossip from a reliable source: Justo Luis del Pozo was at the Columbia Barracks on the night of December 31, 1958. He went there to wish the tyrant a happy new year, share a drink with him and get a sense of the national situation. Although this man was by no means a fool, as he abandoned the presidential house in Columbia nothing led him to suspect that the end was so near. And, so he headed home.

At this time, he was no longer living with his wife Emelina Jiménez at the family residence in 47th and Ulloa streets, in the heights of Vedado. They were separated but not divorced, although he had already moved in with his mistress to the 9th floor of the building on Línea and O streets. A phone call interrupted his sleep and someone told him that Batista had run away. With the certainty that the tyranny would collapse, Justo Luis packed up and took the elevator. It was a short ride. He got off on the second floor and exiled in the Paraguayan Embassy.

A ghost library

One of the most popular stories of the days of the republican Cuba is the one associated to Antonio Beruff Mendieta, a City Mayor from 1936 to 1942.

The Trillo Park is at the center of Havana, specifically in the neighborhood of Cayo Hueso. It was named after the man who donated the grounds to build the community. And, it was there that Beruff Mendieta decided to put up a municipal library for the people of Havana to enjoy and learn.

One of the minutes of the city hall meetings registers the Mayor's resolution and the allocation of the budget. But, Oh, great mystery! It was said that when the building was supposedly completed the neighbors rejected the library and instead claimed back their park. It would be necessary to demolish the building and reconstruct the park, so the city hall voted the two budgets to undertake the works. What's funny about this story is that the library was never built, therefore, there was no need to demolish it, and the park remained untouched all along. It was a huge scam that the people called '*the ghost library of Trillo Park*.' On the other hand, Beruff Mendieta enthusiastically welcomed the initiatives of Emilio Roig, the City Historian from June 1, 1935. Dr. Roig had been working in a very small room at the City Hall General Archives located at the Captain Generals' Palace, but Beruff Mendieta had a larger area in the ground floor of the building adapted to accommodate the Office of the Historian, an entity that emerged then and there with the initial sections of Publications, Municipal History Archive and Library of the History of Cuba and the Americas. This way Roig had access to all of the volumes of the chapterhouse minutes that the Mayor decided to place in his custody.

The wise historian worked at the City Hall since 1927, when Miguel Mariano trusted him with the examination and study of the chapterhouse minutes. Later on, in 1931, he was laid off due to his contribution as a journalist to the campaigns against President Machado's tyranny. But by this time, Dr. Roig had had the first seven volumes of the chapterhouse minutes typed and had published a book with those corresponding to the British occupation of Havana. Upon Machado's collapse in 1933, Dr. Roig was reinstated in his job.

The Mercado Único

Although until now we have only talked about mayors, some aldermen did not lag far behind them in terms of misdeeds.

For instance, Alfredo Hornedo y Suárez started his political career as an opportunist alderman and then went on to the House of Representatives and later to the Senate, several times, and to the Constitutive Assembly of 1940. Elected an alderman in 1914, he joined the so-called *Cenáculo*. This was a group of liberal politicians who ruled the municipality. The *Cenáculo* supported General Machado and Mayor Varona Suárez. By 1916, Hornedo was the chairman of the town council, a position that allowed him to obtain in 1918, through a straw man, a lease on the area of the Mercado General de Abasto y Consumo (General Market of Supplies and Consumption) opened in 1920 in the block limited by the Monte, Cristina, Arroyo and Matadero streets. This marketplace, –popularly known as the Mercado Único (the Only Market) de la Habana— devised to sell farming products, was really a monopoly because its leasing contract prevented the establishment of any similar market in an area of more than half a mile and the opening of butcheries in a seven-hundred meters radio.

The construction of the Mercado Único required an investment of 1,175,000 pesos and Hornedo was granted a license to exploit it for thirty years. Later, when this period was about to expire, the shrewd politician spent a fortune to have his nephew Alfredo Izaguirre elected Mayor of Havana, which would ensure him an extension of his leasing contract. The nephew couldn't win but Hornedo's leasing was extended with few changes. It was only in 1957 that the monopoly began to fall apart with the opening of the Public Market, built in the area limited by Carlos III, Arbol Seco, Estrella and Pajarito streets, tellingly almost in front across the house (in Carlos III and Castillejo streets) where Hornedo had lived for years.

Still, the most incredible Mayor was a character that never reached that office: Antonio Prío, whose brother Carlos, then President of the Republic, tried to impose him in the 1950 elections but lost to Nicolás Castellanos. A few hours after the elections, somebody asked Antonio how he had done in the ballots. *"Good,"* he answered. *"I ended up second."*

June 22, 2008

THE TOOHBRUSH CONSPIRACY

In the three first years of his term, President Ramón Grau San Martín had to face three conspiracies that included plans for his assassination. At the time, the press doubted these plots and even ridiculed them and turned them into laughingstocks by giving them such pejorative names as T*he Toothbrush, The Dead Mule* and *The Black Raincoat* conspiracies. But there is no doubt that these plots were real. The Batista loyalists, ousted from power by the crushing electoral victory that took Grau to the executive mansion on October 10, 1944, wanted a return to the past, and made every effort to pave their way back. Many of the civilian and military men involved in theses plots (Tabernilla, Pilar García, Ernesto de la Fe, Ramón Vasconcelos, Carrera Jústiz and others) were appointed to senior positions when Batista returned to power in 1952.

Even to Batista, who was then in exile, such conspiracies *"showed the decline (of the government), the absence of order and the lack of authority prevailing in Cuba."* These were the same arguments he used to justify his coup d'état of March 10, 1952. One of these plots included the assassination of an outstanding leader of the opposition to provoke a national state of shock. This was the case in 1952, when Ernesto de la Fe was able to persuade some members of the Revolutionary Insurrectional Union (UIR) to carry out an attempt on the life of Alejo Cossío del Pino, an ex Secretary of the Interior and, at the time, the owner of a radio network (Radio Cadena Habana), who was shot to death at the *Strand Café* on Belascoaín Street. As a minister of Information in Batista's government, De la Fe even visited Cossío's assassins at Castillo del Príncipe's penitentiary and it was not long before Batista pardoned them.

Pedraza, with three stars...

In the morning of March 16, 1945, ex Colonel José Eleuterio Pedraza alongside various ex officers of the Army and the National Police, and some civilians accused of plotting to overthrow the government were taken to La Cabaña prison.

Pedraza, one of the sergeants that took part in the coup d'état of September 4, 1933, would later be the most hated man in the capital of the country when as Chief of Police he enforced the martial law sending the people in Havana to bed at 9:00 in the evening and driving the detainees to dark isolated places to make them drink, at gun point, one liter of a laxative known as *Palmacristi* or one liter of aircraft oil. Later on, he replaced Batista as Army Chief but was dismissed in 1941when he tried to deal his own coup d'état. It was at this point that the people made fun of him in a popular song with the lyrics, *"Pedraza with three stars/never made it to General..."*

Bent on carrying forward his coup against President Grau San Martín, Pedraza had come to Cuba from Mexico through the Cabo San Antonio two weeks before and sent emissaries to Havana to contact senior officers of the Armed Forces.

His presence in Cuba was known through General Abelardo Gómez Gómez who received a communication from ex Commander José Manuel Fajardo that Fredesvindo Bosque, a man implicated in the business of slot machines for which he was wanted in the United States, was interested in meeting with him about a message from the ex Colonel. Gómez found it strange that Pedraza was interested in him but agreed to receive Bosque. Then Fajardo said that he would have to take him to the place where he was hiding the conspirator. But instead Gómez took the ex Commander to the presence of Major General Genovevo Pérez, chairman of the General Staff, and the man, utterly worried about his predicament, admitted that he was a messenger.

Immediately, Genovevo contacted Undersecretary of Defense Luis A. Collado and alongside him, Gómez Gómez, Fajardo and thirty police agents he moved to Bosque's house. The residence was surrounded and searched with much noise and drama. Genovevo then took Bosque to a nearby farm and, at gun point asked him about the hiding place of the leader of the conspiracy. Bosque did not speak.

This happened on March 12. President Grau, although apprised of the situation, left on a previously scheduled trip to Isla de Pinos with the assurance of coming back earlier than planned. Pedraza made contact with Colonel Ruperto Cabrera and invited him to join the plot, but Cabrera informed the chairman of the General Staff who then told President Grau. At this point, the President took an oath of allegiance to Cabrera and authorized him to meet with Pedraza.

They met and after providing details of his objectives, Pedraza, in the presence of Lieutenant Epifanio Hernández Gil who accompanied Cabrera, said that Genovevo would be murdered and the conspirators would take over the commanding post at the Columbia Barracks. After this they would send an envoy that, with the pretext of reporting the situation to Grau, would assassinate the President. He also said that Belisario Hernández, an ex assistant to Batista (who also forced the detainees to drink *Palmacristi),* would seize the Aviation Command while Pilar García took over the National Police headquarters. Cabrera affirmed that he might be the one chosen to murder the President of the Republic.

Hey, men, here's the bully!

The authorities had no idea of the exact day of the coup and were afraid of a surprise, thus they decided to arrest the main leader and those closer to him. This anticipated action allowed them to know the extension of the plan and the identity of all the civilian and military men implicated. An impressive operation was mounted to capture Pedraza at the Santa Rosalía farm in San Antonio de las Vegas, while in Havana other alleged plotters were detained.

At the farm, alongside the ex Colonel and his assistant, they detained the tenant farmer, Julio Rodríguez a.k.a. *El Mulato*; Hilario Pedregal and his two sons; and, a motorist by the name of Rodríguez. Meanwhile, in Havana, Colonel Carreño Fiallo, Chief of the National Police, with Commanders Meoqui Lezama and Mario Salabarría, and thirty patrol cars proceeded to arrest numerous ex officers of the Army as the Secret Police did likewise.

On Thursday March 15, at 11:30 pm, troops commanded by General Abelardo Gómez surrounded the Santa Rosalía farm. Pedraza and *El Mulato* hid under a stack of dry palm leafs, but Sergeant Mena, one of Colonel Carreño Fiallo bodyguards, noticed that the dry leafs were moving and aimed at them with a machinegun. Then, he saw in astonishment as the ex colonel got up with a pistol that he soon dropped to the floor. A soldier who saw the scene and Pedraza's submission turned to his comrades saying: *"Hey, men, here's the bully!"*

After Pedraza's detention on the 16th, there was a huge demonstration in support of the government at the Plaza del Pueblo, in front of the Presidential Palace. Grau appeared on the north terrace surrounded by his closest civilian assistants and the high military command, and said: *"Here are the leaders of an Army fully supportive of the Government. The others are in La Cabaña (prison)."*

That same day, the President declared to the press that it was not a recently hatched plot but a movement organized before his inauguration. He added that the Government had exercised self-control avoiding the suspension of guarantees or the declaration of a state of war, and announced that the conspiracy had been triggered by the press campaign some journalists had unleashed inciting a revolt and violent actions against the official government institutions. He was making an allusion to liberal Senator and journalist Ramón Vasconcelos, who had distinguished himself by his incisive attacks on the Government. Asked about Batista's likely participation in the events, Grau answered that he had no evidence to confirm or refute that. From San Francisco, California, Batista denied any involvement.

Chibás speaks his mind

In his radio program of April 1st, Chibás hinted that the three pillars of the conspiracy were Batista, Vasconcelos and Pedraza, who had planned the coup during a meeting in Mexico. On that occasion, Batista had advocated the idea of waiting until a propitious climate had been created for the coup, but Pedraza, who felt that the time had come, left for Cuba on a schooner. In the case of Vasconcelos, Chibás said, he was incriminated by two notes found in the ex colonel's briefcase.

Pedraza's and his accomplices' trial finished on April 13, 1945. They were sentenced to one year in prison. Was this chapter closed?

On November 25, 1945, *Bohemia* published that the 18th of that month had been the date chosen to deal a coup d'état. The main action consisted in the assassination of President Grau as he watched the military parade at La Cabaña commemorating the anniversary of Máximo Gómez's birth, and dedicated a park and a gazebo. One or two tanks would shoot on the President and simultaneously there would be an attack on the barracks of the 7th Regiment where the officers involved would seize command. The Presidential Palace and other public buildings would be occupied and power would be placed in the hands of Pedraza, who according to *Bohemia* had worked out the details from prison and even had a uniform made for the occasion with the ranks of General.

The article ran in *Bohemia* also indicated that all the officers implicated had been arrested in March and that the privileged conditions enjoyed by the ex colonel in jail –a large cell, a refrigerator, a radio, comfortable furniture, a rich diet and permits to visit his home— had allowed him to reestablish contacts and carry on with the conspiracy. The *Bohemia* article pointed out that aware of the plan the Government had suspended the parade with the pretext that the Chilean President would be visiting the country. The military parade was moved to the 25th and President Grau attended. He visited the prisoners and talked to Pedraza. On the 27th, General Genovevo Pérez denied this alleged coup, but *Bohemia* insisted that it was true. Nothing was confirmed in one sense or the other.

Pedraza's attempt was the first action against Grau's Government recognized by the President. The contradictions, the lack of evidence in the hands of the government and those issues that were not clarified by the investigations aroused the suspicion of the public and some journals made a mockery of it. The sarcastic reports published by Vasconcelos, known as the Golden Pen of journalism in Cuba, contributed to stirring up the passions. He was the one who named the conspiracy because a harmless toothbrush was one of the few things found on ex Colonel José Eleuterio Pedraza.

The battle of 'The Dead Mule' and 'The Black Raincoat' conspiracy were yet waiting to happen as well as the attempt to bomb the Presidential Palace and murder the President.

(With documents from Enrique de la Osa
and Humberto Vázquez García)

November 2, 2008

THE BATTLE OF THE DEAD MULE

In the early morning of May 17, 1946, the noise of a thundering shootout alarmed the military community. At 11:00 pm the previous night, the general alarm had sounded at the Columbia Barracks. The troops didn't know the reason but three hours and several grenade explosions later, the shootout spread through the military facility, –seat of the Army General Staff— which woke up to action. But that was it. Soon afterwards everything was quiet and the only noise heard was that of the vehicles arriving at the place. In fact, when the news broke out senior army officers, ministers and members of parliament rushed to the barracks, including Senator Eduardo Chibás accompanied by acting Secretary of the Interior and journalist Enrique de la Osa who would report the developments.

Genovevo in his undershirt

"The Movement is over! We control every road!" Army Chief Major General Genovevo Pérez Dámera claimed, still in his undershirt, as he distributed glasses of the best Spanish cognac and Montecristi cigars among his visitors, generals and assistants on duty. He was sweaty and out of breath, looking haggard as if he were still under the impression of a terrible battle. He spoke as if he had just fought the Ardennes Battle, remembered De la Osa. However, there were no reports of any dead, injured or prisoner and from the windows of the General Staff all that could be seen in the barracks' training field were a small war tank and the vehicles that had just arrived.

What had happened? De la Osa confessed that he felt more at ease in the barracks than in the car driven by Chibás who was a lousy and bold driver. As soon as Secretary of Agriculture Germán Álvarez Fuentes –'the man of the Ipecacuana'— learned that something was going on at Columbia, he phoned a colleague and together they headed for the Defense ministry, where they assumed the Secretary was receiving the war reports. But, at that time, Commander Menéndez Villoch was sound asleep in his home at La Víbora suburb while Foreign Minister Alberto Inocente Álvarez found out about the new developments through the press. The following night President Grau was approached at the Auditorium Theater by some journalists who questioned his silence. It was not his fault, he said, but the reporters' who didn't ask, if they had he would have told them what he declared to the US journal *The New York Sun*.

Grau offered his own version. News had reached him that a 'revolutionary leader' would be arriving at the military airport and so special guards were sent to reinforce Columbia. The plane did not arrive but a car had come close to the walls of the Barracks and thrown several grenades. The vehicle had run away at full speed so it was impossible to catch up with it. In his statement to the same newspaper, Primer Minister Carlos Prío was less eloquent than his boss and mentor. He said: *"The Movement has been suppressed. We took especial precautions and everything is over now."*

As General Pérez Dámeras spoke of *"an aborted conspiracy"* and Chibás defined the events as *"a frustrated uprising,"* Enrique de la Osa, published his report in the *In Cuba* section of *Bohemia* magazine under the headline *The 'Show' in Columbia*. Many people felt that it had been no more than a trick used by Genovevo to make merits while others thought it was a government's move *"to close ranks, raise its popularity and shift the public's attention from the problems facing the nation."*

Bad luck again

The fact is that ordinary Cubans referred to the events both in a dramatic and humoristic way. Because just like during José Eleuterio Pedraza's conspiracy in March 1945, when a harmless toothbrush found on the ex colonel ended up giving a name to the plot and minimizing its significance, bad luck hit again the military high command.

Enrique de la Osa wrote: *"During the shootout of the frustrated coup d'état, a humble member of the army supporting services died: a mule that was killed by machinegun fire. This served to baptize the seditious action as 'The Battle of the Dead Mule" and so the new conspiracy was discredited, too..."*

However, things were not that simple. Some experts today believe that '*The Dead Mule*' conspiracy was much more serious than that headed by Pedraza because unlike that one, which involved only civilians and retired members of the army, this one included mostly active military men, even if at the end of the day only a humble corporal was arrested.

It has been said that the separatist action started in a Regiment when its leaders were informed of their transfer to the San Antonio de los Baños military base. Also, that Commander Mario Salabarría, from the National Police, was not alien to this plot hatched under the wing of Professor Pablo Carrera Jústiz who would have been raised to the country's highest office if the movement had succeeded. This individual, one of the masterminds behind the coup d'état of March 10, 1952, would be Secretary of Communications in Batista's 1952 cabinet.

As the press approached him in his exile in New York City, President Batista declined to comment on the events. He only said to the journalists: "*I don't know the source of the developments. There is nothing I can say.*"

But, in Miami, General Manuel Benítez assured the press that "*the aborted military uprising is only the prelude to a 'great revolution'.*"

It is precisely with this dark character that the other attempt at a coup d'état is associated. On October 24, 1946, the government of Dr. Ramón Grau San Martín was the target of another putsch: '*The Black Raincoat*' conspiracy.

Benítez, a clever boy

The coup of September 4, 1933, led by corporals and sergeants, deprived from their commands the army officers who ended up concentrating in the Hotel Nacional de Cuba following their natural chieftain, General Julio Sanguily, still convalescing from a delicate surgery.

Very few officers chose to stay with the army taking orders from and willing to support that previously unheard of Sergeant Batista who headed the military putsch and dismissed them. Two of those who stayed were First Lieutenant Francisco Tabernilla and Captain Manuel Benítez.

Tabernilla would accompany Batista up until the end of his political life in Cuba, on December 31, 1958. It was Batista who gave him his rank of Brigade General and command of the 7th Regiment stationed at La Cabaña. When President Grau dismissed him from active duty in 1944, Tabernilla exiled with Batista and returned to active service with the coup of March 10, 1952. At that time, the tyrant rewarded him with the rank of Major General and the position of Chief of the Army General Staff. This was not well received by young officers truly committed to the putsch, however, Batista not only kept him in that position but also resorted to the Army Organic Law of 1957 to appoint him chairman of the recently created Joint Chiefs of Staff and successively promoted him to Lieutenant General and General in Chief. Still, so many stars –five stars had 'old Pancho' aligned as a diamond on his epaulettes and on the lapel of his army jacket— failed to prevent the victory of the Ejército Rebelde (the Rebel Army). The two men left the country hastily the same morning; Batista for Santo Domingo and Tabernilla and his clan for the United States of America.

Benítez was nicknamed 'El Bonito' (*The beauty*) from his days as a supporting actor in Hollywood. He was promoted to General in 1942, when the Cuban Army again approved of this rank. He had accumulated plenty of merits to justify the promotion. For instance, he had showed no scruples in 1933 when he recommended Batista to bomb the Hotel Nacional to flush out his former colleagues and there are many indications that it was him that in 1934 machine gunned Lieutenant Colonel Mario Alfonso Hernández, chief of the Rius Rivera Regiment from Pinar del Río, who had dared ask Batista to honor his promise of rotating the leadership of the Army, which had been one of the agreements struck by the sergeants who dealt the coup of September 4.

As of 1942, Benítez became Commissioner of National Police. Much has been said of his complicity with the so-called Fifth Nazi Column in Cuba. At the very least, he was incapable of putting under control the ring made up by over four hundred men, some of them well known figures in sports and radiobroadcasts, that every weekend stole large amounts of fuel from the Shell deposits in Havana and carried it on trucks from a milk-delivery company to the province of Camagüey as German submarines waited camouflaged on the islets off the coast.

Of course, it's rather naïve to blame only one man who, regardless of his position, must have been only a piece of a large network. At that time, more than a few officials in the high circles of Batista's Government sympathized with Adolf Hitler and his policies. Just to mention one case: Foreign Minister José Manuel Cortina was forced to resign after being challenged in Parliament for his antidemocratic behavior and for doing business with the passports of the Jewish émigrés.

Batista had to get rid of General Benítez when in June 1944 he threatened with controlling the Armed Forces and becoming the strong man in the country. He then left for the United States. Some time later he was accused of embezzling half a million pesos belonging to the National Police and of appropriating one-hundred million more destined to the construction of the Pinar del Río-La Palma highway. He was also charged with drug-trafficking and murder.

Actually, when he headed the National Police, General Benítez made no less than seven thousand pesos a week with the illegitimate export of slot machines, and some three thousand pesos daily with the control of illicit games, from gambling houses to the local private lottery. His unbridled hunger for easy money led him to sell, for his own benefit, five hundred beds that belonged to the police, at 20 pesos a piece. He was also charged of this crime, but as usual nothing happened.

(Sources: Texts by Enrique de la Osa and Eduardo Vázquez García)

November 9, 2008

THE BLACK RAINCOAT CONSPIRACY

With the arrest of some fifty people in Havana, Mariano and Pinar del Río the Cuban officials dismantled on October 24, 1946 the third conspiracy faced and suffocated by President Ramón Grau San Martín.

The conspirators had planned to take over the Columbia Barracks in the days following the stabbing to death of all the soldiers on duty and do likewise with the headquarters of the Rius Rivera Regiment, in the capital of the province of Pinar del Río, where ex General Manuel Benítez was supposed to have landed after traveling from Miami. The General would then move to Havana to take on the national government.

The plan included the murder of the main leaders of Grau's government and of the ruling Authentic-Republican Alliance Party as well as what the conspirators defined as *"seventy-two hours of wanton killing"* aimed at getting rid of all those opposing Batista's return to power. The plotters carried modern US weapons that the Cuban Army had not yet received.

But just like the previous conspiracies of *The Toothbrush* and *The Dead Mule* against President Grau, the name given to this one nailed it down for history as a tragicomic episode. Someone who heard that the only thing found by the police on one of the main culprits was a black raincoat baptized the plot as '*The Black Raincoat*'. In *Bohemia*, Enrique de la Osa wrote: *"And the new and brilliant military action also fell to the ground under the weigh of the popular jokes. It was impossible to take over the Columbia Barracks with a raincoat as the only weapon...regardless of how black and waterproof it might be!"*

However, in the opinion of Blas Roca, Secretary General of the Popular Socialist Party (PSP), *The Black Raincoat* conspiracy had posed *"a real danger."* It was only an example of the activities of adventurous groups bent on overthrowing the constitutional government to be able to dismantle what the people had conquered with much pain and blood.

"The Black Raincoat is an attempt that cannot be underestimated," said the communist leader, and added: *"We*

have evidence that the core of the conspiracy was not a black raincoat since some of our party members happened to see several modern weapons in the hands of some conspirators; and these were not arrested, nor were their weapons confiscated," Blas concluded.

It was not the first time that the PSP alerted on terrorist groups that intended to take advantage of the growing popular discontent to build a certain mood and climate among the people and the indispensible political background to deal a coup d'état. These groups had plans to unleash a wave of murders against the leaders of the PSP, among others. Cuban Historian Humberto Vázquez has written: *"American agents and spies known as G-Men were disseminated throughout the Island working actively in a plan to destabilize the political situation and create the proper atmosphere for the coup. Their actions focused on the Armed Forces where they developed schemes against the government and used the pretext of communism to set off violent trends."*

Shootout at La Coronela

Actually, in a farm owned by Nena Benítez, the ex general'sister, located at La Coronela suburbs, in Marianao, the Army and the Police found more than 'a black raincoat'. They found ten hand-machineguns, four rifles, twelve revolvers, automatic pistols and other military supplies. Military personnel and police officers surrounded the farm and urged the people gathered there to surrender but these responded with a barrage of fire. Soon, however, they gave up and were arrested. Shortly afterwards other people were detained in different parts of the capital and in Pinar del Río, where journalist Ernesto de la Fe was captured. This man had links with the gangster groups or *action groups* as those happy-trigger gangs were called at the time.

An Army report revealed that the military high command was aware of the conspiracy and that for a month it had been trying to connect the dots, when an officer stationed in Pinar del Río informed his superiors that some men close to ex General Benítez had invited him to join their movement. This information was followed by other similar reports. Every informant was instructed to pretend to agree with the proposal and join the plot in order to learn about its scope and the means to implement it. But, the Army said it knew more; it said that as from October 7 or 8 it had information that the military action would be carried out on the 24th or the following days.

It was said that, according to reports from the Military Intelligence, ex General Benítez was the head of the movement. The farm at La Coronela was the property of one of his sisters and among the detainees there were many personal friends of his. One of them, Rafael Montenegro, introduced to Grau by a gangster named Orlando León Lemus, a.k.a. *El Colorado*, assured the President that the plotters intended to carry out the assassination of a relevant figure of the opposition to win the sympathy of his political loyalists and that after this they would take over Pinar del Río, the place Benítez would arrive in, to come to Havana and occupy the Columbia Barracks.

At this point, Manuel Benítez had already fled from Havana. Right on the 24th, when La Coronela was assailed, he was flying undisturbed to Miami. From his residence in Florida he declared that he had nothing to do with the plot, and from his house in Daytona Beach, Batista also denied any involvement in the conspiracy and warned that *"the news on the attempted coup simply exposed the lack of order, the decay of the country and the absence of a responsible authority in Cuba."*

In government circles there were contradictory views on the conspiracy. Captain Jorge Agostini, head of the Secret Service in the Presidential Palace, stated that the aborted movement was not significant. However, Prime Minister Carlos Prío said that the political actions of the opposition were aimed at *"creating a violent climate conducive to the seizure of power by some lunatics who would later pass it on to people from obsolete regimes,"* meaning Batista loyalists. He accused the press of trying to bring confusion to the public opinion making it believe that the conspiracy had not existed and informed that the plotters had been arrested when they were already organized in groups and ready to use

President of the Republic; his face was deadly white. They heard him say: *"If you order it, Mr. President,"* and then as a boy taken aback by a reprimand he added, *"But, why?"* As he hung up the phone he said to those around him: *"Get ready, we're leaving for Havana,"* and remained strangely quiet. No one dared ask him. Fifteen minutes later the phone rang again, and this time Genovevo rushed to get the call himself. It was his main staffer to tell him what he already knew. The situation became unbearable in the living room of the house at *La Larga*, and Genovevo offered only one explanation. He said: *"You are talking to the ex Army Chief."*

During the short, tense but respectful dialogue in which the President addressed Genovevo as General, Prío said: *"I am dismissing you because you have lost confidence in me and things must go terribly wrong when a subordinate loses confidence in his chief."* There was no need to say anything else. Two signatures sufficed to remove the strong man.

May 19, 2006

NO MORE GUNS!

The owner of Radio Cadena Habana and of the country restaurant Topeka, Alejo Cossío del Pino, had every reason to feel depressed. For some time he had forgotten the death threat made against him in the days of the Orfila Massacre, September 1947, when Emilio Tro's loyalists had accused him of favoring Mario Salabarría's followers and written his name on a stone plaque placed at the tomb of the leader of the Revolutionary Insurrectional Union (UIR) as a warning that the organization had already put a price on his head.

But something more pressing was weighing heavily on him. A communication received that morning had come to add to his recent discrepancies with the Mayor of Havana Nicolás Castellanos. Although in the 1950 legislative elections he had ended up as a first substitute with over ten thousand votes, the Higher Electoral Tribunal had recognized the right of José

Pedraza had to respond to eight pending charges against him, but the Court didn't want to find him guilty of any of them, even though there were plenty of reasons for that, thus, after he had served his sentence for *The Toothbrush Conspiracy* he was released from La Cabaña, on April 24, 1947. De la Fe didn't serve his full sentence, he was freed in 1952 and Batista rewarded him with the position of Secretary of Information. Pedraza, a wealthy man with over four thousand cattle heads, used this time to care for his private businesses until at the end of 1958 Batista, putting behind their discrepancies of 1941 when Pedraza tried to oust him, appealed to his buddy whom he felt was the right man to suffocate the insurrection in the central region of the country. So, Pedraza returned to active service with the rank of Brigade General in the position of Army Inspector General. He then took pleasure in slapping in public General Alberto Ríos Chaviano calling him a coward for his failure in Las Villas. There is no proof that Pedraza ever saw combat. By then, Batista's army was incapable of winning a skirmish against the revolutionary forces.

Ernesto de la Fe was arrested in Havana in the first days of January 1959 and sentenced by a revolutionary tribunal to fifteen years in prison for his complicity with the tyranny. Pedraza abandoned the country in the last plane leaving from Columbia military airport in the morning on January 1st, 1959.

In Santo Domingo, where he settled, he became the chief of the legion that President Rafael Leónidas Trujillo planned to use in the invasion of the Island to finish off the Revolution. The Dominican satrap demanded Batista's help and the ousted tyrant promised to finance a plan to murder Fidel. To that end, the ex tyrant appealed to Rolando Masferrer, head of the notorious *Tigers*[12], who lived in Miami and recommended two individuals of his confidence. The two assassins arrived in Havana where they were backed by a counterrevolutionary organization whose strings De la Fe pulled from his prison cell. Then, an agent of the burgeoning State Security Corps who had

[12] *The Masferrer Tigers*, a group of thugs who murdered many revolutionary Cuban youths.

infiltrated the counterrevolutionary outfit reported the arrival of the two characters although he was unsure of their mission. An order was given to casually stop them in the street, ask for their identifications and take them to the nearest police station, but the two men responded the law enforcement officers' request with fire from their machineguns and managed to leave the country on a boat waiting for them at the mouth of the Almendares River; needless to say that they failed to accomplish their mission.

(Sources: Texts by Enrique de la Osa, Eduardo Vázquez and Fabián Escalante)

November 17, 2008

THE ORFILA MASSACRE

It's been over half a century since the Orfila Massacre, a development that shook up Cuba on Monday September 15, 1947, when the residence of Commander Antonio Morín Dopico was assaulted by forces under Commander Mario Salabarría. The attack, resisted by those under siege, extended for nearly three hours and halting it required the intervention of army troops that came to the place with twenty tanks and armored vehicles. It was an open battle which resulted in the death –outside the house and after surrendering— of Commander Emilio Tro and a pregnant woman, Mrs. Aurora Soler de Morín. An eyewitness later said to the press: *"I had always believed that the phrase 'a fire screen' was just a literary expression, but now I know it can be a terrible reality."*

Like so many others, Tro and Salabarría became known after Ramón Grau San Martín obtained the presidency in 1944, when a number of anti-Machado fighters demanded the Authentic Party's government to compensate them or to materialize the political aspirations for which they had fought. Soon, the country saw the reproduction of the so-called *'action groups'* which resolved their differences shooting each other and killing their adversaries. Grau encouraged these groups, armed them and boosted their rivalries.

the military man's Kukine farm. At that time, the General had tried to attract Alonso Pujol –despite his senior position in the government— to the coup d'état he was brewing against Prío. It is fair to say that the smart politician did not go along with the putschist's plan but chose to keep quiet and not to inform the government he served.

In those talks over breakfast, Batista offered the reasons that in his view justified a coup d'état mentioning gangsterism as one of them. *"It's an evil leading to anarchy and it's the Army's duty and our own to save Cuban society,"* he said, to which Pujol responded that it was, in fact, a national embarrassment and an evil that should be eradicated. And added, *"But so far its victims are mostly insignificant members of supposedly revolutionary clans and such events have failed to touch public sensitivity. I don't think that these blood crimes and the reprehensible attitude of the authorities that have let them go unpunished might be enough to justify a military uprising in the eyes of history... A major event would have to occur, something as stunning as the death of Calvo Sotelo in Spain, the prelude to the uprising of Generals Sanjurjo, Franco and Mola."*

Vice-President Alonso Pujol thought he had struck a cord in Batista and dissuaded him of his conspiracy. But, the murder of Alejo Cossío del Pino alerted him to the mistake. It was not just one more victim but a man who had become known for his civic protests and who could become the Calvo Sotelo that Batista needed. That's why he decided not to wait and at 11:00 pm he entreated a phone conference with the President. At that point, the differences between the President and his Vice-President were notorious and irreconcilable, to the point that Prío had withdrawn Alfonso Pujol's bodyguards and house protection.

During that telephone conversation, however, although he spoke vehemently he observed the consideration he owed the authority of the head of State. He said, *"As a member of the government you preside, I feel entitled to urge you, with due respect, to act immediately and with maximum energy. I suggest the immediate replacement of the Chief of Police and the suspension of the constitutional guarantees. Also that you personally assume command of the Armed Forces and issue other measures that would allow you to strongly fight the criminals that with their excesses are about to provoke a catastrophe."*

As Vice-President Alonso Pujol later said, President Prío shared his views and, after thanking him for his observations, said that he would leave for the Palace right away where he would meet with his council of ministers. Having said this, the Vice-President felt that he had done the right thing as far as Prío was concerned, and as to Batista he had kept silent. He had disclosed to the President *'only half the secret.'*

On the way to Columbia

But reports from the Military Intelligence Services informed the Army high command of Batista's hectic conspiratorial activity. Since he knew he could not win power through the elections, he intended to get it by force.

During his meetings with a large group of retired officers, at the headquarters of his Unitary Action Party (PAU), at No. 306 on 17 Street, in Vedado, and in his own countryside residence, he insisted on the necessity to create an atmosphere of national turmoil to show that Prío's government was unable to preserve order, keep public peace and secure the rights to property and to free enterprise. His interest was to make the public opinion believe that only Batista could bring back order and balance. That's why the members of PAU were encouraged to commit murder and to promote disturbances conducive to a state of anxiety and alarm in the population that would justify Batista's actions.

After his telephone conversation with Alonso Pujol, President Prío left his *La Chata* farm, in Arroyo Naranjo, determined to suspend the constitutional guarantees and to resolutely fight the gangs with the appointment of a new Chief of the National Police. Once in the Palace, he called his closest assistants. Soon, he was surrounded by Prime Minister Oscar Gans, and the ministers of Defense and the Interior, Segundo Curti and Rubén de León, respectively. Also present were the Army and Navy chiefs, the to the Military Hospital as a detainee and Lieutenant Colonel Landeira arrested Salabarría. It was over six in the evening and a heavy rain was falling on Havana. The victims' blood, thinned down by water, tainted the pavement.

Tro's mother was the first to accuse President Grau of the tragedy, and the same did many political leaders who called the government *"irresponsible, incompetent and undisciplined." "Under the current regime there are no guarantees for women or children who had been respected even at the worst moments of terrorism in Cuba,"* said Senator Chibás while others accused the Executive of promoting disturbances and violence, and there were some who clearly and resolutely identified the President as *"the great culprit, the great fraudster, the great murderer, and the great simulator."*

The truth is that Grau shut himself in his private room in the Palace and refused to receive those who went to the executive mansion to demand the army's intervention in the melee for it was a known fact that Tro and his men would never surrender to Salabarría's forces. A lot has been said about Grau's behavior at the time. Many years later Salabarría disclosed an unknown detail: the President suffered from unexpected lapses of memory and he was going through one of these while the Orfila events unfolded which was the reason why he was not informed. Someone communicated with General Genovevo Pérez who was visiting Washington and the obese and well-fed military man ordered from there the use of the tanks to put an end to the massacre.

The government seized the copies of the documentary made by the *National Newscast* showing the combat minute by minute. Fidel Castro, then a student, accused President Grau, the Minister of the Interior and the Chief of Police of that illegal action aimed at suppressing evidence.

The end

Morín Dopico passed away in Havana in the late 1980s, and around the same time his daughter Miriam left the country and settled in the United States where she died. *Cucú* Hernández Vega was killed on July 1948 at the Cuban Consulate in Mexico City. Roberto Meoqui died of tuberculosis in 1950 at *La Esperanza* sanatorium. In 1951, *El Turquito* escaped from the Castillo del Príncipe prison as part of a spectacular break away staged by Policarpo Soler and arranged from outside the prison by *El Colorado*. On February 1955, forces led by Lieutenant Colonel Lutgardo Martín Pérez shot *El Colorado* to death at 211 Durege Street, in the Santo Suárez suburbs. General Querejeta died in Havana in 1984; he was over ninety years old. Mario Salabarría, sentenced to 30 years in prison, was released from the Model Prison in Isla de la Juventud after the victory of the Revolution before serving his full sentence, but in 1963 he was arrested for his proven implication in a frustrated attempt on the life of Commander in Chief Fidel Castro Ruz, to be carried out on July 26 of that year at the Revolution Square. Again he was released before serving his full sentence and left the country. He died in the United States on April 2004. Emilio Tro is a legend.

September 15, 2002

THE CAPITOL'S DIAMOND

This is really a great story. On Monday March 25, 1946, the 25-carat diamond built-into the National Capitol to mark the zero kilometer of all distances on the Island disappeared mysteriously. That day, at 7:00 am, after the change of guard, agent Enrique Mena from the Senate police, who was checking the *Hall of the Missing Steps*, noticed the diamond was missing and immediately informed his superiors.

The jewel was considered one of the best protected treasures of the Republic. It had been set in Agatha and platinum before its introduction in a block of andesite, the hardest granite in the world, which was then introduced in a concrete block to be built into the floor at the center of the room. A cut glass, so solid that it was considered unbreakable, reinforced the diamond's protection; however, the thieves apparently needed only half an

The "Groups Pact"

In midyear 1951, the boys of the happy-trigger who settled their differences with endless vendettas, are convened by the government of President Carlos Prío to strike a peace accord. Facilities would be given to the members of the *action groups* to reincorporate to a normal life or "arrangements" made for them to stay outside of the country if that was their decision. It was thanks to this pact, of which there is no written record, that Policarpo Soler –following instructions from Orlando Puente, the President's private secretary— settled in Matanzas City with assurances of not being disturbed. He then started working on his campaign for House Representative in the elections of June 1, 1952.

But Policarpo is arrested in Matanzas by the Rural Guard after his loyalists attack a UIR group that torn apart the posters announcing the gangster's race for Parliament. Rather than as a detainee, he is treated as a guest of honor at the Matanzas prison. He is accommodated at the leisure room of the penitentiary chief guards and allowed to receive as many visitors as he wants. Some visitors come straight from the Presidential Palace and upon returning they convey to the executive the threatening messages sent by the gangster. If taken to a court of justice, Policarpo will make sensational revelations.

"For God's sake, don't go"

One night, after meeting at the warden's office with some visiting friends, Policarpo took off his jacket and said, "*Let me hang it here because I'm not planning to go out tonight.*" Everybody laughed, even the guards, and Policarpo added: "*I am sleepy. I've not slept well for six years. I'm tired of this hectic life. People are wrong about me.*" Shortly before, he had said to the press with great insolence that "*I've been the victim of my enemies' schemes to make people believe I'm a monster, to blame me for everything that happened during the six years in which it is said that I was a fugitive of the law. But, I'm sure that the truth will come out.*"

At the same press conference he raised his concern over the destiny of the two to three hundred families that he supported economically and that could be hurt by his detention, thus he would insist on his political aspirations. According to the accusation filed with the Provincial Court on March 4, 1952 by attorney Fidel Castro, Policarpo's group had some six hundred sinecures or '*botellas*' –as they were locally known— in various ministries.

Policarpo also claimed that he had given Prío his word that he would not be involved in violent actions again, and insisted: *"The President of the Republic is my friend. I promised him to put an end to the war among the different groups. Hevia is my presidential candidate; he is a good and honest Cuban. I'm a House candidate for the Authentic Party and I'm one of the "dieguitos" (that is, a loyalist of Senator Diego Vicente Tejera)."*

One afternoon Policarpo tells Florencio Sáenz that he would receive the visit of Tony Varona, a Senator and Primer Minister, along with an army officer. But, these would not be his visitors that day. Carlos Gil, a workers leader in the rigging factory, and others ask for permission *"to say hello to their friend Policarpo."* They are denied admission but they insist making a lot of noise and are finally allowed in. As Gil is entering the prison and Policarpo is walking toward the outside fence, which is opened, a woman who had also requested permission to visit him gets close to the thug and passes on a .45 caliber pistol. Already armed, Policarpo pushes the guard accompanying him and leaves the penitentiary. Then, something incredible happens. A grotesque scene; Florencio Sáenz, the prison warden, embraces the fugitive saying: "Policarpo, for God's sake, don't go! You'll make trouble for me..." But Policarpo insists, heedless to the plea. *"Look, man, I don't want to go, it's my friends who are taking me."*

I am *El Colorado*

Policarpo settles in Havana undisturbed. In his house at La Sierra suburb he receives the visit of ministers Sergio Megía and Ramón by a revolutionary commando in 1932 and that, according to legend, roamed the place at night. That's why it must have been easy for the thief or thieves to hide behind the paintings or the monumental Statue of the Republic before the building was closed and then wait for the right time to act.

Near the empty niche of the diamond, the expert investigators of the National Bureau of Identification found the inside lining of a hat with blood stains, several used matches and a curious inscription on the floor made with a pencil that read: "*2:45 to 3:15 – 24 carats.*" Apparently, this pointed to the time it took the thieves to do their job. No fingerprints were found. The experts determined that the robbery had been perpetrated by specialists. Miguel Suárez Fernández, the President of the Senate, fired the police platoon that had been on duty in the building that night and placed its members under investigation.

An anonymous return

As months passed, the diamond robbery seemed to have fallen in the category of the perfect crimes when on June 12, 1947 President Grau called into his office some of the most conspicuous people in his regime: the President of the Senate; Senators Carlos Prío and Caíñas Milanés; Senator Guillermo Alonso Pujol, the Republican Party chairman; the ministers of Justice and Healthcare; Alejo Cossío del Pino, recently appointed minister of the Interior… But, everybody looked at Dr. Arturo Hevia, the judge in charge of the investigation of the missing jewel. Grau broke the silence: "*Gentlemen, I have summoned you to bear witness to my delivering of a diamond that I have anonymously received and that, apparently, is the same one stolen from the National Capitol some time ago. I'm giving it to Dr. Hevia…*"

The diamond was inside a small and crumpled yellow envelope. A journalist inquired about the way it had reached the President's hands and Grau repeated: "*Anonymously…*" and when a similar question was asked again he said: "*I have already said that it was anonymously returned to me. That's all.*

It's as if you were told to lift up this paper and find something underneath, and in fact, there was the diamond."

The diamond passed from one hand to another. Caíñas Milanés said that it looked clearer than that of the Capitol to which Grau responded that if it was not the stolen jewel it must be returned to him *"because I was the person it was sent to."* But Suárez Fernández, afraid of losing it for a second time, categorically said that it was the missing diamond.

Who cares?

Shortly before noon of that June 2, President Grau had a long interview with minister of Education José Manuel Alemán, a millionaire and the President's protégé. It is said that it was he who took the jewel to the President after paying five thousand pesos for it. This was confirmed by Grau himself in his statement: *"I don't mind what people say about the return of the diamond. The fact of the matter is that it is here. As to the rest, who cares? Alemán consulted me before he brought it and I agreed; it was good publicity."*

Still, it would be too farfetched to derive from this that Alemán was the mastermind behind the robbery. It was said that the smart minister wanted to present the jewel to Paulina Alsina, the President's sister in law and first lady of the nation. Where and under which circumstances would she have been able to wear the stolen jewel? Notwithstanding the fact that such an action on the part of a man so close to the President would have placed his distinguished friend and protector in an awkward situation.

I'm willing to consider that the robbery was the work of the opposition. Tempers frayed as time passed and the President did not even have a majority in Congress. In his well-documented book *El gobierno de la kubanidad*[14] (2005) Humberto Vázquez García affirms that many people felt at the time that the thieves were members of the power circles and adds that there were all

[29] *Kubanity's Government*

easier. The group slipped away through the fortress angle on G Street, crossed the patios of some nearby houses and took the vehicles that waited for them only a few feet from the Ninth Police Station.

This is treason!

Soon, Segundo Curti, minister of the Interior in President Prío's cabinet, arrived in El Príncipe. Arrogant, haughty and with a touch of histrionic he moved his hands in desperation and repeated: *"This is treason! This is treason!"* adding, *"This people couldn't escape without inside help. There was never such a scandalous jailbreak, and so absurd, in the light of day. And the safety measures were fantastic!"*

In his article for the *In Cuba* section of *Bohemia* Enrique de la Osa, whose data I'm using, said that rather than fantastic measures real measures were required to prevent the jailbreak. The truth is that the prison guard was reduced in those days. Over fifteen guards had been laid off and of the twenty three soldiers guarding the facility, only two were on duty. Of the more than one hundred prison guards in the payroll, many were on assignment elsewhere and others looked rather unfit for their job, basically due to their advanced age.

Minister Curti accused Commander Ismail, head of the prison police, of complicity in the jailbreak, and something similar said Federico de Córdoba, superintendent of the penitentiary who also recalled that a few days before Ismail had informed him of a fifteen thousand pesos offer to let Policarpo escape that he had rejected. *"I think that Ismail was preparing the ground to have an alibi,"* Córdoba insisted, while Segundo Curti repeated that there had been complicity and connivance, and Commander Ismail said the same, for he did not think they were talking about him. Curti and Córdoba submitted their resignations right away, but President Prío did not accept them.

In his jailbreak Policarpo was accompanied by José Fallat, a.k.a. *El Turquito*, who had murdered Emilio Tro and Aurora

Soler during the Orfila Massacre; *El Guajirito* Salgado and Luis Matos Silbes that also took part in the attack on the house of Morín Dopico following orders of Mario Salabarría; Wilfredo Lara García, serving a 30-year sentence for the assassination of the student Justo Fuentes Clavel and pending a death sentence for the murder of Wichy Salazar; and Juan Díaz Acanda, a common criminal. From the group, only José Ríos Vence, also a participant in the Orfila affair didn't manage to escape because he broke both legs in the adventure.

In a statement to the press, *El Colorado* immediately denied any involvement in the getaway from El Príncipe, but didn't conceal his joy over the fact that his friend Policarpo was now free. Policarpo also spoke to the press. He said that he had escaped thanks to a group of his political activists and it would have been a discourtesy to refuse to go along. He stated: *"This forces me to defer the clarification of my situation with the law. Now, I'll go back to combat..."*

Death of Policarpo Soler

After his escape Policarpo, who like a local Houdini had the gift to appear and disappear at will, vanished. After President Prío was ousted, he showed up in Spain. In this connection, Raúl Aguiar writes in his book *El bonchismo y el gangsterismo en Cuba*[16] that *"...The coup d'état of March 10, 1952 did not seem to affect Policarpo Soler's good star. When it was assumed that he was hunted, persecuted and running for his life due to an effort to present his capture as a trophy, his extensive circle of friends facilitated his travel to Spain in midyear 1952. The travelers coming from Madrid said that the gangster looked like a tourist walking near the Puerta del Sol. In an article with the title Frente a todos, ran by Bohemia on January 8, 1956, Fidel Castro stated: 'Batista's regime stuffed Policarpo Soler with money and put him on a ship to Spain.'"*

[16] *Bunchism and Gangsterism in Cuba*

Seemingly, Genovevo had the upper hand in Prío's government; some even said that there were two powers in the nation. Genovevo's assistant, Commander Trujillo, referred to President Prío with absolute disrespect for his position calling him "*the Presi*" and brazenly asked in the Palace if there was anything important to report to his boss. Meanwhile, Genovevo felt threatened by Segundo Curti's appointment as Secretary of Defense and his concern grew when he learned that the new minister intended to exercise all the powers of his office even when the President had specifically asked him to avoid making trouble for him with Genovevo.

At this point, and with the aim of strengthening his own standing, Genovevo sought an ally whom he thought he found in Orlando Puente, the President's own private secretary. Soon, and almost without thinking, he announced the man a surprise and took him to see a fifty thousand dollars yacht. It would be a gift to Puente. The man said there that he accepted the present but as soon as he was back home he informed Genovevo that he declined. However, he did it in writing and giving a copy of the note to President Prío who took it as a signal that Major General Genovevo Pérez Dámera was brewing something –writes historian Newton Briones Montoto— even if he still did not know what.

The next victim

On July 19, 1949, *La Voz del Yuna*, a radio station in the Dominican Republic broadcast a message addressed to Genovevo: "*General Pérez Dámera, General Pérez Dámera, beware! You'll be the next victim! There is a plot to murder you!*"

A murder, whose perpetrators have remained unidentified until this day, had taken place on the eve of that radio message; the target was Colonel Francisco Javier Arana, Chief of the Guatemalan Army. The same radio station, a docile instrument of the satrap Rafael Leónidas Trujillo, had previously broadcast a similar warning addressed to him. Thus, the reiteration of the message was a source of concern to Genovevo who, despite

President Prío's recommendations to dismiss it as a deception, sent two envoys to Santo Domingo –behind the President's back— to hear what Trujillo had to say. According to *Bohemia* magazine, Genovevo's distrust became obvious following the return to Cuba of the second envoy. He only moved in the company of a group of assistants in addition to bodyguards armed with machineguns. It was an impressive show, particularly when he traveled with President Prío Socarrás, who watched that exaggerated protection with increasing concern which made the tension grow between the men.

It was on August 22 that the President understood the General's motives, for that day he was informed that on Genovevo's instructions Colonel González Chávez, chief of Cuba's military aviation, had met with Trujillo –an enemy of Prío from the days of the Cayo Confites expedition arranged by the Cuban government to topple the Dominican dictator, an expedition that Genovevo had helped to derail. The next day, the President had in his hands a detailed report of that meeting forwarded to him by the clandestine anti-Trujillo movement. Thus, Genovevo went from distrust to disloyalty, and down that road –indicated Enrique de la Osa— no one could guess how far the wealthy and pudgy General would go. At this point Prío, risking his own neck, decided to act. The President said to those in his inner circle: *"The Army is either an institution or a political entity. If the former is true, my sole presence in Columbia will solve the problem; but, if it is the latter the country is lost and I will suffer the same fate."*

At mother's house

In the morning of that same day, Defense Secretary Curti urged Prío to act quickly and vigorously. *"If you don't dismiss that man today, tomorrow you won't be President,"* he asserted. At 5:00 pm the President, without offering an explanation, ordered the National Police agents to be confined to barracks. At 7:00 pm he met with Curti again and summoned General Ruperto Cabrera, the second chief of the General Staff, to the Palace to inform

General Regreso

I read in a single sitting Newton Briones Montoto's latest book published by Ciencias Sociales Publishing House. The title is *General Regreso*[17]. In over four hundred pages the author examines Prío's government from the economic, political and social angles and delves deep into the sources of the March 10, 1952 coup d'état. It's a good read and a very enjoyable book, like his previous works, and the same as those it's based on an exhaustive research of documents and of numerous oral sources.

One of Briones Montoto's sources is journalist Luis Ortega, a Cuban living in the United States, who was the first person that on that distant year of 1952 received an offer from Batista to be a minister in his cabinet. But Ortega declined the offer, and was included in what was later known as the Consulting Council, which the dictator set up to replace Congress since this legislative body was dismissed by the putsch.

In the early hours of morning, Ortega got news in his house in Arroyo Arenas that something was going on in Columbia so he went there. He could not enter, or didn't dare to because as he put it a tank came to his car threateningly. Thus, he rushed to the house of Sergio Carbó, editor of the *Prensa Libre* newspaper, and from there they phoned Army Chief Major General Ruperto Cabrera.

The call was taken by the General's wife Arminda Burnes, who was confined to the bathroom of her house; an hour before, ex Commander Manuel Larrubia Paneque, retired in 1944, had broken into the Cabreras' bedroom armed with a machinegun and arrested him. But before taking Cabrera to the house of Batista's mother-in-law on 86 and 5thB streets in Miramar, the men with Larrubia pulled off every phone in the house missing only the one in the bathroom. It was through this phone that Arminda could inform Lieutenant Colonel Vicente León, chief of military force in the Presidential Palace, of the developments

[17] *General Return*

President of the Republic; his face was deadly white. They heard him say: *"If you order it, Mr. President,"* and then as a boy taken aback by a reprimand he added, *"But, why?"* As he hung up the phone he said to those around him: *"Get ready, we're leaving for Havana,"* and remained strangely quiet. No one dared ask him. Fifteen minutes later the phone rang again, and this time Genovevo rushed to get the call himself. It was his main staffer to tell him what he already knew. The situation became unbearable in the living room of the house at *La Larga*, and Genovevo offered only one explanation. He said: *"You are talking to the ex Army Chief."*

During the short, tense but respectful dialogue in which the President addressed Genovevo as General, Prío said: *"I am dismissing you because you have lost confidence in me and things must go terribly wrong when a subordinate loses confidence in his chief."* There was no need to say anything else. Two signatures sufficed to remove the strong man.

May 19, 2006

NO MORE GUNS!

The owner of Radio Cadena Habana and of the country restaurant Topeka, Alejo Cossío del Pino, had every reason to feel depressed. For some time he had forgotten the death threat made against him in the days of the Orfila Massacre, September 1947, when Emilio Tro's loyalists had accused him of favoring Mario Salabarría's followers and written his name on a stone plaque placed at the tomb of the leader of the Revolutionary Insurrectional Union (UIR) as a warning that the organization had already put a price on his head.

But something more pressing was weighing heavily on him. A communication received that morning had come to add to his recent discrepancies with the Mayor of Havana Nicolás Castellanos. Although in the 1950 legislative elections he had ended up as a first substitute with over ten thousand votes, the Higher Electoral Tribunal had recognized the right of José

Basterrechea, with only two thousand votes, to take the seat left open by Benito Remedios in the House of Representatives. The Tribunal argued that Cossío was no longer a member of the Republican Party for which he had run, albeit the document affirmed that the final decision on the issue must be made by the House Drafting Commission; but Cossío understood that he would not be returning to the Capitol's right wing, at least not this time.

Everything is going wrong for me, he thought, and made several phone calls to share the bad news with his friends. He then agreed with Representative R. Cremata to meet that night at the door of the radio station. Cremata arrived on time, and alongside José R. Mérida, the President of the Cuban National Party at the Arsenal neighborhood, they crossed the Belascoaín Ave. and walked toward San José Street. At the coffeehouse-restaurant *Strand Café*, Ceferino Duque and one of Cossío's brothers were already waiting.

Nothing could predict the tragedy. There were few costumers at the *Strand* at that hour and everything seemed quiet that night of February 11, 1952. The group sat around a table and only after the waiter had served them Cossío, with his back to San José Street, started reading aloud the ruling of the Higher Electoral Tribunal.

The five friends were still listening to the monotonous and boring legal arguments when a red Oldsmobile momentarily stopped near the café and four individuals got off the car. The vehicle drove on, turned to San José Street and pulled off half-way into the block, keeping its engine running as the four men walked slowly on the sidewalk, went around the *Strand* and opened fire on the group. Cossío fell backwards dragging Mérida who was gravely wounded. The attackers then ran to the car shooting in the air to scare bystanders. At the Marqués González Street, a police agent on patrol risking his own life exchanged shots with the men in the car but could not stop them. At the *Strand Café*, Cremata, Duque and Cossío's brother, recovering from the confusion created by the assault, wanted to help the victims who still moved in a pool of blood. It was then that they noticed that both Duque and Cremata were injured, too. With sixteen bullet holes in his back, Alejo Cossío del Pino died before reaching the Emergencias hospital.

Only half the secret

Since Cossío was an outstanding personality his death aroused a wave of justified indignation. To many, the UIR had delivered on its pledge made during the funeral of its leader Emilio Tro. To others, the frequency and impunity of such actions pointed to Carlos Prío's government as the main culprit since it was incapable of controlling the gangsters despite the so-called "Groups Pact" sponsored by the Executive with the aim of putting an end to the actions of the happy-trigger boys. Some went still further and accused ex President Grau of being the major responsible for the murder. In this token, they remembered that "the old hypocrite" had been bent on making Cossío's life impossible during the five and a half months that he was minister of the Interior. On accepting that position Cossío had said *"No more guns!"* and announced an extensive plan to eradicate the organized political crime. But it was useless because as the Minister took the measures he saw fit to end the gangsters' actions, President Grau continued receiving in the executive office the most renowned happy-triggers.

For the time being, the three men arrested immediately after the homicide had to be released. The two members of the UIR caught by the police had perfect alibis. At the time of the shooting they were peacefully drinking at the Bodegón de Toyo with Commander Luis Varona, from the Bureau of Investigations. The third man arrested was no other than Basterrechea who had been home celebrating the Electoral Tribunal's ruling in his favor. He was arrested for no reason since nothing connected him to the incident.

However, somebody knew how to get to the real culprits. As soon as the Vice-President of the country, Guillermo Alonso Pujol, was informed at his residence in the Miramar suburbs that Cossío was dead, he recalled the private conversations he had had almost a year before with General Fulgencio Batista in the military man's Kukine farm. At that time, the General had tried to attract Alonso Pujol –despite his senior position in the government— to the coup d'état he was brewing against Prío. It is fair to say that the smart politician did not go along with the putschist's plan but chose to keep quiet and not to inform the government he served.

In those talks over breakfast, Batista offered the reasons that in his view justified a coup d'état mentioning gangsterism as one of them. *"It's an evil leading to anarchy and it's the Army's duty and our own to save Cuban society,"* he said, to which Pujol responded that it was, in fact, a national embarrassment and an evil that should be eradicated. And added, *"But so far its victims are mostly insignificant members of supposedly revolutionary clans and such events have failed to touch public sensitivity. I don't think that these blood crimes and the reprehensible attitude of the authorities that have let them go unpunished might be enough to justify a military uprising in the eyes of history... A major event would have to occur, something as stunning as the death of Calvo Sotelo in Spain, the prelude to the uprising of Generals Sanjurjo, Franco and Mola."*

Vice-President Alonso Pujol thought he had struck a cord in Batista and dissuaded him of his conspiracy. But, the murder of Alejo Cossío del Pino alerted him to the mistake. It was not just one more victim but a man who had become known for his civic protests and who could become the Calvo Sotelo that Batista needed. That's why he decided not to wait and at 11:00 pm he entreated a phone conference with the President. At that point, the differences between the President and his Vice-President were notorious and irreconcilable, to the point that Prío had withdrawn Alfonso Pujol's bodyguards and house protection.

During that telephone conversation, however, although he spoke vehemently he observed the consideration he owed the authority of the head of State. He said, *"As a member of the government you preside, I feel entitled to urge you, with due respect, to act immediately and with maximum energy. I suggest the immediate replacement of the Chief of Police and the suspension of the constitutional guarantees. Also that you personally assume command of the Armed Forces and issue other measures that would allow you to strongly fight the criminals that with their excesses are about to provoke a catastrophe."*

As Vice-President Alonso Pujol later said, President Prío shared his views and, after thanking him for his observations, said that he would leave for the Palace right away where he would meet with his council of ministers. Having said this, the Vice-President felt that he had done the right thing as far as Prío was concerned, and as to Batista he had kept silent. He had disclosed to the President *'only half the secret.'*

On the way to Columbia

But reports from the Military Intelligence Services informed the Army high command of Batista's hectic conspiratorial activity. Since he knew he could not win power through the elections, he intended to get it by force.

During his meetings with a large group of retired officers, at the headquarters of his Unitary Action Party (PAU), at No. 306 on 17 Street, in Vedado, and in his own countryside residence, he insisted on the necessity to create an atmosphere of national turmoil to show that Prío's government was unable to preserve order, keep public peace and secure the rights to property and to free enterprise. His interest was to make the public opinion believe that only Batista could bring back order and balance. That's why the members of PAU were encouraged to commit murder and to promote disturbances conducive to a state of anxiety and alarm in the population that would justify Batista's actions.

After his telephone conversation with Alonso Pujol, President Prío left his *La Chata* farm, in Arroyo Naranjo, determined to suspend the constitutional guarantees and to resolutely fight the gangs with the appointment of a new Chief of the National Police. Once in the Palace, he called his closest assistants. Soon, he was surrounded by Prime Minister Oscar Gans, and the ministers of Defense and the Interior, Segundo Curti and Rubén de León, respectively. Also present were the Army and Navy chiefs, the

Supreme Court Prosecutor, and Orlando Puente, the President's personal secretary and promoter of the "Groups Pact."

When the decree suspending the guarantees, drafted and typed by Puente was ready, the President submitted it to those present. The Prime Minister, the military chiefs, Rubén de León and the prosecutor of the Supreme Court opposed the measure arguing that the opposition would accuse the President of using Cossío del Pino's death to favor the electoral position of the government candidate, Carlos Hevia, from the Authentic Party. On the other hand, Prío and Curti believed that the suspension of the constitutional guarantees would deter the conspirators, at least for the time being. Historian Newton Briones Montoto wrote that *"The view of the majority prevailed and the constitutional guarantees were not suspended."*

However, Lieutenant Colonel Juan Consuegra, from the Army, was appointed chief of the Central Division of the National Police. The new leader, a strong and even tough man, according to the press of the time, had joined the Armed Forces in 1937 and as of 1944, had swiftly climbed to the highest rank of the military, under the protection of General Genovevo Pérez. His designation meant the militarization of the police force. Members of the Special Company that Lieutenant José Ramón Fernández y Alvarez had helped train thoroughly for this very purpose would serve with the radio-motorized section. Consuegra ordered the arrest of more than thirty gunmen. But the same thing happened all over again; they were released after the courts argued that there were not enough proofs against them.

It is said that there is evidence confirming that Batista paid the assassins of Alejo Cossío del Pino. It is also said that once in the highest office, Batista pardoned them. The death of the owner of Radio Cadena Habana paved the way for Batista to get to Columbia on March 10, 1952.

(Sources: Texts by Enrique de la Osa,
Alonso Pujol and Newton Briones Montoto)

November 30, 2008

LIFE AND DEATH OF POLICARPO SOLER

Those who met him have said that he did not seem an aggressive man but rather a professional politician, a successful businessman, an easy going person and a good buddy, who covered his huge body with a guayabera shirt of fine linen and impeccable pants; his hair and moustache were always well groomed and his beard properly shaved...His peaceful and jovial face was not that of the typical thug, but Policarpo Soler was a thug and a fearsome one.

A long list of crimes marked his life from the early 1940s when he was accused of homicide in his native Camagüey. But far from being sentenced for that, Policarpo, with the false name of Domingo Herrera started to exhibit his ranks of lieutenant of the National Police. Actually, he remained with this force until the end of Batista's first government in 1944. Two years later, another bloody event forced him to leave the country for Mexico. It was there that he became a close friend of Orlando León Lemus, a.k.a. *El Colorado*, and other adversaries of the UIR –the group of the by now dead Emilio Tro— who had exiled there after the Orfila Massacre, on September 15, 1947.

He returns to Cuba and on September 1948 he is involved in the assassination of Noel Salazar, police chief at the ministry of Education, and in the death of Justo Fuentes Clavel, a vice-president of the University Students Federation and member of the UIR, on April the following year. On the 19th of that same month, Policarpo carries out his first attempt on the life of Wichy Salazar, also linked to the UIR, who had been seeking him out to avenge his brother's death. As from this moment, Wichy lives the life of a man sentenced to death on an undetermined date. Policarpo stalks him and on the Ayestarán and 20 de Mayo Streets he kills Wichy with a machinegun at close range. On July 1950, on the corner of San Rafael and San Francisco streets another action against UIR members results in two dead and several wounded. Eyewitnesses see Policarpo shooting with his machinegun through the window of a speeding car.

The "Groups Pact"

In midyear 1951, the boys of the happy-trigger who settled their differences with endless vendettas, are convened by the government of President Carlos Prío to strike a peace accord. Facilities would be given to the members of the *action groups* to reincorporate to a normal life or "arrangements" made for them to stay outside of the country if that was their decision. It was thanks to this pact, of which there is no written record, that Policarpo Soler –following instructions from Orlando Puente, the President's private secretary— settled in Matanzas City with assurances of not being disturbed. He then started working on his campaign for House Representative in the elections of June 1, 1952.

But Policarpo is arrested in Matanzas by the Rural Guard after his loyalists attack a UIR group that torn apart the posters announcing the gangster's race for Parliament. Rather than as a detainee, he is treated as a guest of honor at the Matanzas prison. He is accommodated at the leisure room of the penitentiary chief guards and allowed to receive as many visitors as he wants. Some visitors come straight from the Presidential Palace and upon returning they convey to the executive the threatening messages sent by the gangster. If taken to a court of justice, Policarpo will make sensational revelations.

"For God's sake, don't go"

One night, after meeting at the warden's office with some visiting friends, Policarpo took off his jacket and said, *"Let me hang it here because I'm not planning to go out tonight."* Everybody laughed, even the guards, and Policarpo added: *"I am sleepy. I've not slept well for six years. I'm tired of this hectic life. People are wrong about me."* Shortly before, he had said to the press with great insolence that *"I've been the victim of my enemies' schemes to make people believe I'm a monster, to blame me for everything that happened during the six years in which it is said that I was a fugitive of the law. But, I'm sure that the truth will come out."*

At the same press conference he raised his concern over the destiny of the two to three hundred families that he supported economically and that could be hurt by his detention, thus he would insist on his political aspirations. According to the accusation filed with the Provincial Court on March 4, 1952 by attorney Fidel Castro, Policarpo's group had some six hundred sinecures or '*botellas*' –as they were locally known— in various ministries.

Policarpo also claimed that he had given Prío his word that he would not be involved in violent actions again, and insisted: *"The President of the Republic is my friend. I promised him to put an end to the war among the different groups. Hevia is my presidential candidate; he is a good and honest Cuban. I'm a House candidate for the Authentic Party and I'm one of the "dieguitos" (that is, a loyalist of Senator Diego Vicente Tejera)."*

One afternoon Policarpo tells Florencio Sáenz that he would receive the visit of Tony Varona, a Senator and Primer Minister, along with an army officer. But, these would not be his visitors that day. Carlos Gil, a workers leader in the rigging factory, and others ask for permission *"to say hello to their friend Policarpo."* They are denied admission but they insist making a lot of noise and are finally allowed in. As Gil is entering the prison and Policarpo is walking toward the outside fence, which is opened, a woman who had also requested permission to visit him gets close to the thug and passes on a .45 caliber pistol. Already armed, Policarpo pushes the guard accompanying him and leaves the penitentiary. Then, something incredible happens. A grotesque scene; Florencio Sáenz, the prison warden, embraces the fugitive saying: "Policarpo, for God's sake, don't go! You'll make trouble for me..." But Policarpo insists, heedless to the plea. *"Look, man, I don't want to go, it's my friends who are taking me."*

I am *El Colorado*

Policarpo settles in Havana undisturbed. In his house at La Sierra suburb he receives the visit of ministers Sergio Megía and Ramón

Zaydín, widely known as *Mongo Pillería* (Tricky Ray). Every night, Policarpo is on the streets with a machinegun hidden in a bag. Someone angrily challenges the Director General of Customs for allowing Policarpo's access to drugs and hand grenades but the director denies the accusation saying that he has only allowed in propaganda material for Policarpo's political campaign.

An impressive piece of information comes to light at this point. Policarpo goes to the Municipal Election Board of the East to claim for his identity card. This he does in the company of the President's private secretary and with the acquiescence of legal officials and law enforcement agents guarding the place. He declares that his name is Policarpo Soler Cué and that he is forty-one years old. He also gives his address as No.14 on Santa Clara Street, in the Havana suburb known as San Francisco.

Members of the UIR provide the Military Intelligence Service (SIM) with information on Policarpo's whereabouts that the police claim to ignore. After much consideration, the officials detain him and confine him to the Castillo del Príncipe. But he also escapes from there the day that the guard in one of the sentry boxes on G Street suddenly finds himself surrounded by three men who showed up out of the blue and ordered him to hit the floor. One of them, a tall, skinny and redheaded man says to the sentry, *"Don't you know me? I'm El Colorado, and I've come to get my brother. Don't you move or you're a dead man..."*

Medical certificates

Policarpo was sent to the Castillo del Príncipe prison under rigorous security measures; he was not allowed visits or walking under the sun at the penitentiary terrace. But very soon his isolation was broken by the lengthy conversations he had in prison with minister Megía, Senator Diego Vicente Tejera and others from government circles. As for the prohibition to go out to the terrace, Policarpo himself claimed for that right of all inmates, and after that he could be seen there every morning.

His friends did not abandon him to his fate. The magistrates from the Provincial Court were under pressure from high government circles to dismiss the two charges pending at that judicial level and as the judges refused to cave in and resisted the harassment, Policarpo's friends changed tactics; his appearance in court was delayed by submitting one medical certificate after another. The first two certificates referred to a hepatic colic and the third to a nasal polyp. It was argued that he required surgery to remedy that condition so he was admitted to the prison's infirmary. This was an indispensible tactical move prior to his jailbreak. The infirmary was located at the roof-terrace, near the row of cells number twenty one where some of the inmates charged in the Orfila Massacre had been confined since 1947.

Hurry up, fatso!

It was impossible to escape from the Castillo del Príncipe without the guards' complicity or negligence. It was first necessary to enter deep into the facility and then come down a one-hundred feet wall guarded by one sentry. After that you had to cross the fosse, climb a high outside wall with a sentry box in every angle and finally climb down the one-hundred feet separating the fortress foundations from the street. But Policarpo and his friends performed such a complicated and risky operation in a few minutes of that now distant morning of November 25, 1951.

After *El Colorado* and his men immobilized the guard covering the 5th and 6th sentry boxes that looked out on G Street –mind you, only one guard for two sentry boxes— Policarpo's group, which had been watching the events from the terrace, went into action. They reached the platform closer to the fosse and tied up to a window there the long rope ladder they would use to descend smoothly to the fosse and once there, the escapees ran through it. They still had to cross over the last wall, the one adjacent to the street, but they did it relatively easy thanks to the ladder that *El Colorado* and his friends had left there. However, Policarpo kept sliding down due to his voluminous anatomy.

So, *El Colorado* shouted to him, *"Hurry up, fatso!"* to which Policarpo responded that he couldn't go faster because of his weight and concluded, *"It's my good life, man!"* The rest was easier. The group slipped away through the fortress angle on G Street, crossed the patios of some nearby houses and took the vehicles that waited for them only a few feet from the Ninth Police Station.

This is treason!

Soon, Segundo Curti, minister of the Interior in President Prío's cabinet, arrived in El Príncipe. Arrogant, haughty and with a touch of histrionic he moved his hands in desperation and repeated: *"This is treason! This is treason!"* adding, *"This people couldn't escape without inside help. There was never such a scandalous jailbreak, and so absurd, in the light of day. And the safety measures were fantastic!"*

In his article for the *In Cuba* section of *Bohemia* Enrique de la Osa, whose data I'm using, said that rather than fantastic measures real measures were required to prevent the jailbreak. The truth is that the prison guard was reduced in those days. Over fifteen guards had been laid off and of the twenty three soldiers guarding the facility, only two were on duty. Of the more than one hundred prison guards in the payroll, many were on assignment elsewhere and others looked rather unfit for their job, basically due to their advanced age.

Minister Curti accused Commander Ismail, head of the prison police, of complicity in the jailbreak, and something similar said Federico de Córdoba, superintendent of the penitentiary who also recalled that a few days before Ismail had informed him of a fifteen thousand pesos offer to let Policarpo escape that he had rejected. *"I think that Ismail was preparing the ground to have an alibi,"* Córdoba insisted, while Segundo Curti repeated that there had been complicity and connivance, and Commander Ismail said the same, for he did not think they were talking about him. Curti and Córdoba submitted their resignations right away, but President Prío did not accept them.

In his jailbreak Policarpo was accompanied by José Fallat, a.k.a. *El Turquito*, who had murdered Emilio Tro and Aurora

Soler during the Orfila Massacre; *El Guajirito* Salgado and Luis Matos Silbes that also took part in the attack on the house of Morín Dopico following orders of Mario Salabarría; Wilfredo Lara García, serving a 30-year sentence for the assassination of the student Justo Fuentes Clavel and pending a death sentence for the murder of Wichy Salazar; and Juan Díaz Acanda, a common criminal. From the group, only José Ríos Vence, also a participant in the Orfila affair didn't manage to escape because he broke both legs in the adventure.

In a statement to the press, *El Colorado* immediately denied any involvement in the getaway from El Príncipe, but didn't conceal his joy over the fact that his friend Policarpo was now free. Policarpo also spoke to the press. He said that he had escaped thanks to a group of his political activists and it would have been a discourtesy to refuse to go along. He stated: *"This forces me to defer the clarification of my situation with the law. Now, I'll go back to combat..."*

Death of Policarpo Soler

After his escape Policarpo, who like a local Houdini had the gift to appear and disappear at will, vanished. After President Prío was ousted, he showed up in Spain. In this connection, Raúl Aguiar writes in his book *El bonchismo y el gangsterismo en Cuba*[16] that *"...The coup d'état of March 10, 1952 did not seem to affect Policarpo Soler's good star. When it was assumed that he was hunted, persecuted and running for his life due to an effort to present his capture as a trophy, his extensive circle of friends facilitated his travel to Spain in midyear 1952. The travelers coming from Madrid said that the gangster looked like a tourist walking near the Puerta del Sol. In an article with the title Frente a todos, ran by Bohemia on January 8, 1956, Fidel Castro stated: 'Batista's regime stuffed Policarpo Soler with money and put him on a ship to Spain.'"*

[16] *Bunchism and Gangsterism in Cuba*

From Spain, Policarpo moved to Venezuela and from there to Santo Domingo, where he was a hit man in the service of General Trujillo. After January 1959, the different versions turn confusing. It is said that Trujillo was not fond of Batista's relations with Policarpo. Others have said that the Cuban thug wanted to rob the Dominican satrap some money; one million dollars of the three demanded by Trujillo that Batista paid for his stay and that of his men in the Dominican Republic.

Their differences of opinion grew and Policarpo, aware that his position was weakening, decided to get out quick. Trujillo would have none of that, and so one day he arrived in Policarpo's house without bodyguards and with a white handkerchief in his hand as a sign of peace. They chatted and drank like in the old times and said good-bye with a hug. Then Trujillo's men, who had positioned outside during the visit, opened fire on Policarpo and his people.

They were riddled with bullets. Only Caridad, Policarpo's wife, survived to tell the story. At this point, the stories get confusing again, because Delio Gómez Ochoa, an expeditionary on the *Constanza* and a Commander with the Ejército Rebelde, affirms that he watched the execution of Policarpo Soler in the Dominican prison known as La Cuarenta.

(Unpublished)

ANOTHER COUP D'ÉTAT

I have previously discussed the two coups d'état on March 10, 1952, one orchestrated by young officers headed by Captain Jorge García Tuñón that toppled President Prío, and the other dealt by Batista against those young officers.

Among other sources, I referred to a document ran in those days by *Bohemia* magazine under the signature of Guillermo Alonso Pujol relating how in March 1951, –that is, one year before the putsch— Batista, his usual cunning and resourceful self, had asked how he would react *"if Dr. Prío suffered a mishap, like a fatal plane accident."* Of course, Alonso responded that as Vice-President of the Republic he would do as the Constitution provided and assume power. And concluded: *"Unless the Army prevents it."* Batista then said that they needed to prepare, just in case, *"and start monitoring the Armed Forces."* The conversation proceeded and Alonso realized that his interlocutor was inviting him to join a plan intended to forcibly dismiss President Prío and promote him to the highest office in a government where Batista would secure full political and military control.

They met again the following day and Batista exposed his secret to Alonso as far as he felt it was convenient. *"There is this movement of young army officers intended to topple President Prío and replace him with the Vice-President of the Republic. They consider me the right person to give this movement a historical character. If we remain heedless, they might go ahead on their own and this could be very dangerous given the lack of a political orientation common to the military."* Alonso argued that the military high command would support Prío but according to Batista these officers could be easily dismissed. *"They are not in my plan. It's the command of the units that counts and these will side with us."*

During this second conversation, Batista asked him to immediately extend him his official appointment as Secretary of Defense, a document he would take to Columbia at the right moment. *"Although he would not say it clearly, he spoke as if the coup were to take place within a few hours."* Despite Batista's insistence, Alonso refused to go along with him in this adventure. He chose to leave Havana and to not respond the General's phone calls. When they met again Batista said: *"The sick man is better now and the operation has been suspended. We were worried that we couldn't reach you yesterday. We had a hard time halting the coup for everything was ready. It was not easy to call it off..."*

A year would pass before those young officers –nearly fifty of them in the force— dealt a coup d'état with the help of a group of retired military officers.

General Regreso

I read in a single sitting Newton Briones Montoto's latest book published by Ciencias Sociales Publishing House. The title is *General Regreso*[17]. In over four hundred pages the author examines Prío's government from the economic, political and social angles and delves deep into the sources of the March 10, 1952 coup d'état. It's a good read and a very enjoyable book, like his previous works, and the same as those it's based on an exhaustive research of documents and of numerous oral sources.

One of Briones Montoto's sources is journalist Luis Ortega, a Cuban living in the United States, who was the first person that on that distant year of 1952 received an offer from Batista to be a minister in his cabinet. But Ortega declined the offer, and was included in what was later known as the Consulting Council, which the dictator set up to replace Congress since this legislative body was dismissed by the putsch.

In the early hours of morning, Ortega got news in his house in Arroyo Arenas that something was going on in Columbia so he went there. He could not enter, or didn't dare to because as he put it a tank came to his car threateningly. Thus, he rushed to the house of Sergio Carbó, editor of the *Prensa Libre* newspaper, and from there they phoned Army Chief Major General Ruperto Cabrera.

The call was taken by the General's wife Arminda Burnes, who was confined to the bathroom of her house; an hour before, ex Commander Manuel Larrubia Paneque, retired in 1944, had broken into the Cabreras' bedroom armed with a machinegun and arrested him. But before taking Cabrera to the house of Batista's mother-in-law on 86 and 5thB streets in Miramar, the men with Larrubia pulled off every phone in the house missing only the one in the bathroom. It was through this phone that Arminda could inform Lieutenant Colonel Vicente León, chief of military force in the Presidential Palace, of the developments

[17] *General Return*

for him to communicate them to Prío who at the time was at his *La Chata* farm, in Arroyo Naranjo. Unknown to her, other Generals had been detained too. Such were the cases of Generals Otilio Soca LLanes, Assistant General, and Quirino Uría, Inspector General, both arrested in their houses located inside the Columbia area, by Captain Hernando Hernández and Lieutenant Victorino Díaz, respectively. Captain Pilar García was designed to arrest Colonel Eulogio Cantillo, but this one escaped through a window and took shelter at the Aviation Command subordinated to him.

An hour later, Luis Ortega returned to Columbia where he accidentally came across his friend 'Silito' Tabernilla, the son of the "old Pancho" and Batista's secretary who let him in and had him driven by jeep to the headquarters.

Briones Montoto offers an account of what Ortega related to him: "*...Batista looked extremely nervous but still he welcomed the journalist. Some future ministers were there. The orders were given by Jorge García Tuñón...he was on the phone giving instructions and monitoring the situation. Other people there were Andrés Rivero Agüero, Ramón Hermida, Colacho Pérez and Oscar de la Torre; Luis Ortega approached Batista and asked him what was going on. "Look, man, we've had to seize power..." Batista said. You could sense fear in the room because the coup had not been accomplished yet and command was in the hands of the main officers. Batista remained at a corner; he was not giving orders, García Tuñón was...*"

Background

On May 1959, when the culprits of the March 10 putsch were tried in a court of law, at least two of the defendants described chapter and verse the complicity with the coup of Ruperto Cabrera, who attended the proceedings of Case No. 50 as a witness. Anyway, this was not proven. Segundo Curti, the minister of the Interior under Prío, who passed away in Cuba in 2001, called Cabrera "*an incompetent*" and spoke of the man's "*clear negligence that at times looked like complicity or complicit acceptance*" of the coup d'état. But, when directly asked by Briones Montoto on the attitude of the ex Army Chief, he said that he did not consider the man a traitor, although he added with malice: "*Remember that Cabrera entered the stage on September 4, 1933.*"

The truth is that during Prío's government some retired and active officers perceived Cabrera as a possible choice to head the government. As Briones Montoto indicates, "*The only problem was that Cabrera refused to head the movement, and then Batista cropped up as an alternative.*"

In 1944 Batista, a Liberal Party Senator for Las Villas, was back in Havana from his self-imposed exile ('the long winter') in Florida. By this time, he had founded his own political organization –the Unitary Action Party (PAU)— to support his race in the presidential elections of June 1st, 1952.

But, unaware of the undertakings of Batista and his loyalists, another group of officers had their own plans. This conspiracy had been born at the Military Academy where three professors –Roberto Agramonte, Herminio Portell Vilá and Rafael García Bárcenas all of them civilians with political ties with Orthodox Party leader Eduardo René Chibás— were encouraging a coup d'état in collusion with a group of military men, the most important of which was Captain García Tuñón.

The journalist Luis Ortega, who had obtained this information from García Bárcenas and García Tuñón himself, said to Briones Montoto who wrote it in his book that these professors had talked Chibás into leading the movement and that he had agreed because he was embittered for his defeat in the 1948 presidential elections. That is, he was not directly involved in anything, says Ortega, but he gave his consent.

Lacking an attractive leader

But Chibás stepped back after the midterm elections of 1950 when again he was elected Senator. In view of the possibility to win the presidency in 1952, he decided that he wanted to pursue the electoral path. He then communicated this to professors Roberto Agramonte, Portell Vilá and García Bárcenas who were working to that end with a group of officers, particularly Captain Jorge García Tuñón.

"To the professors and the party members involved Chibás withdrawal was a hard blow. They were left without an attractive leader...the three professors ceased promoting the rebellion but the military were by now obsessed with the idea of saving the republic from chaos..." writes historian Briones Montoto in his book *General Regreso* elaborating on the testimony offered by journalist Luis Ortega. Thus the conspirators were looking for a leader when they came across Batista.

You mean Batista? Some would ask. The man has changed, insisted other conspirators and designed García Tuñón, the one who hated Batista the most, to contact him. Ortega said. *"He was an excellent officer, not very savvy in terms of politics but with a high professional morale...unfortunately, he was also easy to influence and given to take things seriously. Batista's interview with Tuñón was lamentable. A devious Batista persuaded Tuñón that he was a different man, that he had changed and that all he wanted was the best for the country. He then laid out a great government plan and Tuñón left the meeting a believer, and very excited offered his comrades an optimistic appraisal; Batista was the man they had been looking for. He was not interested in money but in glory, and he had a following in the lower echelons of the army. He had leverage in national politics and was in good terms with the United States. In summary, the military men involved in the putsch chose Batista as the leader of the regeneration movement."*

At the end of the day what the young officers wanted was to topple Prío and put in his place a regime of absolute administrative honesty, one respectful of constitutional succession and bent on the eradication of the gangsters that infested the country. At least that's what those officers said who wanted to deal the coup, even with Batista, in order to take over the top positions in the army. Later we'll see what happened to them.

The third man

In 1951, during the run up to the elections, Batista's Unitary Action Party ended third with 227,457 registered votes, preceded only by the Authentic Party with 689,894, and the Orthodox Party with 358,118. But it fared better than such traditional parties as the Liberal, the Democratic and Republican, the Communists; the Cuban National Party headed my Mayor Castellanos and the Cuban Identity Party of ex President Grau. According to surveys on the intention of vote, Batista was third with 14.21%, following engineer Hevia (the Authentic Party) with 17.53%, and Agramonte (Orthodox Party) with 29.29% who led the polls. At the same time, 33% of those surveyed supported the performance of the Authentics while 50.54% opposed it. Meanwhile, half a million potential voters, what sociologists call "the spiral of silence," was not affiliated with any party.

In the 1952 elections, Batista was a long shot. He thought, however, that other political parties, including the Cuban Identity Party headed by Grau, who was now distanced from Prío, would support his nomination, alongside the Cuban National Party. When he had confirmation that these two organizations would endorse Hevia, the government candidate, and that Alonso Pujol's Republican Party would not put up his candidacy either, he felt that he had little chance and commented to his closest friends that he was stepping out of the race. This resolution alarmed Prío. He knew that with Batista running the opposition vote would be divided while with Batista out of the race all of his potential votes, a lot or a few, would end up supporting the Orthodox candidate.

Before this, Batista and Prío had secretly met in one of the President's private residences –of course, not so secretly that the Orthodox loyalists could not find out— to strike an agreement on Batista's presence in the elections. In that meeting, Batista offered Prío to decidedly help him to split the opposition; therefore, when Batista announced that he was out of the race, the President's advisors felt that perhaps the offer had been too low and decided to add two more million pesos plus juicy amounts for some members of his inner circle. Prío's men were willing to do anything to keep him in the race.

"This event, whether true or not, is the reason for which a long time later...journalists and researchers misread him. The alleged offer made by Prío to Batista was interpreted in a different way giving rise to the comment that Prío had negotiated with Batista a coup d'état," writes Briones Montoto in his book *General Regreso*.

In plain clothes

Election Day was now closer and the conspiracy in the military institutions was underway. On instructions from higher up, the Military Intelligence Service (SIM) kept a constant and discreet surveillance on General Batista's every movement for they had news that he had political relations with army members on active service. The SIM recommended its superiors *"that the chiefs of the 5th, 6th and 7th Regiments keep a special surveillance on the access of retired officers to their respective areas, limiting such movements as much as possible, the same as the visits of civilians to military facilities."*

The Secret Police also kept an eye on the plotters, particularly their contacts with relatives of men on active service, and journalist Mario Kuchilán wrote in his column *Babel* in *Prensa Libre* newspaper on January 30, 1952: *"Last January 9, we received a piece of information that now we are getting from other sources: 'I've overheard a conversation taking for granted a conspiracy among military in plain clothes. The date, May or June...'"*

Actually, neither the SIM nor the Secret Police ever had any concrete evidence of the conspiracy, underlines Briones Montoto in his book. In a document on the conspirators worked out by the SIM it is specifically stated that *"...the clever way they act... has prevented us from getting clear proof."* The reports produced by both institutions reached the President but he failed to systematically pursue the issue and made the mistake of leaving the investigation in the hands of General Ruperto

Herrera, the Army Chief. When Commander Jorge Agostini, the chief of the Palace Secret Service, told Herrera of certain rumors he had heard, the General responded: *"You're nervous. Go to the shooting tournament and try to relax."*

However, at a lunch with army officers President Prío admitted he was aware that something out of the ordinary was going on, and added that Batista was scheming and that the military were placing themselves in a ridiculous position. The officers responded that they did not like the idea of taking orders from Batista, who was totally discredited, and that no one in the army would root for him. He also heard the names of the civilians implicated –Colacho Pérez, Hermida, Carrera Jústiz…— people that he gave too little credit to even think about them twice. *"The President,"* concluded Briones Montoto, *"heard what he wanted to hear, that's why again he did nothing."*

To act or not to act

President Prío was faced with a dilemma: to act or not to act against Batista. It's not that he lacked determination. He was unaware of the true dimension of the movement against him that would end up removing him from power. His priority at the moment was the election, and more than that, the defeat of the Orthodox candidate. But acting against Batista at this point on account of the conspiracy would mean pushing him out of the electoral process and his withdrawal from the public stage whether voluntary or forced might lead the opposition to close ranks in support of Agramonte. He had no choice. In his book *General Regreso*, Briones Montoto writes: *"Politics and safety fought for the President's attention, and the former came on top. Prío understood politics better than he did conspiracies."*

A tacit agreement?

Was there really an agreement between President Prío and General Batista that paved his way to the coup d'état?

In his book *General Regreso*, historian Newton Briones Montoto denies this assumption. However, Martín Díaz Tamayo, one of the protagonists of the coup of March 10, 1952, an ex Captain and employee of the Havana Bus Terminal that the putsch raised to the rank of General, died fully convinced that there was at least a tacit agreement and that Prío decided *"to leave it at that and do nothing given the possibility of a coup."* The promoter of this thesis argues that the defeat of the President's brother, Antonio Prío, in the race for Havana Mayor –at a time when the Authentics' slogan was *"Says Pomponio that our mayor will be Antonio"*—made it clear that in the presidential elections of June 1st, 1952 the government candidate would be swept away by the Orthodox wave.

Then, in light of the Orthodox promise to confiscate what they considered unearned goods in the hands of the Authentics, whom they planned to try as thieves, Prío chose the safety of a government headed by Batista. It is also said that Prío was so determined to prevent Roberto Agramonte from reaching the highest office that he was willing to alter the results of the elections to benefit another opposing candidate, Batista perhaps. But someone very close to his brother in law Roberto Fernández Miranda, –one of those most favored by the putsch— wrote in his book *Mis relaciones con el General Batista* (1999): *"Of course, many people...will say that Prío would have never made that shady deal, and it's their right to think that. As for me, I can only say that Batista never gave as much as a hint on such a deal, neither then or later. To me it's merely an assumption."*

The pretext

During the republic, the political climate became more strained every day. Batista was scheming with a bunch of retired officers whereas Jorge García Tuñón headed a group of military on active service. The rough behavior grew common in public life while confusion and anarchy gained ground. Seemingly, the rumors on the likely resignation of the President were false but it was true that Prío was anxious for the day when he could transfer power; something unheard of in Cuban politics. The President was worried and overwhelmed by the problems within his own party and the opposition's attacks on him. The freedom of expression that he insisted on protecting was used against him. The country was in disarray. The names of gunmen and terrorists showed up in the ballots of the Authentic Party and its allies as candidates to elective positions while *'the happy-trigger boys'* gathered together in the so-called *action groups* were back in the streets as mischievous as ever. *"The government loads the pistols and the delinquents shoot,"* Batista said, perhaps forgetting that by encouraging the university *bonche* years back he had become one of the promoters of the gangsters' actions so common during the Authentics' governments. Actually, at that time 50% of the population was unemployed and the growth of the Cuban economy failed to match its necessities...

The deadly action on Alejo Cossío del Pino that provoked a wave of indignation was attributed to the Insurrectional Revolutionary Union (UIR) bent on punishing him for his statements in favor of Salabarría after the Orfila Massacre (September 1944) although others blamed Batista's loyalists who a few days before, on February 7, had agreed to urge young members of the Unitary Action Party to conduct assassinations and provoke all sorts of public disorder to justify a coup d'état.

The outstanding historian Newton Briones Montoto also says that Batista emphasized the issue of anarchy and portrayed himself as the guardian of order. He even announced that once in power the first thing he would do was to take strong and effective measures against the gangsters to eradicate *"once and for all the disturbing actions of these enemies of public tranquility."* Although he hammered the government on this issue, he knew that this pretext fell short of justifying a coup d'état, affirms Briones, an action that would not be politically welcomed. Thus, as he could not find a plausible justification he invented it: Prío would lead a putsch against his own government.

On April 13, 1952, Batista declared to *Bohemia*: *"We have reliable evidence that they were planning the coup for April 15...*

an informal conversation of Carlos Prío and Anselmo Alliegro gave us a clue..."

According to Batista this is how things happened. The President was watching a baseball game at the Grand Stadium in Cerro, and Alliegro –one of Batista's cronies in the military before and after coup of March 10—came to say hello. Then, Batista says, Prío told Alliegro: "*...I've decided that unless the situation improves for the elections by April 15 I'll adopt the necessary decisions, and I swear to you...that they will not be allowed to seize power.*"

Prío denied that he ever said such thing and even that they met at all although apparently he did use Alliegro to send a message to Batista: He feared a coup d'état so he was alert and watching a certain military chief. But Batista interpreted the message as he found fit and used it as the justification he had been seeking.

"This was the new narrative...Prío intended to deal a coup on April 15, the ex General acted first and saved the Republic from the danger posed by the Authentics," Briones affirms.

On the eve

On March 9, Batista attended an election rally in Matanzas. He returned to Havana in the evening and in a house at the Kohly suburbs he met with some of those involved in the coup before heading for Kukine where other plotters waited for him. That same day President Prío, who had spent the weekend at *La Chata*, enjoyed the carnivals and drove along the Prado Boulevard in a convertible with his two little daughters. His brother Antonio danced all night at the Sans Souci night club, and Segundo Curti, the minister of the Interior, had dinner at the Río Mar restaurant. The President planned to make the announcement of his new cabinet with Curti as Prime Minister the following day, but he didn't have a chance to do it.

Without a shot

In Columbia, Captain Dámaso Sogo, the senior officer on duty, waited for the putschists to let them in through the sentry box number six, but at the last minute Batista, always distrustful, decided to use sentry box number four in front of the Finlay monument, but this delayed his arrival a few minutes because the sentry, unaware of the plot, halted the five-cars caravan guarded by as many patrol cars and Captain Tuñón had to get off the car with a pistol in his hand and remove the chain that prevented access. Sogo, who was there by now, indicated that Batista should take an armored vehicle to move to the commanding post of the 6th Regiment where the other officers of the 'Revolutionary Military Junta' were waiting. Before this, First Lieutenant Rodríguez Ávila, considered by many the most daring of the putschists, had deployed the tanks in combat formation.

With the detention of the senior chiefs, Columbia fell in the hands of the putschists without a shot. There was no resistance at La Cabaña, the headquarters of the 7th Artillery Regiment, or La Punta, which sheltered the Navy headquarters. The leadership of the National Police was also seized without a shot by Lieutenant Salas Cañizares who immediately ordered the occupation of The Workers Palace and the offices of the Popular Socialist Party; the telephone exchange offices on Aguila Street; the energy plant of Tallapiedra and its ancillary plant of Melones; and, the radio stations. In the provinces, except for Colonel Fernández Rey in Pinar del Río, the chiefs of regiments disagreed with the coup but none opposed it. They simply chose to resign their positions.

When Colonel Vicente León, the head of the Palace Military Guard, called *La Chata* to inform Prío that Batista had crashed Columbia, the President already knew and after some comments on his efforts to thwart the putsch he ordered that while he drove to the Palace, the colonel must shoot on any force trying to seize the executive mansion. By this time León, acting on his own, had detained Captain Juan V. Mendive, the dentist of the presidential family, who had tried to occupy the building with a group of marines.

"We're the law!"

At 4:30 am, almost two hours after Batista had entered Columbia, President Prío arrived in the Presidential Palace. He was accompanied by his wife, his brothers Paco and Antonio, and Rafael Izquierdo, one of his assistants. The civilian collaborators present there at the moment included Segundo Curti and Félix Lancís, ministers of the Interior and Education, respectively, the Chief of the Navy, officers of the Palace guard and military aides de camp. Someone suggested that the President should move to a province where the troops remained loyal. He communicated over the phone with the chiefs of several regiments in the provinces and spoke with Colonel Eduardo Martín Elena, chief of the 4th Regiment in Matanzas, inquiring about the military's positions concerning the coup. The officer responded that he would stay in his position while he could discharge his obligation of defending the Constitution and the laws of the Republic. Before this, in response to a message received from Columbia, the senior officer had said that he would not take illegal orders wherever they came from and that he would limit himself to discharge his obligations in compliance with the oath he had taken. These words pissed off Batista who retorted: *"We're the law! Take these orders or resign your command!"*

In his book *General Regreso*, historian Newton Briones Montoto explains that Martín Elena met with the main officers in his Regiment and then with his troops with the intention to sound them out and if conditions were favorable, *"he would work out a plan to oppose with weapons the consolidation of the coup."* But only one officer was willing to support him; most of those gathered there were neither in favor nor against the coup. Thus, *"he considered it was useless to resist it,"* writes Briones Montoto.

Colonel Cantillo, the Aviation Chief, who joined Batista even when everybody expected that he would do the opposite, had become the Assistant General of the Army. It was with him that Colonel Martín Elena communicated to express his disagreement with the coup. They had the following exchange: *"I felt just like you," Cantillo said, "but they have convinced me of the opposite." "I'm sorry they have convinced you..."* responded the colonel. *"Look, Columbia and La Cabaña have already joined the coup and you could be left alone,"* Cantillo insisted. *"I'll never feel alone while reason and justice are with me,"* Colonel

Martín replied. *"So be it,"* said Cantillo. *"So be it; let history be the judge,"* ended Martín Elena.

It has often been said that Prío left the Presidential Palace for Matanzas with the aim of leading the resistance and that it was in that province where he learned that the colonel had been dismissed. As a witness in the putschists' trial, on May 1959, Martín Elena said that he did not recall the President ever mentioning the possibility of moving to Matanzas. *"It was not to Matanzas that he should go, but to Columbia and if he had needed me I would have gone with him. I didn't tell him because he didn't ask,"* he stated.

In La Víbora suburb

On the third floor of the Palace, Paco and Antonio Prío were as pessimistic as they could be. Others urged the President to resist. The leader of a group of fifty soldiers that arrived to supposedly defend the President was arrested when it was clear that his intentions were quite the opposite. Two members of Prío's security detail fought the crew of a patrol car arriving in the building by the gate looking out on Monserrate Street; both sides sustained fatal casualties as a result of the shootout. Alvaro Barba went to the Palace to offer the government his sympathies on behalf of the University Students Federation; he asked for orders and weapons. He had wrongly believed that the Executive had by now a defense plan. Prío gave instructions to send the weapons requested to the University, but this was impossible because they first had to be removed from the San Ambrosio barracks and the facility was under control of the putschists.

About 8:00 in the morning, Prío left the Palace in a Buick with a private license plate and, by his own decision, accompanied by a limited number of bodyguards who left him a few blocks away from the Palace. The car driving the man who still was the President of the Republic moved on unprotected. Briones Montoto questions the theory that he went to Matanzas. A report published in those days by *El Crisol* newspaper informed that he went with his wife to the residence of engineer Jarro, in La

Víbora suburb and that at 1:00 am the next day the Mexican ambassador driving his own car picked them up there to take them to that country's diplomatic mission on Línea and A streets. President Prío left the country without resigning his position.

According to Briones Montoto, *"The surrender of the Presidential Palace and the military barracks, and Prío's subsequent asylum, marked the end of the operation. In the pretended race between Chibás and Aureliano...Fulgencio Batista had won." "The event that had just taken place was rather the result of Batista's analytical capacity than of his courage,"* concluded the historian.

Let's recall our previous description of Batista in a corner of the Army General Staff during the first minutes after the coup while Captain Tuñón gave the orders. But the roles changed at noon when many civilians came to Columbia hailing the ex General. At this point, the putschist officers, García Tuñón included, were cornered. *"As of this moment, Batista was in control of the coup. It was a well conceived and executed maneuver since what had begun as the coup of a few military discontents with a civilian leader, Batista had turned into Batista's coup, and from then on he would make the decisions,"* Briones writes. He appointed old Tabernilla Chief of the General Staff putting aside García Tuñón, the real architect of the coup, who would have to do with the rank of colonel and the leadership of Columbia. It's true that a few months later, attending the request of his peers he was promoted to General, but his days in the army were numbered.

January 15, 22 and 29, and February 5, 2006

THE HONEST

More than five decades back, a group of army officers wanted to overthrow Fulgencio Batista. The movement, baptized by the people as *The Conspiracy of the Honest,* was thwarted but it served to prove that the Armed Forces were not a 'monolithic unit' as the tyrant boasted. The opposition to Batista in the military academies had started the first day of the coup, that is, March 10, 1952. Four years later, over one-hundred and twenty regular officers, of the some five hundred the army had at the moment, –not including those promoted after the coup by pulling strings—were directly involved in the conspiracy. The cowardice of one of them frustrated the movement whose main leaders were tried and sent to jail.

These were the events of that April 4, 1956.

Removing Batista

The movement emerged and structured spontaneously. There were discontent officers at the Columbia Barracks, the headquarters of the Army General Staff, at La Cabaña fortress, the Aviation, the Artillery Academy at Atarés, and the Cadets School in Managua; but the disgruntled in one institution were unaware of those with the same feelings in another. It was Commander Enrique Borbonet, who first headed a platoon and later an entire company of paratroopers that contacted them and brought them together. He became the soul of the conspiracy.

Prior to March 10, the young and honest officers looked up to colonels Eduardo Martín Elena, Eulogio Cantillo Porras and Ramón Barquín López in the belief that if any of these was promoted to Army Chief, they would make this a more professional institution, distinct from illegitimate political interests, and devoted to the service of the Constitution and the Republic. But Martín Elena left the force the day of the coup d'état and Cantillo, acquiescent to Batista who made him a general, helped with his name, prestige and authority to consolidate the putsch. As to Colonel Barquín, he was a military attaché at the Cuban embassy in Washington and a deputy president of the Inter American Defense Junta. He was not a Batista loyalist and he did not owe his rank to the March 10 coup. He did not enjoy special benefits and showed the same discontent as the conspirators with the situation in the country. Some of these contacted the colonel and asked him to join the Movement. The idea that to be successful the Movement must be led by somebody with the proper rank and name, with public recognition and international credentials convinced the plotters of offering the leadership to Colonel Barquín, with Borbonet's consent.

The group lacked a homogenous mentality. Most of the officers held a conservative thinking and exhibited a prudent behavior. Practically nothing or very little was written about the social projection of the movement. They all agreed on the necessity to remove Batista from power and restore the Constitution of 1940. But their coincidence practically ended here for some felt that Batista's expulsion from the country was enough while others wanted to try him in a Court of Justice alongside murderers, henchmen and the white collar thieves who had stolen the treasure from the public coffers. They advocated a reorganization of the army and a streamlining of its payrolls inflated after the coup of March 10 as well as turning public service into an independent career to prevent public servants from being affected by changes in the government, when the ghost of unemployment hovered on them. There were differences concerning the implementation of a land reform; some wanted all of the land included while others wanted to affect only the unproductive and state land. The proposal to confiscate the unearned goods also had opponents. They all agreed that elections should be convened as soon as possible. These were, in general, the ideas of the conspirators. They were all willing to act but they disagreed as to the way of resolving Cuba's dramatic situation.

If they could seize power, the plotters planned to appoint Dr. Clemente Inclán, the rector of the University of Havana, as provisional President of the Republic and Dr. Herminio Portel Vilá, a man known for his probity, as Attorney General. Neither of the two heard of that intention at the time. Many felt that Barquín should be Secretary of Defense and Borbonet the Army Chief. Soon it was known that the colonel wanted this position for himself so a final decision remained pending. It was agreed that none of those involved in the plot would be promoted and that once the provisional government called the general elections, they should all apply for retirement and abandon military life.

Revolution! Revolution! Revolution!

As months passed, the efforts of those opposed to Batista, –such as Aureliano Sánchez Arango, the minister of Education and foreign minister under Prío, ex Senator Emilio Millo Ochoa from the Orthodox Party, and members of the Association of Friends of the Republic headed by Cosme de la Torriente— failed and merely led to the so-called Civic Dialogue. And, so it was that delegates of the government and the opposition met for discussion in the Continental House of Culture (currently the House of the Américas). Such discussion had the effect of slowing down the plans of the military who still believed it was possible to find a political solution, however, the shouts of *"Revolution! Revolution! Revolution!"* of the people attending the rally of the *"fragmented and demanding"* political opposition at the Luz Plaza in Old Havana on December 1955, left no doubt about the true solution to the Cuban problem.

Thus came the month of March 1956. The conspirators in the army believed that conditions were ripe to unleash their actions and decided to take advantage of the imminent arrival of Colonel Barquín in Havana. He had been summoned by Major General Francisco Tabernilla, the Chief of the General Staff, to inform him of a conference on the sea bed in Santo Domingo that he would attend as a member of the Cuban delegation and ask him that aside from the international meeting he tried to find out if Trujillo thought that he (Tabernilla) was implicated in an alleged weapon smuggling operation in favor of the enemies of the satrap or if this was just a smoke screen designed to cover up other plans.

This story Barquín revealed in an interview with *Bohemia* magazine, on February 8, 1959. He added that during his stay in Cuba, Batista had invited him for lunch and announced his immediate promotion to Brigade General and his appointment as Quarter Master General of the Army to replace retiring General Díaz Tamayo. In the same interview, Barquín said that he returned from the Dominican Republic convinced of the danger of Trujillo's conspiracy against Cuba which involved the worst of Batista's loyalists.

Sunday 1st, in the evening

With Barquín back in Havana, the final arrangements were made for the uprising, and the plotters informed that the warning would be given 24 or 48 hours in advance for everybody to get ready.

On Sunday April 1st, in the evening, a group of conspirators met at Barquín's residence in Tarará beach. Those attending the meeting included Commander Borbonet, Lieutenant Colonel Manuel Varela Castro from Columbia's Tank Division, Commanders Orihuela Torra Director of the Artillery School and Enrique D. Ríos Morejón from La Cabaña, and Captain Hugo Vázquez among others.

The final details of the uprising were discussed and the date agreed; it would be in the evening of April 3 to 4. Later, Borbonet conveyed the message to the most important officers involved for them to act accordingly in their units and take the necessary measures.

According to the plan, Lieutenant Colonel Varela and Commander Borbonet would seize the Infantry Division and assume command of Columbia while Barquín with two officers would take over the General Staff. These actions aimed at beheading Batista's high command. Meanwhile, Lieutenant Manuel Villafaña would take care of the Aviation neutralizing the airstrips with a group of officers and using the planes if necessary. On orders of Borbonet, the troops stationed in Columbia would seize the Presidential Palace and Kukine, Batista's farm in Arroyo Arenas., as Commander Ríos Morejón secured La Cabaña.

Then, with the great force of the disciplined cadets, First Lieutenant José Ramón Fernández Alvarez, currently a Vice-President of the Council of Ministers, would secure command of the School and Barracks at Managua and march on Columbia, where the senior officer of the guard that day would let them in. The cadets, divided in groups commanded by School officers committed to the Movement and on board an armored vehicle would detain the chiefs of the army in their own houses located inside the Military Zone. Once these detentions were accomplished, the conspirators would inform the troops of the developments. The military were not planning to resort to the structure of the workers' movement controlled by Batista's loyalist Eusebio Mujal although they did plan, once the operation was completed, to call on the university students and invite them to release a proclamation to the people explaining the role that the army was starting to play.

The traitor

Given the number of those involved and the positions they held, the April 4 conspiracy had great possibilities of success; but there was a traitor among *The Honest*.

Everything seemed to go according to plan when Commander Ríos Morejón turned up at the infirmary of La Cabaña Fortress and asked First Lieutenant Dr. Jordán Desquirón to give him a sedative because he was too nervous and had not been able to sleep all night. As it is only natural, the doctor asked him the cause of his distress and Ríos responded, *"It's because we'll topple Batista tomorrow. We are preparing a coup..."*

Doctor Jordán Desquirón could barely conceal his surprise at the revelation that the following day an uprising would try to overthrow Batista, as Ríos Morejón, the Commander of La Cabaña, had just told him in the infirmary. The doctor was not part of the conspiracy but he was not a Batista loyalist either so he decided to keep the secret and sent the officer off but not before recommending that he did not repeat such thing to anyone. Once outside the infirmary, Ríos Morejón came across First Lieutenant Bienvenido Fuentes to whom he repeated the story. Fuentes owed his ranks to the March 10 coup d'état, so he did not keep the secret but instead ran to Colonel Julio Sánchez Gómez, chief of the 7th Regiment based in the fortress. He couldn't find him so he passed the information on to the second in command, Lieutenant Colonel José de la Campa Méndez who rushed to Columbia where he reported to General Cantillo Porras, Assistant General of the Army. Cantillo did not waste a second and summoned Ríos Morejón to the General Staff. The officers of the Military Intelligence Services (SIM) waiting there detained Commander Morejón and took him to their own headquarters.

At that time, Commander Borbonet and Second Lieutenant Reynaldo Pérez Figueiras were at the cadets' school in Managua. Borbonet was discussing with First Lieutenant José Ramón Fernández, a deputy director of the center, the final details of the mission assigned to him during the uprising, when alongside other officers of the Academy and a group of cadets he would take into custody the high military command in Columbia. The officers were also checking the Thompson machineguns they would use in the operation to which the cadets would carry rifles.

At the SIM, Ríos Morejón wouldn't stop talking, to the extent that they practically had to tell him to shut up. He said that he was lured into joining a movement supposedly aimed at consolidating Batista in power but that he was denouncing now because he felt it intended exactly the opposite. Soon his detention was known and also how he damaged with his statement all the officers he knew. The news got out because one of the SIM officers was involved in the plot and from a public phone he called an officer in Columbia who was also a member of *The Honest*.

One of the agreements reached at Barquín's residence in Tarará on April 1st was that if any of the conspirators was arrested, he would resist the interrogation and even torture while those still free brought forward the actions scheduled for the next evening. Ríos Morejón was arrested on April 2. Barquín said that he was arrested the next day, April 3. He had gone to the Military Hospital for a diathermia treatment, ran some errands and on his return home he learned that Colonel Ramón Vidal Cruz was summoning him to the General Staff. He complied and Cruz Vidal welcomed him at the lobby. *"Colonel, you've been denounced for conspiracy and should come with me to the SIM,"* he said.

Later on, from his cell, Barquín heard the strong voice of Borbonet and then Lieutenant Colonel Varela Castro who were also arrested. Upon hearing of these and other arrests, Lieutenant Pérez Figueiras turned himself in. He said to his chief that although he was not plotting he sympathized with the conspirators and as such he requested to be dismissed from the army. He was arrested.

"Get out the tanks!"

When Borbonet heard of the arrests of Ríos Morejón and Barquín, he wanted to proceed as agreed in Tarará and bring forward the uprising. At 2:00 or 3:00 in the afternoon of April 3, he urged Varela Castro to act. Varela was the chief of the Mixed Regiment of Tanks based in Columbia, the main force in the country for its impact and moving capability. Varela hesitated and eventually refused to get out the tanks. He said that acting at that moment would provoke a slaughter, that it was more convenient to wait for the evening when he would be the Senior Officer on Duty in the barracks.

At this point, General Batista, on a fishing expedition in Isla de Pinos, was informed of the conspiracy. He returned to Havana and established his military high command at the headquarters of the Infantry Division in Columbia. With Batista at the Columbia Barracks, Borbonet insisted in unleashing the full operation right away. Again, he urged Varela to get out the tanks, use them to surround the Division Headquarter and force the tyrant and the other chiefs to come out hands up; Varela refused again. It was better, he said, to wait for the night. But the conspirators would not have another chance.

Borbonet was arrested in Columbia. At his house in Buena Vista, he had incriminating documents, including a roster of the army officers where he had check-marked one by one the names of the one-hundred and twenty men involved in the conspiracy. He requested permission to go home promising on his honor to be back in two hours to be arrested. He was allowed to go home and he burned all those papers.

The rumors that something out of the ordinary was going on at the tyrant's lair reached the cadets school. There were all kinds of news about arrests at the Columbia Barracks. In order to determine what was really happening, First Lieutenant José

Ramón Fernández took his car, a 1954 blue Ford, and went to his house on 9th Street, in the Almendares suburbs. Everything was quiet there. He wanted to make sure and as the use of a telephone seemed dangerous to him he simply drove on to Columbia. Near the obelisk he saw an old acquaintance, a soldier. Pretending a casual encounter, he asked the man where he was going and the soldier said that in Columbia they had called all soldiers to their quarters and that several officers were arrested including Borbonet and Barquín.

At the Cadets School

First Lieutenant Fernández restarted his car, picked up two or three officers who lived near Columbia and were also involved in the conspiracy and told them what he knew. He said that they should all wait at the Cadets School for news of the developments because despite the arrests the Movement still had a chance to anticipate to the events.

He then drove along the Boyeros Avenue to reach Managua via Santiago de las Vegas. Beyond Mazorra Psychiatric Hospital, before entering the small town of Boyeros, to the right, he pulled out the car in front of a house. There lived Second Lieutenant Angel Sánchez Mosquera, a professor of Tactics and his colleague in the Teaching Department of the Cadets School. Mosquera was also a conspirator. This officer had obtained the best grades of his class and was considered an honest and loyal officer, not compromised with the March 10 coup d'état. The man would change much with the passing of time and in the days of the fight on the Sierra Maestra Mountains, by then a lieutenant colonel, Che Guevara defined him as *"the bravest, but also the worst murderer and thief"* of all of Batista's military chiefs.

Sanchez Mosquera came out to meet Fernández shirtless, wearing only his pajama pants. Fernández was acquainted with the man's wife and family whom he considered decent people, and particularly Sanchez Mosquera was a neat and tidy person. Fernández quickly told him about the latest events and asked him to take to the School all the officers affiliated with the Movement that he could find. About eighteen officers in the Cadets School were part of the conspiracy along with Fernández.

April 4, at 6:00 am

Everything seemed normal that midnight in Managua. So far the news on the conspiracy had not leaked beyond the military quarters, and apparently those arrested had not mentioned the Cadets School during the interrogations. In his room, First Lieutenant José Ramón Fernández, the deputy director of the school, contemplated the possibility of being killed. He also thought that he could be arrested. He would have had enough time to seek asylum in an embassy that afternoon; he could have done it if he wanted but he rejected the idea. Perhaps nothing happened…and there was still the possibility that the Movement succeeded. With these thoughts in mind he went to bed. It was already April 4, 1956.

At six in the morning someone knocked hard on his door. It was Commander Pedro Foyo, the director of the school, and First Lieutenant José de Jesús Castaño, from the Bureau for Repression of Communist Activities (BRAC) who were coming to arrest him and take him to the SIM. They searched the room and in the closet they found the detainee's personal weapons and two grenades. No one else in the School was arrested despite the numerous officers involved in the conspiracy.

At the SIM offices, he was interrogated by Lieutenant Colonel Antonio Blanco Rico, head of the Military Intelligence Services, and Colonel Orlando Eleno Piedra Neguerela, head of the Bureau of Investigations of the National Police. Fernández said he knew nothing about the conspiracy nor anyone related to it. He assumed that attitude because the important thing was to save what was left of the Movement preventing the arrest of all those involved. They found nothing incriminating him, not even a document. They could blame him of having the machineguns but he had the authority to have them and the grenades they found were not important.

During the interrogation, Blanco Rico was inquisitive but professional, calm and businesslike. For an hour, he kept asking questions while Orlando Piedra waited for his turn to ask. Then he told Fernández that several arrested officers had admitted their culpability and that he should do likewise because the others had incriminated him in their statements.

Fernández did not move an inch from his statement. *"I don't know anything, I don't know anyone, and I don't know what you're talking about..."* At some point, Piedra Neguerela seemed to have lost his patience and said to the detainee that he would have to resort to other methods to freshen up his memory and make him talk. *"Well, that's up to you,"* Fernández said.

The chief of the Bureau of Investigations of the National Police did not act on his threats. Actually, none of the officers arrested in connection with the conspiracy of *The Honest* was tortured or ill-treated. The Military Intelligence investigated more than one hundred officers. A number of them had nothing to do with the April 4 Movement but the slightest suspicion was enough to put them under the microscope. From the over one hundred officers investigated only some seventy were arrested, whether implicated or not in the conspiracy, and of these only thirteen were brought to trial. More than thirty men involved in the conspiracy were not subjected to any action, either because they went undetected or because it was not convenient. The others were either reincorporated to their units or transferred to other less important barracks; some were discharged or retired. This purge deprived the army of many of its best cadres. Of those conspirators who remained in service after the failure, some were ready to join any other effort against Batista while others didn't want to hear of any Movement, and there were still some, like Lieutenant Colonel Sánchez Mosquera, who renounced his dignified attitude of April 4, 1956 and became a war criminal.

Anyway, Batista with his characteristic shrewdness chose not to admit the scope of a conspiracy that involved the artillery, tanks, aviation, Columbia, the Cadets' School... and more than one-hundred and twenty officers, that is, one fifth of the regular army.

The conspiracy, even when thwarted, dealt a huge blow to Batista. That much he acknowledged in some of the books he published outside Cuba. It actually gave rise to a fissure in the armed forces and revealed the presence of a group of officers bent of rescuing the decency and prestige of the army, setting distance from petty politics, crime and corruption, and restoring institutionalism to the country to carry forward certain social transformations.

A mockery of justice

The Summary War Council would be held at the War Jurisdiction of the Supreme Court to judge a crime of conspiracy to rebel. The Council would be presided over by Colonel Dámaso Sogo, that captain who opened the gates for Batista to enter Columbia in 1952. The prosecutor would be Commander Fernando Neugart and the defense attorneys would be doctors José Miró Cardona, Segismundo Paret, José J. Fernández and José Emilio Ferrer while Commander Aníbal Ortega from the Navy would be the court-appointed counsel to the defense. The thirteen officers indicted coordinated their strategies for the trial through their attorneys. Only those that could not avoid their implication would plead guilty and use the opportunity to expose the reasons for the conspiracy.

On April 11, at 8:00 am, the defendants were brought to court. The first to enter, given his highest rank, was Colonel Barquín followed by Lieutenant Colonel Varela Castro and Commanders Borbonet, Ríos Morejón and Orihuela Torra. Then came captains Travieso, Vázquez and Despaigne, first lieutenants Planas, Villafaña, Travieso and Fernández Alvarez, and finally Second Lieutenant Pérez Figueiras. Neither the press nor the defendants' relatives were allowed in the courtroom. The rear seats accommodated hostile soldiers, corporals and sergeants.

As soon as the trial started, Miró Cardona attacked the proceedings. He said that Neugart could not be the prosecutor because he had taken part in the investigations. It was an anomalous situation, a wrong procedure running contrary to legal process as established in Criminal Law. Neugart argued that he was covered by the code on War Jurisdiction, but the other defense counselors insisted and the president of the Council, not knowing what to do, declared a recess to resolve the matter. Nothing was solved and the tribunal returned to the courtroom with the prosecutor still in his bench.

Then the evidence of confession was presented. The statement made by Commander Borbonet raised the temperature in the room. Colonel Sogo had to call him back to order several times, *"Lower your voice," "Limit yourself to answer the question," "Don't use an affected voice," "Don't proselytize here," "You must show respect for this Court or I'll be forced to penalize you."* Eventually, Borbonet ignored the specific accusations of the prosecution and pleaded guilty to the crime of conspiracy. He said that the conspirators did not intend to kill President Batista but simply restore the democratic institutions, hand power over to a group of better Cubans and call for elections. Then he added, *"Our plans were designed to defend our homeland and the army. We wanted to return the Armed Forces to their barracks and set them apart from any interference with the country's political leadership. We wanted to eradicate forever the gangs that take turns to assault power..."*

That was too much for the soldiers watching the trial in the courtroom. From the back of the room they fiercely shouted *"Viva Batista!"* Sogo ordered the arrest of the man who had shown such contempt of his court and asked to clear the courtroom. The prosecutor protested and lied when he said that *"The man who shouted, Your Honor, has already left this courtroom,"* and adding with a mellifluous voice *"Let not the just pay for the sinner. Don't deprive these soldiers of their right to be here."*

Confusing and contradictory

The traitor of April 4, Ríos Morejón, offered a confusing and contradictory statement. He admitted his participation in the Tarará meeting and repeated his picturesque version of the events: he became involved in the conspiracy because he was told the intention was to consolidate Batista's power and he realized too late that the opposite was true. He reiterated his accusations against all the defendants, and incriminated others that had been exonerated and quite a few retired officers. At this point, Sogo asked his words to be considered a testimony but Miró Cardona protested since according to the Supreme Court, the military in a passive situation are considered civilians for any legal proceeding; therefore, the court would have to suspend the trial and transfer it to civilian jurisdiction. This time it was the prosecutor, Neugart, a lean man with a long and angular face, who jumped like a tiger.

"This is just a technicality aimed at jeopardizing the proceedings of this court, this is a summary war council and the issue of competence is out of place," he said.

"But I insist that the court decides this now," said Miró Cardona.

"You, civilian lawyers, should study military law not to make a mockery of yourselves with absurd positions..."

But Miró interrupted him, *"I demand respect for the toga I'm wearing!"*

Again at a loss, Sogo did as usual, he declared a recess. The session was resumed without the issue of the jurisdiction incompetence solved.

Cuba in the dock

The court insisted in clarifying some specific points. Were the conspirators planning to establish a Military Junta? Would they have killed Batista? Would the presidential family have been in danger? Would *The Honest* have unleashed a bloodbath?

Varela Castro denied these accusations. *"We did not intend to act against the life of the President or that of our comrades in arms, nor did we plan to establish a Military Junta. We were only moved by an idealistic sentiment."* When his time came to speak, Colonel Barquín confirmed the words of his colleague. *"Our objective was to bring about a transformation without violence...we wanted to bring democracy back to our country. In that meeting in Tarará, my comrades offered me the political and military leadership of the Movement. I decided to take part in these efforts because these were prestigious members of the Armed Forces...I accepted my comrades' offer. There, we agreed on avoiding bloodshed. This was an indispensible requisite. It was not our intention to climb to higher positions..."*

Having heard the defendants' statements, the court listened to the witness for the prosecution. Then the prosecutor presented his report and the defense attorneys spoke. The presentation of the case by Miró Cardona was brilliant. He was the president of the Bar Association and a professor of Penal Law, and although he was representing Commander Orihuela Torra, his nephew-in-law, he spoke in favor of all the defendants. He dismissed the crime of conspiracy because a conspiracy must come out of the mind of those involved before it becomes a crime, and added that it was fundamental to have a concrete agreement as to the means to carry out the rebellion, and as such agreement did not exist, the crime did not exist either.

Finally Miró Cardona said: *"Honorable judges, these men have not really committed a crime against the sovereignty of the State, the safety of its powers or public order. What they wanted, and want, as soldiers of their homeland is a loving Cuba for all of its children. They were doing this neither in favor nor against anyone; they were doing it for the Republic. They were acting against the abuse of power, against the arrogance of those at the top, to put an end to the insane race for wealth, and to give the people, as the sole custodian of sovereignty, the possibility to determine their historic destiny. That is why I ask the members of the Council, chivalrous officers of Cuba's Army, that when the time comes to exercise their judgment to punish their peers avoid the replacement of the rational principles of justice with the macabre blemish of terror and ponder the exemplifying nature of the sentence because at this moment the people feel that Cuba is in the dock."*

The sentence

No way. The following day the defendants were informed of their sentences for the crime of conspiracy to rebel: Barquín,

Varela Castro, Borbonet, Orihuela, Ríos Morejón, Despaigne and Vázquez were sentenced to six years in prison and Captain Travieso and lieutenants Plans, Villafaña, Travieso, Fernández Alvarez and Pérez Figueiras received four years and two months. The punishment included removal of their military ranks and expulsion from the army. The traitor, Ríos Morejón, was soon pardoned. The others would serve their sentences in the Cárcel de la Habana, at the Castillo del Príncipe. But after a few days there they were transferred to the prison in the Isla de Pinos, whose warden was Commander Capote Fiallo, a soldier promoted to officer in 1933 who boasted of being more powerful in that island than Batista in Cuba. And it was true, since to his position of prison warden he added that of chief of the 43rd Squadron of the Rural Guard covering the territory, delegate of the ministries of the Interior and Public Works and *de facto* Mayor.

On the island

They were transferred to Isla de Pinos in two groups. The first one, which included Barquín, Varela Castro, Orihuela Torra, Borbonet, Despaigne, Vázquez, Villafaña and Fernández Alvarez traveled handcuffed and with heavy protection. At the warden's office in the prison they were received by Commander Capote who ironically said to them *"I'm so sorry for you! I'm really sorry for what happened to you, I like you and respect you so much! You don't know, my friends, how sad I am about all this...as time passes I'll improve your conditions here but now I must see after your safety, because it happens that every guard and inmate here now is loyal to Batista and I'm afraid they could hurt you, so I should send you where you are safe."*

And, he did. He placed Barquín in solitary confinement in a cell at the entrance of pavilion No.1; Borbonet and Despaigne in two punishing cells at the entrance of the room assigned to the lunatics in pavilion No.2. Others were sent to the so-called 'Selection' building, all of them in separate cells. Fernández Alvarez was confined to a cell in this same pavilion where he spent four or five months without anyone to talk to, without access to a radio or the press, and without 'recess' time. Eventually, they also sent Vázquez there, and later replaced him with Varela Castro. One day, they took Fernández out of that cell and locked him in another with three of his comrades. From that cell, they could see, sixty or seventy meters away, Barquín's and Vázquez's cells. Fernández communicated with them every night before the lights were turned off through the marine code of signals which he had learned. He stood on a bed and from there transmitted the signals, one letter at a time. It could take an hour to communicate twenty words with this method, but it was something. To submit them to complete isolation, Capote conceived a sinister organization of family visits. The relatives of *The Honest* never coincided and although the families kept in touch and carried messages between the imprisoned officers, a year could pass before a message made it to its destination.

A letter from Fidel

Colonel Capote's replacement as a warden was Colonel Ugalde Carrillo, who some time later was accused by Fernández Alvarez of abusive behavior toward the inmates, and put to trial. A great scandal broke out and the colonel lost prestige with the public opinion. Batista removed him from the prison management but before that Ugalde transferred the officers of the April 4 Movement to circular building No.4. This created a complex situation because the common criminals were precisely in that area. Colonel Ugalde was replaced by Colonel (and later Brigade General) Dámaso Sogo, the same man who had presided over the War Council against *The Honest*, but he spent only one month in that position.

The next warden of the prison was Commander Juárez Rueda, a fearless man that walked along the entire prison unarmed and without bodyguards, but who was abruptly replaced when he tried to enforce the inmates' rights. Time passed and, on January 6, 1958, Lieutenant Colonel Casillas Lumpuy, the murderer of

Jesús Menéndez, the workers' leader, was appointed chief of the penitentiary. It was Batista's gift on the Epiphany. However, in his watch there were no crimes, abuses or beatings in that prison, and the common offenders were taken out of that building. At that point, some one-hundred former military men and members of different organizations opposing the tyranny made up the political penal population. Borbonet assumed leadership of the prisoners in that building and was later replaced by Fernández, who resigned after a violent discussion with Casillas and was succeeded by Hugo Vázquez.

The long months in prison brought to light the truth about each and every one of the officers involved in the April 4 Movement. Some denied the Ejército Rebelde any right to restructure and purge the Armed Forces. Others expressed publicly their sympathies with the guerrilla, but they didn't mean it, and there were those who did not understand that when Batista was defeated they should submit to the leaders now fighting on the Sierra Maestra Mountains. Some let their imperative character show and others their conservative leanings while only a few understood that they should support the Revolution that was in the making. The members of the July 26 Movement –also known as M-26-7— created their military organization in the penitentiary and structured a battalion under the leadership of José Ponce, a participant in the assault on the Moncada Barracks and a member of the *Granma* expedition. The M-26-7 assigned Fernández Alvarez the mission of training that force. In theoretical classes, almost on a daily basis, he showed the men to aim, to hit the ground and shoot, and the steps to follow for a good shot. He taught them about organizational structure and tactics, and also how to dig a fox hole and camouflage. One day, Jesús Montané's family brought the prisoners a letter from Fidel and five thousand pesos. Although the money in fact helped in the solution of pressing problems and improved their living conditions in the penitentiary, they perceived the gesture as an indication that those on the Sierra Maestra Mountains had not forgotten or abandoned them.

The beginning of the end

Batista's situation was shaky and discontent expanded within the armed forces. Conspiracies were common in the army. One of these was called by the regime the *Conspiracy of the Drunk*. Retired General Martín Díaz Tamayo was involved in this conspiracy, and he even met with Commander Camacho Aguilera from the Ejército Rebelde General Staff, but the plot was postponed and exposed, and fifty five officers ended up in jail. In Las Villas province General Ríos Chaviano also had a plan endorsed by the chairman of the Joint Chiefs of Staff. On December 1958, *The Honest* got information that there would be a joint action of the M-26-7 and the military. Major General Cantillo would lead a revolt in Oriente and advance on Havana alongside the rebels, whereas the army troops deployed in Las Villas would join forces with the troops headed by Brigade General Carlos Cantillo, the chief of the Plácido Regiment in Matanzas.

The messenger who took the information to the penitentiary in Isla de Pinos asked the imprisoned officers to join and to send as proof of their allegiance Colonel Barquín's graduate ring but the colonel didn't have it with him so they finally sent Varela's. The messenger also said that the conspirators had a frigate that would take them out of the island and carry them to Manzanillo where they would incorporate to the forces fighting Batista. Among the authors of the message was Colonel Florentino Rosell, chief of the Army Corps of Engineers and of the armored train that he should have commanded but did not and that fell in the hands of Che Guevara in Santa Clara. The train was sent to the frontline under Commander Calderón, second in command to Rosell who fled the country loaded with money on a yacht days before Batista's collapse. The promised frigate never showed up.

Meanwhile, the prisoners got news that Batista's support in the army was definitely declining and that the people's support was eluding him, too. They learned about the fiasco of the *Spring Offensive* that broke the army's backbone; of the rebels victories in El Jigüe, San Lorenzo and Las Mercedes; of the attack on Guisa and Maffo; of Camilo's and Che's victories in Las Villas... Armando Hart, the leader of the M-26-7 in the penitentiary, discussed with Barquín the great deed of the Invasion of the western provinces by the Ejército Rebelde. But Colonel Barquín said, *"It's impossible. It's militarily unfeasible,"* to which Hart responded, *"Colonel, they did it because they didn't know it was impossible."*

On December 25, coinciding with Colonel Casillas' transfer from the penitentiary to the leadership of the Leoncio Vidal Regiment in Santa Clara, the prisoners found out that the town of Cruces was now in the hands of the rebels. First Lieutenant Fernández Alvarez analyzed the information and realized that the collapse of Batista's regime was imminent. To his comrades he said: *"The man won't make it to January 6."*

Securing the island

It is said that before leaving the country Batista warned Cantillo not to release the officers involved in the April 4 conspiracy, so in the morning of January 1st, the latter informed the officers that they would be pardoned *in due course*. Cantillo had been left in command of a disrupted army, which had lost the capacity to win even a skirmish against the rebels but was still well armed, and in charge of organizing a civilian government to be headed by Judge Carlos M. Piedra y Piedra. The Supreme Court declined taking the oath to the chimerical President and Cantillo was left empty-handed. Fidel did not accept the ceasefire, denounced the putschist maneuver and called a revolutionary general strike. There would not be a civilian government headed by Piedra and Columbia, the most important fortress in the country, was in chaos. Amidst this complex situation, a group of officers asked Cantillo to release *The Honest*, because these were the only ones with the necessary prestige to solve the problem in the army, and so they went for them.

The release of only the officers of the April 4 conspiracy meant leaving the members of the other organizations in prison.

Some of these military understood the maneuver and Hart, on behalf of the M-26-7, suggested to Barquín to appoint a military chief for Isla de Pinos. The colonel came up with a proposal but Hart didn't accept it. Instead, he proposed First Lieutenant Fernández Alvarez who said he would only take on this responsibility if he could release the political prisoners and take orders only from the M-26-7. Hart would be the political leader of the territory.

Thus, Fernández left the penitentiary and took over the Rural Guard headquarters, then went back to the prison and ordered the battalion made up by members of the M-26-7 to leave the prison building in perfect military formation. Everything seemed to be going well when they saw that the common offenders in circular building No.3 were running away towards the prison outer fence, because someone had inadvertently left the gate to their cells open. A soldier opened fire against them with a .30 caliber machinegun and Fernández ordered him to stop but the man did not obey so the officer had no choice but go to him, open the weapon's ammunition chamber and pull out the cartridge belt. There were no casualties but three hundred inmates escaped from the prison center; later, all but three or four were captured.

Supporters of the Revolution assumed control of the military facilities. It was important to Fernández to secure Isla de Pinos, which had an airport, a harbor and a radio station, and Batista's loyalists now running away could try to turn it into a bulwark. So, he ordered the detention of ex Commander Capote and the guards implicated in crimes and abuses, and started to take action against those involved in dirty businesses with Batista. He also detained Captain Patrocinio Bravo Moreno, second chief of the penitentiary. This was a rough man, extremely loyal to the tyrant whom he had protected after his entrance in Columbia on March 10, 1952, but Fernandez later helped him to clarify his situation and get his release. Once in custody Capote said: *"You know me, and you know I'm against Batista." "That's not the problem," Fernández said. "The problem is that the people who live in this island believe you are a Batista's loyalist and as it happens that every guard and inmate here now are revolutionaries I should protect you,"* and he sent Capote to the same room where he had sent Fernández in the first months of his imprisonment.

April 8, 15, 22 and 29, 2007

THE SECRET WEAPONS

The last weapons that Fulgencio Batista received to shore up his already shaky regime came from the Dominican Republic and from Somoza's Nicaragua. In the first case, which is widely known, he received San Cristóbal carbines that sometimes failed in the din of battle. As to the second case, it was revealed not long ago, when a host of documents kept in the Cuban Heritage Collection of the University of Miami were declassified.

The ex-dictator was very upset. He had heard the rumor that General Francisco Tabernilla Palmero, a.k.a. *Silito*, whom he had known from birth and that until December 31, 1958 had been his private secretary and chief of the Infantry Division based at the Columbia Barracks, had dared address a letter to Anastasio Somoza Debayle, chief of the National Guard in Nicaragua, to advise him on what to do with regards to the invasion of Olama y Mejillones carried out by Pedro Joaquín Chamorro at the head of nearly one hundred men, on June 1959. Batista learned that Tabernilla Palmero had suggested Somoza to cut off the flow of food, clothing and medicines to the area occupied by the insurgents and, as if Somoza needed to be told, he had added that *"repression against those involved in the conspiracy should be as unbiased and severe as warranted by the circumstances."*

This was not, however, just one more rumor making its way to the distant Funchal, on the Madeira Islands, and Tabernilla Palmero himself set the record straight. *"The letter to Somoza is not a rumor. I'm enclosing a copy. I wrote it when I saw his country invaded to prevent him from making the same mistakes we made,"* the mouthy secretary wrote to Batista in a letter dated November 8, 1959, and added: *"You know that I was his (Somoza Debayle) friend and could not forget that he cooperated resolutely with our Army..."*

And Tabernilla Palmero carries on refreshing the memory of his former boss. He says that when in the final months of Batista's government they only had two thousand .37 mm cannon bullets, he called Somoza Debayle and *"the following day a NICA aircraft was landing in Columbia with four thousand bullets for the tanks. By the way, you gave a forty thousand pesos credit for that material, but the money was not released in time."*

In summary, Somoza, who was defeated by the Sandinistas on July 1979, had sent his colleague in distress thirty T-17 tanks with ninety machineguns, sixteen thousand bullets for the .37 mm cannons, one million .30 mm bullets, napalm bombs and five-hundred-pound cluster bombs; a nice package.

Silito was one of the most conspicuous members of the Tabernilla clan. His father was the chairman of the Joint Chiefs of Staff. One of his brothers was chief of the Army Air Force and the other also held a senior position in the armed institution. General Alberto Ríos Chaviano, *'the butcher'* of the comrades who assaulted the Moncada Barracks in 1953, was married to one of his aunts. Chaviano was at the head of the Columbia Mixed Regiment of Tanks when on March 13, 1957 a group of revolutionaries attacked the Presidential Palace, and he rushed to help the tyrant. This was the cause of his promotion to Brigade General and chief of the Infantry Division, although that day the armored vehicles moved there from Columbia arrived long after the combat was over. But times were different in 1959; Batista and the Tabernillas were in exile and the former tyrant accused them of treason and blamed them to a large extent for the military failure in the fight against the guerrilla. They too pointed fingers at Batista and to prove it they asked (and paid) journalist José Suárez Núñez, a Batista loyalist right to the previous day, to write the book *El Gran Culpable*[18].

Hence the letter on Tabernilla Plamero's conduct forwarded by Batista from Funchal to two mysterious "R and P" (Could it be Irenaldo García Báez and Orlando Piedra?). He qualifies it as interference in the internal affairs of Nicaragua. *"The phrasing*

[18] *The Great Culprit*

and the content of what he tries to say, such as the letter sent to the Somozas, are so out of place that it's better to completely ignore them," he recommends to his former assistants and tells them that he has news that Silito's document was considered "*disgusting*" by its addressees.

Forced to clean his room

No one knows if Batista eventually paid back his debt to Somoza but he did have to pay Rafael Leónidas Trujillo, the Dominican satrap, his arrears and this was one of his main troubles in the Dominican Republic.

Batista arrived in Santo Domingo in the morning of January 1, 1959. At the military base where his plane landed, Ranfis Trujillo stood waiting to offer an official welcome. Ranfis, the General's favorite son (who as rumors go was fathered by a Cuban) had received his ranks of colonel at the age of three and general at nine. Batista was declared an honorable guest of the Dominican Republic and accommodated near the National Palace in a splendid residence destined to distinguished visitors. He then thought that his benefactor would receive him right away; however, he had to wait more than 48 hours to be granted an audience. That same day, January 3, Batista stopped boasting when Trujillo told him that he would give the General twenty five thousand men and the necessary planes and ships to conduct an expedition to Cuba. Batista declined the offer but volunteered to promote and pay for an action to assassinate the leader of the Cuban Revolution.

A few months later, Trujillo summoned General Batista to the Palace. In the previous interview, he had appealed to the man's courage and manliness, now he appealed to his pocket. Batista had a pending account with the Dominican government; he had failed to pay for the last shipment of weapons and Trujillo was demanding reimbursement. The debt amounted to nine hundred thousand dollars.

Batista responded that it was not a personal debt, that those weapons constituted a debt of the Cuban government. Trujillo sarcastically said: *"You are not telling me to ask Castro to pay for the weapons you used against him. Think it through, General Batista. I demand to be paid. Those weapons belonged to the Dominican Army and that money belongs to the Republic. I sent them to help you..."*

"But, I don't have that money," Batista lamented. *"I barely have enough to live. I'm a poor man..."*

Of course, the Dominican General did not buy the story and the following day sent to the other's suite at the Jaragua hotel, where he had been living since the first interview, his main assistant. The envoy, an army colonel, very respectfully and always standing to attention conveyed Batista the greetings of his benefactor and reminded him of his debt. Again the tyrant used the same arguments which he repeated every time the officer visited. This became a very frequent, almost daily occurrence, until the unexpected happened.

Another colonel showed up at the Jaragua hotel alongside two soldiers and urged Batista to accompany them. Trujillo wanted to meet with him right away. Batista complied. The tone of the voice and the tough gestures of the colonel, and the menacing look in the eyes of the soldiers left him no choice. On his way out, he asked Admiral Rodríguez Calderón to come along. The former chief of the Cuban Navy had spent most of the time with Batista since the General's wife Marta traveled to New York.

Batista and Calderón were taken 'on a ride' through Trujillo City and it was getting dark when their car left the capital. Eventually, they ended up in La Cuarenta penitentiary.

There they spent the night and part of the next day in separate cells. In a letter Batista sent a few months later to Rivero Agüero from Funchal and signed with the pseudonym Mateo, he said *"I was forced to clean my room."*

He was rescued from La Cuarenta by the chief of Trujillo's assistants, the man who always addressed him respectfully and standing to attention. He apologized. He said that it had been an excess because Batista had not registered as a foreigner and that Trujillo was very embarrassed over the incident. But the ride and the short stay in jail had an effect and once in the hotel, bathed and properly dressed, he paid the debt in full. The ex tough man of Cuba, the once-favorite son of the United States, the tyrant that in the 1956 Pan American Conference President Eisenhower had addressed as "*my friend*" was ridiculed and that was something he would have to live with for the rest of his life. A few days later he was again summoned by Trujillo who demanded one million dollars to pay for actions against Cuba. Batista signed the check without saying a word.

His future in the Dominican Republic was obviously uncertain. At the end of June 1959, an influential American journalist, Drew Pearson, with good connections in the State Department, wrote in his column "*...it still remains to be seen what will happen to him in the hands of Trujillo or of the former officers of his army.*"

On July 17, an AP cable dispatch informed that the former dictator had been detained at the airport as he tried to leave Trujillo City on a private plane. Another report dated in Washington that same day claimed that Batista had been to the American Consulate in Santo Domingo to apply for a US visa. The information did not say whether he would receive it.

The US government seemed to have forsaken him. The former dictator's wife had not obtained an audience with Mrs. Eisenhower so she appealed to the First Lady in an open letter. Meanwhile, Gonzalo Güell, the ex minister of the Interior in Cuba, visited the European foreign ministries in an effort to obtain political asylum for the tyrant, and Batista's New York lawyer hit the roof: the life of the ex general was in danger in the Dominican Republic.

Finally, the State Department asked the Brazilian foreign ministry to make arrangements to give him asylum in Portugal. But, before abandoning the Dominican Republic, Batista had to give Trujillo two more million dollars to be allowed to leave the country. On October 1959, a photo showed him arriving at the Spanish airport of Barajas. He was bald now.

Admittedly, the money paid by Batista for the months he stayed in his benefactor's Santo Domingo has long been the subject of speculation, as various figures have been mentioned. Two men of the former president inner circle, Orlando Piedra and

Roberto Fernández Miranda, have argued that from the three million dollars demanded by Trujillo, Batista delivered less than one, an amount that obviously does not include payment for the San Cristóbal carbines. However, in the abovementioned letter to Rivero Agüero that he signed as Mateo, Batista complains of his stay in the Dominican Republic where Trujillo *"robbed me of four million dollars and I had to clean my room."*

A Chinese mystery

Let's take now our time-machine and go backwards. This is now December 1958 and a Dominican delegation is at Columbia waiting for Batista. It is sent by Trujillo to make arrangements for the troops that will shore up an army incapable of winning even a skirmish against the rebels. The group is made up by Colonel Johnny Abbes García, head of the sinister Intelligence Services under Trujillo, and by senior Army and Navy officers. The group is accompanied by a Yugoslav and a Chinese coming to solve the problem of the San Cristóbal carbines that sometimes shoot and others get stuck. Batista refuses to give them an audience leaving them high and dry. In his memoirs, Orlando Piedra writes that his men looked all over Havana for the visitors to force them out of the country and couldn't find them, but Abbes García never forgave him for what happened, hence the way Batista's loyalists were received in Santo Domingo. One of them, Captain Juan Castellanos from the Bureau of Investigations, was kidnapped for a few days and tortured with electroshock and pushing his head under foul water.

It's not clear how those men sent by Trujillo left Cuba. It is said that only the Chinese couldn't make it and spent some time in a Cuban jail where he taught his language to other inmates. But there is another version. As it goes, at seven in the morning of January 1st, Porfirio Rubirosa, a playboy who was General Trujillo's ambassador to Havana, knocked on the door of a distinguished lawyer who happened to be his neighbor at the Biltmore suburb and asked to get him an aircraft to take out of Cuba and to Miami Colonel Abbes García, the Yugoslav and the

Chinese. In fact, Abbes and the Yugoslav could enter the US but not the Chinese, but this was not an insurmountable obstacle, for they dropped the Chinese in the waters of the Florida Straits.

In the final months of 1958, two dictatorships, Trujillo's and Somoza's, tried to save another one, and the three eventually collapsed.

January 18, 2009

BATISTA'S LAST NIGHT IN CUBA

Barely six years after the assault on the Moncada Barracks, Fulgencio Batista's dictatorship is overthrown and the Revolution triumphs in Cuba. It is an impressive time record taking into account that during that period Fidel spent almost two years in jail and one and a half years in exile before he could unleash a war that lasted twenty five months.

After the landing of the Granma yacht, the revolutionary combatants suffered a set back in Alegría de Pío. The future Ejército Rebelde was decimated and dispersed. Of the eighty two men who came in the expedition to start the war on the mountains only a few could regroup.

By January 14, 1957, the guerrilla scored its first victory: the La Plata combat attracted the attention of the country to the guerrillas asserting their willingness to fight and potential to succeed. That potential was confirmed on the month of May when the rebels attacked, in full daylight, a significant place like the Uvero barracks. That combat and the subsequent action on the Estrada Palma town marked the coming of age of the Ejército Rebelde and the end of what Che Guevara called their 'nomad' stage. After this the guerrilla settled in a territory and its capabilities multiplied.

Later on, other columns led by Che, Raúl and Almeida were created in addition to the first headed by Fidel. Raúl established the II Eastern Front on the Sierra Cristal Mountains, and Almeida the III Front. In the meantime, the underground movement intensified its actions in the cities.

The mountain fighters' political line

A major development of strategic importance took place on the Sierra Maestra Mountains on May 3, 1958: the leadership of the July 26 Movement ratified Fidel's position as Commander in Chief of the Ejército Rebelde and Secretary General of the organization and entrusted him with the political and military leadership of the war both on the mountains and in the cities. As of this moment, the struggle pursued the political line of the mountain fighters calling for direct armed confrontation and its expansion to other regions until the final victory.

The general strike of April 9, 1958 failed and far from hurting Batista's stability it gave the government the opportunity to mobilize large contingents of troops and send them to the mountains. This was the beginning of the so-called *Spring Offensive* involving ten thousand soldiers of the tyranny in the harassment of the guerrillas' I Front headed by Fidel.

With only three hundred men, one third of them without weapons, the rebel leader put up a strong resistance, and thirty combats and six hard battles later the enemy was either running away from the battlefield or annihilated. The stern resistance had broken the backbone of Batista's regime, but it was not yet defeated, so Fidel unleashed the counteroffensive where Commanders Ernesto Che Guevara and Camilo Cienfuegos played decisive roles. Their mission was to extend the war beyond the boundaries of the Oriente province while Fidel and the other commanders steadily tightened a circle around Santiago de Cuba.

The last month of the war

By this time, the province of Oriente was practically under control of the Ejército Rebelde. In Las Villas province, two thousand troops of the regime were unable to hold back the thrust of Che's and Camilo's forces while fighting was underway in the provinces of Camagüey and Pinar del Río. Batista's popularity continued to fall and those sectors that until then had supported him were now disgruntled. In Havana, where repression was particularly harsh, the people followed the instructions of the M-26-7, which under the slogan of "0 3 C"[19] called on the people to stay home during the Christmas celebrations. The streets of the capital looked empty and gloomy.

The battle of Guisa, from November 20 through 30, 1958, commandeered by Fidel had been fought practically in sight of the city of Bayamo, the headquarters of the operations against the guerrillas in the eastern region. On December 10, the towns of Baire and Jiguaní were freed, and the next day saw the onset of the battle of Mafo, which lasted until the 30th. The city of Palma Soriano surrendered to the rebels and in Las Villas, Che and Camilo took the initiative.

In the central region, the two columns headed by Che and Camilo managed to cut off road and railway traffic into the city of Santa Clara coming from the west. Che laid siege to the town of Fomento, seized it and attacked the towns of Guayos and Cabaiguán where he was equally successful. Subsequently, Placetas, Remedios, Caibarién and Camajuaní surrendered to his troops while Camilo and his forces attacked the army troops stationed in the north of the province and laid siege to Yaguajay, where Batista's army resisted his attacks for eleven days. At the same time, forces mobilized by the Revolutionary Directorate and the Popular Socialist Party that had subordinated to Che Guevara's leadership were also fighting in the area.

Che's strategy consisted in keeping under control the enemy troops deployed in the cities and towns around Santa Clara to prevent them from reinforcing that strong military site. As Fidel prepared for the final assault on Santiago de Cuba, Che unleashed an attack on the troops stationed in Santa Clara, which he conquered at noon on January 1st. By this time, the legendary commander had derailed and captured the armored train.

[19] *'0 3 C', in Spanish, cero compras, cero cine, cero cabarets*, that is, zero shopping, zero movies, zero night clubs.

The devil's reward

As this was going on, Washington moved to try saving the regime without Batista. American Ambassador Earl Smith, serving in Havana until 1959, wrote in his book *The Fourth Floor*; "*The US companies' representatives concurred that it was too late to help Batista and that the best alternative was to promote a civic-military Junta. Those gentlemen felt that a Junta could attract general support from the people of Cuba and weaken Castro if it included recognized members of the civilian political opposition and some of the best elements of the government. Batista would be left out.*"

Overwhelmed by the continuous defeats sustained by his army, on December 9 Batista received the visit of an odd character: William D. Pawley. The old acquaintances met at Kukine, the private farm used by the tyrant for relaxation. The visitor said that he spoke for himself but he was actually following instructions from the US Administration to persuade President Batista of stepping down. Of course, he said that everything he was offering in exchange for the resignation would have to be ratified in Washington. If Batista was willing to relinquish the presidency now he could settle in the United States and his friends and loyalists would not be disturbed. Pawley also announced the names of the members of the Junta that would replace the tyrant. "*We'll make an effort to prevent Fidel Castro from reaching power,*" he assured. In September 1960, in his testimony at a Senate committee hearing, Pawley said: "*I was chosen to travel to Cuba, talk to Batista and try to persuade him to step down. I did not succeed in my mission but if Rubotton (Assistant Secretary of the State Department) had allowed me to at least indicate that what I was saying had the tacit approval and support of the government, I think that Batista would have accepted.*"

Actually, Pawley carried out his mission behind the ambassador's back. Washington was preserving their top diplomat in Cuba for an official mission in case Batista chose not to listen to the envoy's familiar voice. And this was exactly what happened.

A wounded beast

While Pawley was still in Havana, Ambassador Earl Smith was summoned to Washington where he was given the names of the Junta that would replace Batista. It was known later that not every name in that list coincided with those the envoy gave they tyrant.

As soon as he returned, the ambassador forwarded a coded message to the State Department. He wanted to know the result of Pawley's mission. He didn't get a response. A few days later, he sent another message; the sugar harvest would be seriously impaired because the eastern half of the Island was controlled by the rebels. This time he got a swift response. In his book *The Fourth Floor*, Smith wrote: *"In the early morning of December 14, I received my instructions. It was evident that Batista still hoped for the United States support. My mission consisted in making him face the facts."*

When they met on the 17th, Smith made clear that he disliked his mission but his government was skeptical about Batista's possibility to remain in Cuba until February 24, 1959, when he planned transferring the presidency to Rivero Agüero, "elected" on November. Despite the short time passed since Pawley's mission, Smith's terms were quite different: Batista would neither be allowed into the United States, at least not immediately, nor would he have a voice in the composition of the Junta. *"I suggested that he spend one or more years in Spain or any other country and not to stay in Havana longer than necessary for an orderly transfer of power."* In the summary of his meeting with the President, Smith writes: *"Batista breathed like a wounded beast..."*

On December 28, Fidel met with Major General Eulogio Cantillo. The officer, who had been the great looser of the Spring Offensive launched under his command, had requested the interview and the rebel Commander agreed to receive him. The meeting could help shorten the war. Major General Cantillo, by then chief of anti-guerrilla operations, promised to issue a military proclamation on December 31, from the Moncada Barracks, demanding the resignation of the government and the arrest of Batista and his main accomplices. He failed to deliver on his pledge.

General Batista, who was very critical of that interview, wrote in his Memoirs that Cantillo acted on orders of General Tabernilla, chairman of the Joint Chiefs of Staff. *"The meeting itself was more than a defeatist attitude; it was defeat,"* he admonished.

Looking past certain phrases specially intended for history, the tyrant was really behind every step taken by Cantillo, who would demand Batista's resignation and assume command of the armed forces. Simply put: a coup against Batista conceived by Batista himself.

The last minutes

New Years' Eve 1958 was the last day of Batista's regime. Cantillo met with Batista at 10:00 in the evening and urged him to make a quick decision. The capitulation of Santa Clara was now imminent and nothing could prevent the fall of Santiago de Cuba already besieged by the forces headed by Fidel, Raúl and Almeida.

The military and civilian hierarchy of Batista's regime had joined the dictator at the Columbia Barracks for the New Year's Eve party. Many of them were hastily called by the presidential assistants. Others used the celebration as a pretext to see with their own eyes if there was any truth in the rumors about Batista's resignation. Although many assured that the tyrant would resist and fight his final battle perhaps in Havana, his inner circle of friends grew increasingly apprehensive. Despite the New Year celebrations, the atmosphere in the executive mansion in Columbia was not exactly of joy, and the dictator and Cantillo's continuous asides, showing a perfect understanding between the two, had the effect of heightening the strain.

Shortly before midnight, the guests moved to the dinning room and Batista, with a glass of Champaign in his hand, toasted to a happy New Year. Thirty minutes later, however, at the executive office and surrounded by his senior military officers, Cantillo told him: *"Mr. President, in the interest of reestablishing the public peace so badly needed by the country, the Army chiefs and officers appeal to your sense of patriotism and your love for the people in requesting that you resign your position now."* Then Batista said a few words, asked for paper and a pen, and wrote down his resignation.

The only people left in Columbia at that time were his closest assistants and some henchmen. At one in the morning, the chiefs of the National Police and the Bureau of Investigations ordered all of their vehicles back to their units and instructed the drivers to pick up the chiefs and officers in their homes.

Cheers! Cheers!

Batista arrived in the airport at 2:10 am. He was wearing a dark suit. Actually, he seemed calm amidst the surrounding tension. He was accompanied by his wife Marta, four of his children, and some of his closest assistants and paid thugs; fifteen people in all.

Before boarding the plane, he took Cantillo aside again;

"You understand what I've told you and know what you have to do. Call the personalities I mentioned: Doctors Nuñez Portuondo, Raúl de Cárdenas and Cuervo Rubio, and tell them of my intentions."

"Very well, General," Cantillo answered.

"Try to enlist these people's help. They represent large segments of the public opinion and their cooperation is necessary at this point."

"I agree, General," Cantillo replied.

"All right, Cantillo, mind my recommendations. Success depends on the actions you take from now on."

Batista climbed the stairs to board the plane, and from there he turned back to Cantillo and repeated the final phrase of his speeches and remarks, *Cheers! Cheers! Cheers!"*

Immediately afterwards, Major General Cantillo called Ambassador Smith to communicate the latest developments and decreed a ceasefire, then he proceeded to establish the Civic-

Military Junta to be headed by Carlos M. Piedra, allegedly the oldest member of the Supreme Court, but his action failed. Piedra would never be President because the highest court refused to take his oath and he gave up.

Thus, Cantillo's position in Columbia as the head of a totally dislocated army was ephemeral. At 9:00 in the evening of January 1st, Colonel Ramón Barquín, who had just flown in from Isla de Pinos where he had served his prison sentence after the conspiracy of April 4, 1956, claimed command of the armed forces. On the 3rd, First Lieutenant José Ramón Fernández, who had been in the same prison for the same reason, detained him in his residence at the Columbia Barracks.

Meanwhile, Fidel addressed the people through the Radio Rebelde station in Palma Soriano stating that he rejected the ceasefire and did not recognize the Junta based in Columbia. He did not accept Barquín either and called on the people to launch a revolutionary general strike to prevent the derailment of the Revolution. He warned: *"Let's say yes to the Revolution and no to the coup d'état!"*

December 26, 2004 and January 2, 2005

THE FOBS RUN AWAY

The four-engine C-54 aircraft took off and headed for the United States carrying on board Fulgencio Batista and thirty five other people. It was already reaching cruise speed when Colonel Cosme Varas, an assistant, walked to the cockpit and said to the pilot, Lieutenant Colonel Antonio Soto, that the General wanted to talk to him. Batista inquired if the aircraft had enough fuel to get to the Dominican Republic and after receiving a positive answer he ordered the pilot to head for Santo Domingo. Soto was almost back in the cockpit when he remembered that four other planes would be following his, so he returned to Batista and asked if he should let the others know of the change of destination. *"No,"* Batista replied. *"May they go with good wind!"*

A few days before, in the evening of December 22, 1958, the tyrant had dictated to his private secretary the names of those who would run away with him and their distribution in the first three planes. He would be accompanied in his plane by his wife Marta and his son Jorge; several ministers; the henchmen Esteban Ventura Novo and Orlando Piedra, head of the Bureau of Investigations; and four or five bodyguards... The fifty one passengers of the second plane that would land in Jacksonville would include the Tabernilla family and some of Batista's other children; and the third, an executive C-47 plane, the presidential aircraft named *Guáimaro*, would be carrying thirteen more people. Although there were last minute changes of the passengers traveling in each plane, the list included one hundred names. The remaining Batista loyalists were abandoned to their fate.

This is over!

On January 1st, 1959, at 1:00 am, Sergeant Joaquín Tasis from the Bureau of Investigations heard on the radio that the headquarters of that force was calling all cars. When he got there, he was instructed to pick up two persons in their respective homes. Back at the precinct he was ordered to join a thirty vehicles caravan that soon was on its way to the Columbia military airport. In the first car traveled Colonel Piedra: Operation Running Away had started.

Once at their destination, Piedra asked to be accompanied by the "previously summoned" men. These included the cream of the crop among Batista's criminals: Medina and Sarmiento, Calzadilla and Rodríguez, Margoza and Macagüero, Antolín Falcón and Mariano Faget...in addition to those already inside. Incredible as it may seem, some thought they had been taken there for an interview with Fidel Castro, but Piedra soon removed all doubts when he shouted: *"Gentlemen, this is over!"*

Although Tasis was not among those "previously summoned", the already mentioned Commander Medina, second chief of the Bureau, ordered him in and even when his name was not in any of the lists, he crashed and got a seat in the second plane while others, like the henchmen Peñate and Carratalá –who seemed to have aged twenty years in minutes—didn't get any.

The captain of the plane said everybody had to be seated and Tasis that didn't know whether leaving or staying, and that finally left only to return a few days later, on January 16, stood up for somebody else to take his seat. Peñate and Carratalá hurried to take it but somebody else was faster.

Tasis then thought of going home but the guards wouldn't let him leave the airfield. He left a few hours later for the Dominican Republic in the plane carrying José Eleuterio Pedraza, a godfather to one of Batista's children, who had recently been appointed Army Inspector General. That aircraft also carried Peñate and Carratalá, by now Pedraza's shadow, as well as Ventura's wife and daughters.

Lieutenant Colonel Rolando García Báez, Pilar's son and Irenaldo's brother, was not included in the list either but just like Tasis he managed to leave. He was the Air Force Chief of operations and practically lived at the headquarters of that corps. He woke up at 7:00 am and saw from his window some strange people at the airport. He inquired what was going on, somebody told him and he raced down the stairs barefoot and wearing only his uniform's trousers. He stumbled, fell, stood up and climbed back, as if he had just remembered something. Those who saw him thought he was going to get dressed but he was not. He ran to the officers' club and took the money from the bar register: thirty six pesos. He crashed one of the last planes. His brother had left from the same airport a few hours before but didn't care to let him know.

Forcing his way out

Lieutenant Colonel José María Salas Cañizares, the murderer of Frank País, forced his way out. Aware of Batista's runaway, he arrived in Holguín's airport looking for a way out and there he found Colonel Manuel Ugalde Carrillo who was waiting for an army plane to do exactly that. To get rid of him, Ugalde said he was heading for Havana but Salas didn't swallow the story and boarded the aircraft, put his machinegun to the pilot's head and forced him to go to Santo Domingo.

On the other hand, Commander Pérez Chaumont, one of the assassins of revolutionaries at the Moncada Barracks in 1953, hijacked a schooner in Manzanillo.

A serious diplomatic incident with Chile led some of the more notorious individuals involved with Batista's government to seek asylum in that mission at Línea and G streets. Cuba granted the corresponding permits and took them to the airport under the strict custody of Commander Camilo Cienfuegos and a number of rebels. They boarded the *Constellation* that would take them to the South American country but twenty five minutes into the flight, and already beyond our jurisdiction, the plane broke down and it had to return, so the fugitives had to leave the Chilean aircraft.

Camilo and the Chilean ambassador returned to the airport right away. At this point, the chief of the Ejército Rebelde rightly said to the diplomat that those thieves were no longer covered by the right to asylum because they had left the country and returned to it. The Chilean diplomat protested and both spoke over the phone with highest authorities of the government. Eventually, it was agreed that they return to the embassy and wait for a final decision. Cuba recognized the right to asylum but it argued that Batista's loyalists who had taken refuge there and in other diplomatic missions in Havana were really common offenders and since the Caracas Convention granted the recipient country the right to decide on the qualification of the asylum seeker, Cuba would abstain from issuing permits until every diplomatic mission in Havana filed such qualification in writing. Once this requirement was met, these and other asylum seekers left the country, even someone as repulsive as Manuel Calviño Insua, a murderer who took orders from Ventura and who later made the mistake of coming as a mercenary with the Bay of Pigs invaders and paid for his crimes.

But Captain Orlando Tato Rodríguez could not escape. He was a man close to Colonel Pilar García in Matanzas. He had done evil things in that city of the Yumurí Valley. His motto was: *"No wounded and no prisoners; I've no time for detainees."* He was supposed to have left the country although there was no proof that he had arrived in any country, the same as Agustín Labastina, the henchman from Holguín, who had just disappeared off the face of the earth. But a woman recognized Tato's wife on Santa Catalina Avenue, followed her and on the porch of a house on Lagueruela street, in La Víbora suburb, she saw the hated military who pretended to be a shoe shiner, and an invalid at that. She then tipped the police and the authorities took the case in their hands. It was, in fact, Tato pretending to be crippled. Thirteen years had passed since Batista's escape.

November 28, 2004

FIDEL IN HAVANA

For a week, Havana waited anxiously. As of January 2, Fidel could enter the capital any day. It seemed as if he would be here anytime now and the press agencies added to the confusion since their news would have him on board a plane or heading the Freedom Caravan at the entrance to the city. Now that the hero of the Sierra Maestra Mountains, who had defeated the tyranny's forces, was coming from Santiago de Cuba to the west of the Island, he was trapped by an overflowing wave of people who wanted to show their affection.

It was practically impossible to keep schedules. The foreseen routes could not be used. It was hard to make predictions. In Bayamo, the headquarters of the anti-guerrilla forces, two thousand soldiers and officers from the defeated army joined the victorious troops. The rebels were forced to stop at the provincial capitals along the Central Highway. However, twice Fidel insisted on leaving that route. In Las Villas he headed south. He wanted to greet the people from the city of Cienfuegos, which was the stage of the uprising of September 5, 1957. In Matanzas he went north and at the cemetery of Cárdenas City he laid a wreath at the tomb of university students' leader José Antonio Echeverría, killed in the aftermath of the assault on the Presidential Palace. In Camagüey, Santa Clara, Catalina de Güines, San José de las Lajas...the warm popular welcome delayed the advance of the rebels. In cities and towns the people demanded to see and hear the leader of the Revolution.

In his remarks, Fidel barely mentioned the past, the years of sacrifices that were now behind us. Riding the exciting wave of events, he addressed the future and warned against easy optimism. Certainly, the war was over, he asserted, but the Revolution was just starting and a hard path to progress and reforms lay ahead of the nation. The homeland could not be robbed of its destiny, he warned. Every time the Commander in Chief addressed the people he laid another stone in the foundations of the new organizations of the country, called the militias to order and appealed to the army senior officers. Cuba was on its way to reconstruction and it was imperative to commit to this effort. As the tyranny collapsed, he had called to the revolutionary general strike in an effort to thwart the enemy's intention to preserve Batista's regime without Batista. The time had come now to go back to work, to have the businesses start functioning again, to bring the country back to normality.

Visiting the Granma yacht

And, so it comes January 8. The people from Havana, mesmerized in front of the TV sets, waits for the moment to take to the streets to welcome the rebels. Cuban flags are hanging from balconies and windows alongside the black and red flag of the July 26 Movement. The women are dressed in these colors that had been forbidden until now. The town of El Cotorro, some thirty minutes off the capital, has a great surprise in store for Fidel. There is his son, Fidelito, dressed in olive green fatigues, and Commander Juan Almeida lifts the little boy up to the military vehicle carrying Fidel so that father and son can embrace.

The Commander in Chief then travels in a car from El Cotorro to the Virgen del Camino where he takes a jeep to ride into the city. Commander Camilo Cienfuegos is riding with him and their troops follow in lorries, cars, trucks and all sorts of military vehicles. These are mostly young people from the countryside who have never been to Havana and who look in astonishment at the high rise and the avenues, and smile shyly behind their legendary beards.

Fidel is in town and the church bells toll; the cars blow their horns and the ships in the harbor their whistles. All along the way, on both sides of the streets, the people cram to greet him. The victorious caravan drives along the Avenida del Puerto. The Granma yacht is docked in front of the Navy headquarters and the leader of the Revolution orders to stop and boards the sea craft. The Máximo Gómez and José Martí frigates shoot salvos. The caravan is again on its way. At the Avenida de las Misiones it turns right and Fidel asks to make a second stop, this time in front of the Presidential Palace for he wishes to call on President Manuel Urrutia who waits for him in the company of all his ministers at the door of the executive mansion.

They all walk up to the second floor of the building. From the north terrace Fidel greets those who have concentrated in front of the Palace. It's a compact crowd from the building right up to the Malecón and the Castillo de la Punta.

Urrutia introduces him saying, *"Cubans, the Government of the Republic at the Presidential Palace has opened its arms to welcome the great leader of the Americas, Fidel Castro Ruz. Cuban democracy is honored by the presence in the Presidential Palace of the great hero of the struggle against the tyranny. Our people should be very proud that he is one of its children. He is, no doubt, the most dedicated combatant leader in our history... After defeating the dictatorship with admirable effort he has not seized power for himself but rather given it to a man he trusts.*

"Cubans, we promise to honor that gesture of the great leader of Cubans. Now I leave you with Fidel Castro Ruz."

Our unconquered mountains

Fidel must wait for the excited crowd to quiet down to start talking. The same as in Santiago de Cuba and all along the route he doesn't want to make a speech accentuated with bombastic or dramatic gestures but rather converse with the people as you do with a friend and establish a dialogue from one comrade to another.

"I never liked this building; I think nobody really liked it," *Fidel says with a smile. "The highest I had climbed was that wall when I was a student,"* he adds pointing to a canvass depicting a wall near the executive mansion that he once used as a rostrum to denounce official corruption.

And he carries on: *"You might want to know what I feel entering the Palace. I'll tell you that I feel the same as in any other place of the Republic. It doesn't awake any special feelings. It's a building that, at this moment, is valuable because it shelters the Revolutionary Government of the Republic. If it were for reason of affection, the place I would like to live in, because it holds the deepest sentiments, is the Turquino Peak, because to the strength of the tyranny we opposed the strength of our unconquered mountains..."*

Subsequently, he invites the people to move to the Columbia Barracks, the headquarters of the General Staff of the tyranny's Armed Forces and until recently the power center of Cuba. He then indicates: *"...now Columbia belongs to the people. Let the tanks that now belong to the people march ahead of the people, in the vanguard, and open the way for the people; nobody will stop us and we shall meet there."*

The Commander in Chief comments that seeing that crowd gathered in front of the Palace somebody had said that the protection of a thousand soldiers would be required to walk across. *"...and I say it's not true. I'll walk across the people. They say that because they have seeing all the excitement and the enthusiasm and they fear that we might get hurt; yet, the people have come here to protect the revolutionaries.*

"I'll prove again that I know the people. We don't need any soldier ahead of us because I'm going to ask the people to open up a way, and I'll walk down that way with the President of the Republic. Yes, comrades, we'll show the entire world, the journalists present here, the discipline and restraint of the Cuban

people. Open up a way, comrades, and we'll walk through it, so they will see we need no soldiers to walk across the people gathered here."

Fidel and Urrutia walk down the street and the crowd spontaneously moves back opening a path for the Commander in Chief and the President to walk through, and again close ranks after they have passed.

A paper shower

The Freedom Caravan is on the move again. It reaches the Malecón and turns left up 23rd Street on its way to the Columbia Barracks. The number of people following the rebel leader grows since the people watch him pass and follow the impressive parade. The American tourists staying at the Havana Hilton hotel rip out the pages of the phone books, tear them to little pieces and drop them on Fidel, Broadway style.

The foreign correspondents in Cuba are amazed. Although many of them are experienced journalists who have traveled the world no one remembers seeing anything like this in their professional lives. The reporter of the Columbia Broadcasting System, who witnessed the reception Generals Eisenhower and McArthur had at the end of World War II, admits he had not seen such crowd and such a warm welcome. Journalist Jules Dubois who covered the ousting of Juan Domingo Perón in Argentina, Gustavo Rojas Pinillas in Colombia and Marcos Pérez Jiménez in Venezuela is astonished. *"It's the most extraordinary event I've seeing in thirty years as a journalist,"* he affirms, and another American journalist points out that what he is watching largely exceeds General De Gaulle's welcome to Paris after liberation.

There are no soldiers in Columbia to prevent the people from entering. The huge crowd that now crams the military training field is testimony to the scope of the victory. Officers and soldiers of the defeated army join the multitude.

Fidel starts talking. A white pigeon perches on his left shoulder. It's a most emotional instant. The war hero becomes the conductor of his people. *"The people, the people won the war. No one else but the people won this war...therefore, the people comes first."*

In this historical speech, the Commander in Chief describes the duties of revolutionaries, claims for peace and underlines the need for all of the forces that fought against the tyranny to work together for the Cuban people.

Fidel concludes his remarks to a frantic ovation. It is almost dawn and he is asked to stay at the residence that had been Batista's until a few days before, but he declines and instead goes to a modest hotel on the Monserrate street in Old Havana, where he used to stay as a college student.

New Year 1959

At that time, no papers were published on the first day of the New Year and also the radio and TV stations were disturbingly silent. Only some news flashes alluding to "transcendental developments" interrupted the silence, but for hours now the news, as a confusing rumor, had been going around the city, from one house to the next. No one could pinpoint its source or offer any specific details but everybody was convinced that the moment they had all been longing for was here now.

Despite the press censorship it was common knowledge that the tyranny was quickly crumbling down; that Camilo Cienfuegos was operating in the north of Las Villas; that Santa Clara was besieged by Che Guevara; and that the columns headed by Fidel, Raúl and Almeida were ready to lay siege to Santiago de Cuba. Far from paralyzing the rebellion, the Dantesque repression unleashed in the cities had intensified it and the people were increasingly moved by patriotism. Havana and the main cities in the provinces seemed like ghost cities. Even during Christmas, the streets were empty as the people took refuge in their houses to listen to the broadcasts of Radio Rebelde and to comply with the M-26-7 slogan "no shopping, no movies, no night clubs", popularly known as "03C".

Unknown to the people that was starting to feel the taste of their victory, treason was hatching at the Columbia Barracks, the tyranny's main bulwark. To rob the Revolution of its victory, a Civic-Military Junta was established in connivance with the runaway tyrant; but it would soon suffocate in its own stench while the streets filled with popular warmth.

The general strike

The combatants of the July 26 Movement that until then had so zealously concealed their membership, took to the streets with their bracelets and weapons. The churches' bells tolled and windows and balconies exhibited the Cuban national flag and the black and red M-26-7 flag. By seven in the morning, journalist Carlos Lechuga from the *Telemundo* newsreel had broken with the restraint of the news released until then that spoke of the 'Honorable President of the Republic' and started calling Batista a thief and a murderer; and a little later the News on Channel 12, directed by Lisandro Otero, set in motion a transcendental news service.

An endless line of people paraded in front of the cameras; these were mothers claiming for their missing sons, girls carrying pictures of their young brothers murdered, men devastated by torture and incarceration who told hair-raising stories and publicly accused their torturers.

From Palma Soriano, the Commander in Chief expressed through Radio Rebelde his determination to reject the ceasefire decreed in Columbia and his refusal to accept the Civic-Military Junta while calling the people to a general strike. A few hours later, this time in Santiago de Cuba, he told thousands of people from that city gathered in front of the City Hall that "*If a military coup is orchestrated behind our people's back, our Revolution will go on forward. This time the Revolution will not be thwarted. Fortunately for Cuba, this time the Revolution will not be stopped.*"

The troops headed by Camilo and Che entered Havana. The revolutionary general strike was a reality that frustrated the intention of the military to seize power. On January 8, the capital offered Fidel a terrific welcome.

The last night of the year 1958, at midnight, many Cubans threw out of their houses and into the streets the traditional bucket of water that should drag away the old year and all evils with it… The old year had taken away the tyrant Fulgencio Batista, his loyalists and an entire social regime. For the first time in history, the old phrase "a New Year, a new life" became a reality for the Cuban people.

One protagonist: the people

In his speech in Santiago de Cuba on January 2, Fidel announced his objectives with pristine clarity. He indicated that *"Time is of the greatest importance. The Revolution will not be made overnight but you may be certain that we'll make the Revolution, you may be certain that for the first time the Republic will be truly and completely free and the people will have what they deserve…"*

The year 1959 becomes the Year of Liberation. At the time, the structures of the old power start to break down and the economic and social transformation of the country begins. The culprits of the old regime respond for their crimes and the assets stolen from the nation's coffers are recovered. From that early stage it's obvious that Washington is not happy with the nascent Revolution.

Popular laws are passed this year that the people receive joyfully, such as a slash of the house rents, the electric tariffs, the price of medicines and the cost of books. The ministry of Education is given the tyranny's barracks to turn them into schools. Ten thousand new classrooms are opened throughout the country while houses are built for workers and farmers, and tourist resorts are developed.

A new character is definitely entering the history of Cuba: the people. As of this moment, the people will be the center of attention of the Revolution and its main support. The Cuban people, starving, illiterate, lacking medical care and deprived of their land and of the country's wealth now start to enjoy full dignity and to recognize themselves as masters of their own destiny.

Shake-up the tree!

It was the same people Fidel talked about in his court statement *History Will Absolve Me;* the same that on January 21, during a massive rally in front of the Presidential Palace, asked the leader of the Revolution to '*shake-up the tree*' referring to those who opposed the Revolution but still occupied senior positions in government institutions.

This was a year when practically everything remained to be done. It could be said that it was a romantic stage but one that demanded definitions and, sometimes, dramatic and definitive decisions. Very early, the enemy showed its true face. A smear campaign launched by these enemies outside Cuba aimed at discrediting the Revolution when the courts of law passed judgment on the murderers and torturers who killed thousands of Cubans in the seven years of Batista's government.

Before long Cuba became the target of all kinds of actions and pressures from the United States government and Congress and from the Organization of American States (OAS). In light of the unexpected turn of events and supposedly concerned over *"the effective exercise of democracy in the Caribbean,"* they hoped to become arbiters of the nation's internal affairs.

The leaders of the Revolution were under threat; Cuban planes and vessels were hijacked and the economy was the target of terrorist actions and sabotages. In August, a counterrevolutionary expedition sponsored by Rafael Leónidas Trujillo, the Dominican satrap, was captured as it arrived in Trinidad. On October, the military chief of the Camagüey region betrayed the Revolution, and a plane coming from the United States treacherously attacked Havana killing two people and injuring fifty others.

The Revolution must defend itself from its internal and external adversaries. It must fight for survival. Thus, on October 26, the National Revolutionary Militias are created. These would become an invincible force and prove it in the fight against the bandits armed by the United States on the Escambray Mountains, and against the mercenary brigade trained and equipped by Washington and defeated in the sands of Playa Girón[20].

It was also in that year that the nation suffered a painful experience, when Commander Camilo Cienfuegos, the leader of the guerrilla vanguard and a hero of many combats, perished in an aircraft accident on his way from Camagüey to Havana.

Duality of power

From the first days of 1959, a duality of power was evident in Cuba. On the one hand, there was Fidel, the undisputable leader of the Revolution, ratified as Commander in Chief by the people gathered in Columbia on January 8; on the other, there was the Government with mostly principled honest people who had fought against the dictatorship but also with characters whose class origin and interests soon aligned them against the Revolution. These were popularly called *the pretending ministers*.

The President of the Republic was Dr. Manuel Urrutia Lleó, a former judge in the Oriente Provincial Court, who had had the honesty and courage of voting to acquit those accused for the developments of November 30, 1956when the revolutionaries in Santiago de Cuba, headed by Frank País, took to the streets and for almost an entire day kept the city under control in support of the landing of the revolutionaries on board the *Granma* yacht. Before the victory of the Revolution, the July 26 Movement had appointed Urrutia the new President of the Cuba. In the last days of the war he was moved to a place on the hillside of the Sierra Maestra and in the early days of 1959 he took the oath.

One detail can help us understand the personality of this man; while the Cubans claimed for an honest and austere government, he kept receiving the salary Batista had set himself as president amounting to 12,500 pesos a month and did not cut down a penny from the budget allocated by the tyranny to cover the expenses of the Presidential Palace: 2,433,650 pesos a year.

[20] *Playa Girón* was the place where the mercenaries who landed at the *Bay of Pigs* found defeated.

The die is cast

It can be said that with Urrutia and *the pretending ministers* the counterrevolution was crouching inside the government. As the first weeks passed of that year 1959, the President intensified his public anticommunist campaign joining Washington's deceitful propaganda aimed at confusing and dividing Cubans.

Although Urrutia remained in the highest office until July, the dualism in power ended on February 16 when Fidel assumed the position of Prime Minister. Under his leadership, the cabinet started *"issuing laws, decrees and agreements that undermined the foundations of the exploiters' regime bent on surviving under a revolutionary disguise."*

The Revolution did not dismiss the pretending ministers all at once but used a more effective method: it replicated in the National Institute for Agrarian Reform (INRA), headed by Fidel, the most important government functions. The INRA had, among others, an Industrialization Department led by Che Guevara, and a Commerce Department that assumed the powers that until then rested with the ministry of Trade. Later, when some of these departments became ministries, some new posts were added to the cabinet and several people were dismissed. The Council of Ministers ended up in the hands of prestigious leaders who had the confidence of the Revolution.

Meanwhile, the President grew intensively negative. At this point, Fidel showed a commendable political good sense. Actually, with the support of the people, he could have swept away Urrutia with the wave of a hand, but he chose not to. One night, he told Captain Antonio Nuñéz Jiménez, "*alea jacta est*", that is, the die is cast. He resigned from his position as Prime Minister.

Fidel must return

The sixth anniversary of the attack on the Moncada Barracks and the first in a free Cuba was nearing and thousands of farmers were readying to come to Havana to partake in the popular demonstration scheduled for July 26 in the Revolution Square.

President Urrutia would not leave his position; he was inflexible. Fidel Castro remained the Commander in Chief of the Armed Forces. The people were increasingly restless; workers and students took to the streets to protest and paint phrases expressing their support for and solidarity with the abdicating premier.

On July 17, the same day that the *Revolución* newspaper ran the news of his resignation, Fidel went on television to explain to the people the reasons of his decision. As he made his remarks, a large group of people surrounding the Presidential Palace shouted: *"Urrutia should go!"* The President had no option and that same night submitted his resignation to the Council of Ministers, which appointed President Dr. Osvaldo Dorticós Torrado, a lawyer from Cienfuegos who was minister of Revolutionary Laws right up to that moment.

This change put an end to the crisis. Yet, Fidel did not resume the position of Prime Minister. He wanted to leave that decision to the people. In his opinion, the issue should be settled at the Revolution Square, during the July 26 demonstration.

But the pressures for him to resume that position kept mounting by the minute, and the Cuban Workers Confederation called for a one hour strike to demand his return. At this point, the entire country was paralyzed. The industry, trade and services ceased their operations and the vehicles in the streets blew their horns.

On July 26, a great popular referendum brought Fidel back to the position of Prime Minister. The crowd at the Revolution Square rejoiced and thousands of straw hats –a typical accessory among Cuban farmers— were thrown to the air as they raised the machetes hanging from their belts.

The end of latifundia

The proclamation of the Land Reform Law, on May 17, set the tone for the year 1959. In his *History Will Absolve Me* court statement, Fidel discussed "*the land issue*." The peasantry had not hesitated to join the rebels, so it was not surprising that measures were taken very early in the free territories of the Sierra Maestra to benefit this segment of the population. The Peasants'

Congress in Arms, chaired by Raúl in the II Front, examined the living conditions and aspirations of the men who tilled the land. By October 10, 1958, the Law No.3 of the Ejército Rebelde granted the land to those who labored it while in the provinces of Oriente and Las Villas, controlled by the revolutionary forces, the peasants were relieved of their responsibility to pay rent for the land.

It was only natural that the land issue was given a priority from the early days of the Revolution. The Law of May 17, 1959 delivered the land, free of charge, among over one hundred farmers. This anti-imperialist and anti-feudal legislation aroused hatred against the Revolution among the US monopolies. These could not accept that the Revolutionary Government was recovering for the nation the land that they had misappropriated and exploited for years.

It was precisely this law that led to the subsequent US government suspension of the Cuban sugar quota in the American market and the interruption of the oil supplies to the Island; the main reason for the Bay of Pigs invasion and the economic, commercial and financial blockade that right up to this minute when I'm writing this lines has cost Cuba over 82 billion dollars in losses. *"This law,"* Fidel said, *"was the one that brought about imperialism's direct confrontation with Cuba."*

The presence of those peasants in Havana on July 26, 1959 was more than a symbol. Fidel continuously traveled to the countryside; he spent a lot of time with the peasants in Pinar del Río and with the charcoal producers at the Zapata Swamp; he designed *in situ* the future of a remote area in Isla de Pinos, and returned to the Sierra Maestra Mountains…

Following Fidel in his tours of the country and watching his concern for the people, a nation that until 1959 had its eyes fixed on the horizon started looking inside and learning about itself, realizing its strength and courage; this was the beginning of the indestructible bond of the urban and rural areas, of the people and their government that would lead to greater and more resounding achievements.

January 1 and 8, 2006